Papers of the Forty-Sixth Algonquian Conference

Actes du Quarante-Sixième Congrès des Algonquinistes

PAPERS OF THE ALGONQUIAN CONFERENCES
ACTES DU CONGRÈS DES ALGONQUINISTES

46

Papers of the Forty-Sixth Algonquian Conference

Actes du Quarante-Sixième Congrès des Algonquinistes

EDITED BY Monica Macaulay and Margaret Noodin

MICHIGAN STATE UNIVERSITY PRESS | EAST LANSING

∞ The paper used in this publication meets the minimum requirements of ANSI/NISO Z39.48-1992 (R 1997) (Permanence of Paper).

Michigan State University Press
East Lansing, Michigan 48823-5245

Printed and bound in the United States of America.

26 25 24 23 22 21 20 19 18 17 1 2 3 4 5 6 7 8 9 10

ISBN 978-1-61186-250-8 (paperback)
ISBN 978-1-60917-532-0 (PDF)

Book design by Charlie Sharp, Sharp Des!gns, East Lansing, MI
Cover design by Erin Kirk New
Cover detail of a quill box is used courtesy of Julie L. Loehr.

Michigan State University Press is a member of the Green Press Initiative and is committed to developing and encouraging ecologically responsible publishing practices. For more information about the Green Press Initiative and the use of recycled paper in book publishing, please visit *www.greenpressinitiative.org*.

Visit Michigan State University Press at *www.msupress.org*

CONTENTS

PREFACE

The Forty-Sixth Algonquian Conference was held at the Mohegan Sun Casino and Convention Center in Uncasville, Connecticut, from October 23 to 26, 2014. It was cohosted by Doug Whalen of the Endangered Language Fund and the City University of New York and Stephanie Fielding of the Mohegan Tribe, who writes the following:

> At the Forty-Fourth Algonquian Conference Doug Whalen and I got together to talk about hosting the Forty-Sixth annual conference. In all the decades that it had existed, the conference had never been held on sovereign Native lands. The irony was too great. All these forty-plus years anthropologists and linguists had been studying the cultures and languages of Native people, and yet the conference had not been on Native soil. I talked to then-chairman Bruce Bozsum of the Mohegan Tribe, who said, "Let's have it here at the Mohegan Sun!" But the Mohegan Sun was expensive, and anthropologists and linguists always fly economy.
>
> With the encouragement of Daryl Baldwin, though, the Miami Tribe came through with a generous donation, and the Endangered Language Fund likewise came through with a smaller but also greatly appreciated donation to help fund the conference.

The wonderful people in the Cultural Department helped to stuff our conference bags and folders. The people at the Sun were wonderful and helped keep costs down.

Everyone loved the glamour and color and liveliness of the Sun above and beyond meeting new and old friends, and listening to scholarly presentations. One of the highlights of the conference was Friday night, when the newly published book *Dawnland Voices: An Anthology of Indigenous Writing from New England* was premiered. The editor of the volume, Siobhan Senier of the University of New Hampshire, gave an introduction, and several of the contributing authors read passages from the book. The book was well received, as was the special cake made in the Sun's bakery by Chef Lyn.

There are many people to thank. Recent organizers of the conference were quite generous with their advice and their spreadsheets, including Amy Dahlstrom, Marguerite McKenzie, Margaret Noodin, and Monica Macaulay. Another 'thank you' goes to co-coordinator Doug Whalen for his help. He had the idea of honoring Ives Goddard, unarguably the best Algonquianist in the world, and he wrote and delivered the speech for that event. He allowed the Algonquian Conference to be included under the Endangered Language Fund's aegis, making it possible to function as a nonprofit, and he drafted the conference program. Most of all he was there when I needed someone to consult with.

Next, thanks go to Mohegan Chief Lynn "Many Hearts" Malerba, who opened our conference with a greeting and a prayer in Mohegan. A hearty 'thank you' goes to Melissa Tantaquidgeon Zobel, the Mohegan Tribe's Medicine Woman and Historian, for her consultation and assistance throughout the conference's preparation and execution. Many thanks too for her staff, whom she made available for things of both a creative and tedious nature. She saw that all the conference attendees had a copy of the book *Lasting of the Mohegans,* a short history of the Mohegan Tribe. She inspired a bookmark featuring Fidelia Fielding, the last fluent speaker of the Mohegan language, to be put into the conference bags. And last but not least, she was a gracious and informative hostess on the bus tours of the reservation.

Many thanks are extended to David Freeburg and Rachel Sayet for helping with registration. Hannah King of Haskins Laboratories and the Endangered Language Fund was helpful before the conference, and she and Lauren Spradlin, a CUNY linguistics grad student, were on hand the evening of the book readings to sell books.

Huge thanks go to Lauren Mishkin of the food and beverage crew from the

Mohegan Sun for the constant attention and encouragement, and her vast knowledge of how things work. She was the oil that kept the conference moving smoothly.

Thanks also to Jesse and Joe Bruchac, who traveled all the way from upstate New York to entertain at the Saturday banquet. As a special treat they enticed sister/aunt Marge Bruchac into singing with them. Lovely!

And finally, thanks to Phil Cahill and Sue Bergeron, who graciously helped with the finances for the Tribe and the Sun.

In addition to the papers published here, the following papers were presented at the conference:

Antti Arppe (University of Alberta), Lene Antonsen (University of Tromsø), Trond Trosterud (Unviersity of Tromsø), Conor Snoek (University of Alberta), Dorothy Thunder (University of Alberta), Jordan Lachler (University of Alberta), Jean Okimâsi (Independent Scholar), and Arok Wolvengrey (First Nations University of Canada): Linguistic insights from computational modeling of Plains Cree morphology

Akeia A. Benard (Wheelock College): Liminality and prestige: Interpreting the status of seventeenth-century Native American children with burial data

Heather Bliss (University of Victoria) and Martina Wilschko (University of British Columbia): The syntactic composition of Blackfoot demonstratives

Ksenia Bogomolets (University of Connecticut): Arapaho as a stress-accent language

Marge Bruchac (University of Pennsylvania): Following the Wampum Trail

Chris Cieri and Mark Liberman (University of Pennsylvania): Using automatic speech analysis with language archives

David J. Costa (Miami University): The future/desiderative in Miami-Illinois and Old Illinois

Andrew Cowell (University of Colorado): Topic initiation, addition, and control: A multi-modal perspective from Arapaho

Andrew Cowell (University of Colorado) and William C'Hair (Northern Arapaho Tribe): Purposing archiving efforts: Arapaho for the future

Miloje Despeć and Sarah E. Murray (Cornell University): Cheyenne and the typology of person features

Christian DiCanio and D. H. Whalen (Haskins Laboratories): Vowel production in a spoken corpus

Lynn Drapeau (Université du Québec à Montréal): Associative plurality in Innu

Joel Dunham (University of British Columbia): Computationally modeling the morphophonology of Blackfoot: Expediting IGT creation and automating analysis testing

David Ezzo and Michael Moskowitz (Independent Scholars): Shinnecok Indian history and land claims: A historical overview

Inge Genee (University of Lethbridge): A functional discourse grammar account of Blackfoot causative constructions

Inge Genee (University of Lethbridge) and Arok Wolvengrey (First Nations University of Canada): The functional discourse grammar approach to information structure applied to word order in Cree and Blackfoot

Ives Goddard (Smithsonian Institution): Some early Munsee place names from New York, New Jersey, and Connecticut

Douglas Gordon (McGill University): The distribution of *me'* and *gi's* in Mi'gmaq

Michael David Hamilton, Michael Wagner (McGill University), Mary Ann Metallic, Janice Vicaire (McGill University and Listuguj Education Directorate), and Elise McClay (University of British Columbia): Focus in Mi'gmaq: Prosodic and syntactic reflexes

Doug Harris (Narragansett Indian Tribal Historic Preservation Office): Triggered by tribal elders' declarations, new tribal historic preservation research frontiers emerge

Mary Hermes, Jordyn Flaada, Kevin Roach, and John Nichols (University of Minnesota–Twin Cities): Why is this so slow? The Ojibwe movies conversation project

Ruth Wallis Herndon (Bowling Green State University) and Alice Nash (University of Massachusetts): "Come as we meet on common ground": A collaborative approach to Narragansett history

Bill Jancewicz (SIL International/Naskapi Development Corporation): Developing Naskapi grammatical awareness and its effect on adult literacy

Meredith Johnson (University of Wisconsin–Madison): The syntax of *Wh*-scope marking: Evidence from Menominee

Ryan Kasak and Claire Bowern (Yale University): Quiripi verbal inflection

Jeanne Morningstar Kent (Nulhegan Band, Coosuk Abenaki of Vermont): The visual language of Wabanaki art

Kyumin Kim (University of Ottawa) and Elizabeth Ritter (Ben Gurion): The categories of number in Blackfoot

Manuel Lizarralde (Connecticut College) and Jason R. Mancini (Mashantucket Pequot Museum and Research Center): The hisotrical ethnobotany of southern New England: Recovering and repatriating indigenous plant knowledge

Sarah Lundquist (University of Wisconsin–Madison): Semantic contributions of abstract finals in Menominee AI verbs

Victor P. Lytwyn (Independent Scholar): Indian presents: The bounty of the crown and sacred trust reconsidered

Monica Macaulay (University of Wisconsin–Madison): Preparing Menominee material for automatic speech processing

Monica Macaulay and Joseph Salmons (University of Wisconsin–Madison): Menominee deverbal finals in historical context

Jason R. Mancini (Mashantucket Pequot Museum and Research Center): Preserved on the Mighty Waters: Exploring the Indian mariner's project

Jason R. Mancini (Mashantucket Pequot Museum and Research Center): Living between termination and recognition: An Indian neighborhood in Westerly, Rhode Island, 1850–1950

Eric Maynard (Mohegan Tribe): "Reel" or "Real Americans"?: Bringing Algonquian voices to the American Indian Film Gallery (AIFG) archives

Donna L. Moody (University of Massachusetts, Amherst): Anthropology, colonialization, and Indigenous Peoples from the perspective of an Abenaki scholar: How violence to Indigenous Peoples continues

John S. Moody (Independent Scholar): *Alnôbak, Wôbanakiak, ta Alnôbaiwi*: Abenaki language survival from the 18th century to present

Lori Morris (Université du Québec à Montréal): Lessons from language testing of Innu children: The critical need for early intervention

Margaret Noodin (University of Wisconsin–Milwaukee): Critical commentary on stretching creative limits in a re-emerging language

Will Oxford (University of Manitoba): Variation in TA theme signs

Connor McDonough Quinn (University of Maine): Algonquian grammar without all the grammar: Making Algonquian language patterns accessible to all

Bryan Rosen (University of Wisconsin–Madison): Prenouns as adjectives: A case from Ojibwe

Rachel Sayet (Mohegan Tribe): *Wikôtamuwôk Wuci Ki tà Kihtahan* (A celebration of land and sea): Modern Indigenous cuisine in New England

Theresa Schenck (University of Wisconsin–Madison): The St. Croix Chippewa of Wisconsin: A lost tribe?

Douglas Schwartz (New England Antiquities Research Association): Native American archeogeology: Clues to the subterranean landscape

Andrew J. Strack (Myaamia Tribe): *metimankwiki kimehšoominaanaki*—We follow our ancestors' trail: Sharing historical *myaamia* language documents across *myaamionki*

Kathleen Strader (University of Ottawa): Function and position of Michif determiners

Rhonda Telford (Independent Scholar): The Indian Land Management Fund and the Indian agents on Lake Superior to 1913

Lucy Thomason (Smithsonian Institution): A few words and thoughts that didn't make it into the dictionary: Implications of a newly discovered manuscript of Alfred Kiyana's

Irina Vagner (University of Colorado): Language revitalization on the web: Developing Algonquian resources

D. H. Whalen, Christian DiCanio, and Hannah King (Haskins Laboratories): From corpus to corpus phonetics: Challenges in adapting an Arapaho corpus for linguistic research

Martina Wiltschko (University of British Columbia) and Elizabeth Ritter (Ben Gurion): The syntax of animacy and humanness

Arok Wolvengrey (First Nations University of Canada): A functional discourse grammar analysis of Plains Cree constituent order: A beginning

Fanny York (Université du Québec à Montréal): The treatment and categorization of direct and inverse forms in Algonquian grammars before the twentieth century

Patterns of Syncretism in Nominal Paradigms: A Pan-Algonquian Perspective

Heather Bliss and Will Oxford

This paper examines the morphology of nominal paradigms from a pan-Algonquian perspective, focusing on inflectional syncretisms.[1] From an empirical standpoint, our focus on syncretisms reflects their ubiquity: a nominal paradigm without syncretisms is unattested across the family. From a theoretical standpoint, syncretisms have the potential to deepen our understanding of the organization of nominal features. Paraphrasing Jakobson (1962), Caha (2009:17) observes that "syncretism points to the existence of a hidden level of linguistic organization inside an apparently indivisible unit: the morpheme." A pan-Algonquian survey of nominal syncretisms will lay the groundwork for future studies of nominal features such as number, person, animacy, obviation, and absentation. Are these features grammatical primitives or are they derived? How are their exponents handled in the syntax? To what extent is variation possible? These are the types of questions that we can begin to address once we understand the distribution of syncretisms across the family.

The paper begins with a general discussion of the types of contrasts that occur in Algonquian nominal inflection; we then proceed to survey nominal syncretisms across the family. The scope of our investigation is restricted to "nominal categories" in the sense of Goddard (1979), including animacy, number, and obviation, but excluding possession and the "further obviative" marking that occurs in some possessed forms. (Following Wolfart 1978, we regard the "further obviative" as marking an obviative possessor rather than an additional degree of obviation on the possessed noun.) For the sake of simplicity, we also set aside absentative inflection.

Contrasts in Nominal Inflection

Algonquian nominal paradigms are canonically regarded as having two dimensions of contrast: NUMBER, which can be singular or plural, and ANIMACY, which can be animate proximate (3), animate obviative (3′), or inanimate (0) (e.g., Bloomfield 1946:§29). This approach, illustrated in (1), treats the obviative as a special type of animate third person, thus inherently restricting obviation to occurring only on animate nominals.

(1) Two-dimensional system: Obviation part of animacy dimension

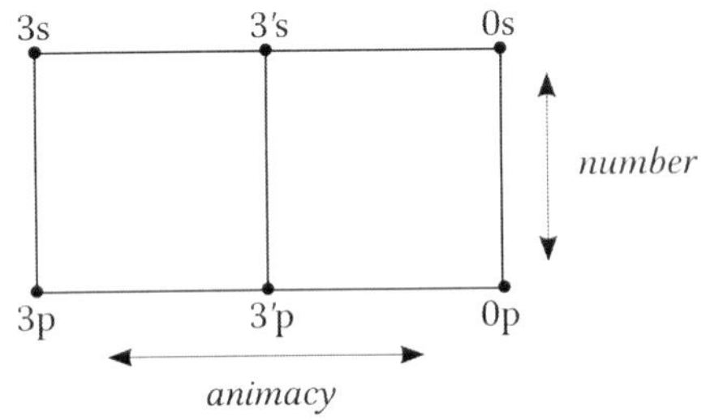

The two-dimensional analysis is widely held, as indicated by the following quotes (emphasis ours). Goddard and Bragdon (1988:493) describe obviation in Massachusett as "a syntactic category marked on ANIMATE NOUNS that can roughly be described as a SECONDARY ANIMATE THIRD PERSON." Costa (2003:215) states that obviation in Miami-Illinois applies "if there are two non-coreferential ANIMATE THIRD-PERSON participants in a clause." Frantz (2009:13) notes for Blackfoot that "when two or more nouns of ANIMATE GENDER occur in the same sentence, only one . . . can be [proximate]."

The two-dimensional analysis does not work for the entire family, however, because some Cree and Ojibwe dialects have developed INANIMATE obviative noun inflection. This is illustrated by the Innu examples in (2) (Clarke 1982:30). In (2b), where the subject is an animate third person, the inanimate object *ûsh* 'boat' carries the obviative suffix *-inu*.[2]

(2) a. ni-mishken ûsh (1—0)
1-find.TI boat.0SG
'I find the boat.'

b. mishkam ût-**inu** (3—**0′**)
find.TI.3 boat-**0′**SG
'S/he finds the boat.'

In addition to Innu, this pattern is also attested in Moose Cree (Ellis 1971), East Cree (Junker 2000–2014), and Oji-Cree (Rogers 1964; Todd 1971). In such languages we must recognize a THREE-DIMENSIONAL system of nominal contrasts in which obviation cross-classifies with both number and animacy rather than being part of the animacy dimension, as illustrated in (3).

(3) Three-dimensional system: Obviation cross-classifies with number, animacy

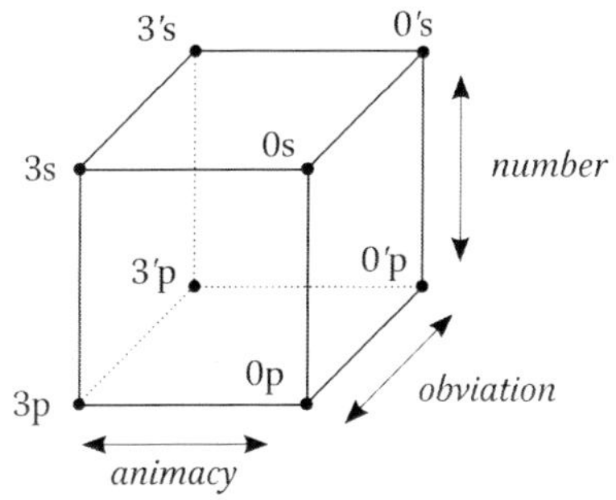

Based on noun inflection alone, we might conclude that the three-dimensional system is an innovation limited to certain Cree and Ojibwe dialects. However, this cannot be the case: although inanimate obviative noun inflection is an innovation, inanimate obviative verb agreement is widely attested across the family. This is illustrated by the Plains Cree examples in (4) (Joseph 1980:168). In (4b), where the subject is an animate third person, the inanimate object *cîmân* 'canoe' does not inflect for obviation, but the conjunct-order II verb that agrees with it does.

(4) a. ni-wâpahten cîmân ê-misâ-k (1—0)
1-see.TI canoe PVB-big-3SG
'I see a canoe which is big.'

b. okimâw wâpahtam cîmân ê-misâ-**yi**-k (3—**0′**)
chief see.TI canoe PVB-big-**OBV**-3SG
'The chief sees a canoe which is big.'

The occurrence of inanimate obviative verb agreement can be taken to indicate that in the relevant contexts inanimate nouns are covertly obviative despite the total absence of obviative noun inflection. The idea of a covert obviation contrast on inanimate nouns is not new. Hockett (1966:60–62) considers the proximate-obviative contrast in Potawatomi to apply to inanimates but states that it "is not shown" in the inflection of inanimate nouns. For Plains Cree, Wolfart (1973:29) observes that "while . . . there is no inflectional distinction for obviation in inanimate nouns, this category is nevertheless present as shown by concord with verb forms." For Ojibwe, Rhodes (1976) states that "the obviation of inanimates is left unmarked" (p. 199) but "by associating a relative clause with an inanimate noun we can see where it is obviated" (p. 203). Drapeau (2014:337) makes the same observation for Innu. All of the above languages, then, must underlyingly have the three-dimensional system in (3).

As for the distribution of the three-dimensional system throughout the family, inanimate obviative verb agreement is widely attested, occurring in Cree (Wolfart 1973), Ojibwe (Rhodes 1976), Meskwaki (Goddard 1994), Cheyenne (Goddard 2000), and early records of Delaware (Goddard 1979) and Arapaho (Cowell et al. 2014);[3] it has also been reconstructed for Proto-Algonquian (Bloomfield 1946:94; Pentland 1996:349; Goddard 2000:98). The three-dimensional system is thus not an innovation. Rather, the innovation is the two-dimensional system, which may exist in languages that lack evidence for an inanimate obviative contrast in either noun inflection or verb inflection, such as Shawnee, Miami-Illinois, Menominee, and most Eastern languages.[4]

Recognizing a three-dimensional system forces us to acknowledge a deep syncretism in the nominal inflection of many of the languages. Except in the Cree and Ojibwe dialects that have developed inanimate obviative noun inflection, the obviation contrast is robustly neutralized in the inflection of inanimate nouns. The result is the paradigm in Table 1, with the cells outlined in bold indicating the syncretism.

TABLE 1. Obviation Syncretism (all languages except some Cree and Ojibwe dialects)

	ANIMATE		INANIMATE	
	PROX	OBV	PROX	OBV
SG	3SG	3′SG	0(′)SG	
PL	3PL	3′PL	0(′)PL	

In order to know whether a syncretism can inform us about the nature of nominal features, we must first distinguish between accidental and nonaccidental syncretisms. Accidental syncretisms result from phonological processes and hence provide no deep lessons for grammar. Nonaccidental syncretisms are properties of the morphological system rather than phonological artifacts. In what follows we apply Caha's (2009) diagnostics for accidental syncretisms to the inanimate obviation syncretism. The unanimous result is that the syncretism is nonaccidental.

The first diagnostic is that accidental syncretisms are confined to a single paradigm while nonaccidental syncretisms occur across all paradigms for a given category. As illustrated in (5), the obviation syncretism occurs across various inanimate stem types in Plains Cree, suggesting that the syncretism is nonaccidental.

(5)	C-stems	*maskisin*	'shoe'	(0SG and 0′SG)
	Cw-stems	*pihko*	'ashes'	(0SG and 0′SG)
	Vy-stems	*askiy*	'land'	(0SG and 0′SG)
	Vw-stems	*meskanaw*	'road'	(0SG and 0′SG)

The second diagnostic is that accidental syncretisms are limited to a single exponent while nonaccidental syncretisms are repeated across multiple exponents. The obviation syncretism most obviously affects the nominal peripheral suffix (PA **-i* 0SG and 0′SG, **-ali* 0PL and 0′PL), but in many of the languages it also affects demonstratives that do not use the nominal suffix. This is illustrated by the Plains Cree inanimate demonstratives in (6) (Wolfart 1973:33), which are each syncretic for obviation. This is another indication that the syncretism is nonaccidental.

(6)	*ôma*	'this'	(0SG and 0′SG)
	ôhi	'these'	(0PL and 0′PL)
	anima	'that'	(0SG and 0′SG)
	anihi	'those'	(0PL and 0′PL)

TABLE 2. Obviation Syncretism is Nonaccidental

ACCIDENTAL SYNCRETISM DIAGNOSTICS	OBVIATION SYNCRETISM
Confined to a single paradigm	✗
Limited to a single exponent	✗
Does not target a morphosyntactic class	✗

The third diagnostic is that nonaccidental syncretisms target a morphosyntactic class while accidental syncretisms do not. The obviation syncretism clearly targets a morphosyntactic class, namely inanimate nominals, including nouns, demonstratives, and pronouns. Again, this suggests that the obviation syncretism is nonaccidental. A summary of the three diagnostics is given in Table 2.

We conclude that the obviation syncretism is nonaccidental. It is also perhaps the most deep-rooted of all the nominal syncretisms, so much that its existence often goes unacknowledged (as evidenced by the pervasiveness of the two-dimensional analysis).

Survey of Nominal Syncretisms

All Algonquian languages have at least one syncretism in their nominal inflection, and several syncretisms recur in multiple languages. Establishing the range of variation in syncretisms is important, as a theory of Algonquian nominal features must not rule out any attested system; it should also capture which syncretisms are natural and which are not. To this end, the following section surveys the syncretisms in noun inflection that are attested across the family. The survey is based on a compilation of Algonquian nominal paradigms, which is included as an appendix to this paper; see the appendix for complete data and sources for any of the languages mentioned in the survey.

We begin with syncretisms in which obviation is neutralized. The first syncretism of this type was discussed above: obviation is neutralized in the inflection of inanimate nominals. This syncretism is attested in Proto-Algonquian, Meskwaki, Kickapoo, most Ojibwe dialects, Plains Cree, Delaware, Cheyenne, and Blackfoot.[5]

A second obviation syncretism occurs in Blackfoot and in some animate stem classes in Mi'gmaq. In this pattern, obviation is neutralized not only on inanimate nominals but on animate plural ones as well, as illustrated in Table 3.[6]

TABLE 3. a. Blackfoot Animates

	ANIMATE	
	PROX	OBV
SG	*-wa*	*-yi*
PL	*-iksi*	

b. Some Mi'gmaq Animates

	ANIMATE	
	PROX	OBV
SG	-Ø	*-l*
PL	*-k*	

TABLE 4. Innu Inanimates

	INANIMATE	
	PROX	OBV
SG	-Ø	*-inu*
PL	*-a*	

Illustrative examples from Blackfoot are given in (7); the same plural inflection appears on the object regardless of whether the subject is first or third person.

(7) a. Nitsikáístsimmayi omiksi aakíí**ks**. (1—3p)
nit-ik-a-istsimm-a-yi om-iksi aakii-**iksi**
1-INTNS-IMPF-respect.TA -DIR-PL DEM-PL woman-**PL**
'I respect those women.'

b. Anna Anna iikáístsimmiiwa omiksi aakíí**ks**. (3—3'p)
ann-wa Anna iik-a-istsimm-yii-wa om-iksi aakii-**iksi**
DEM-PROX Anna INTNS-IMPF-respect.TA-3:4-PROX DEM-PL woman-**PL**
'Anna respects those women.'

A third obviation syncretism occurs in Moose Cree, East Cree, Innu, and Oji-Cree. These are the dialects that have developed inanimate obviative noun inflection. However, the obviation contrast is marked only on inanimate singular nouns; obviation is neutralized on inanimate plural nouns, as in the Innu forms in Table 4.

The Innu sentences in (8), from Drapeau (2014:38), illustrate this syncretism. While the 0SG and 0'SG forms of the noun *min* 'fruit' are distinguished by the obviative suffix *-inu*, the 0PL and 0'PL forms are both marked by the same plural suffix *-a*.

TABLE 5. Menominee Animates

	ANIMATE	
	PROX	OBV
SG	-Ø	*-an*
PL	*-ak*	

(8) 1–0SG *nimitshin min* 'I eat a fruit.'
3–0′SG *mitshu minnu* 'S/he eats a fruit.'
1–0PL *nimitshin mina* 'I eat fruits.'
3–0′PL *mitshu mina* 'S/he eats fruits.'

To this point, we have considered three different syncretisms in which obviation is neutralized. We turn now to a syncretism that neutralizes number. In Menominee, Ojibwe, Cree, Delaware, Massachusett, and Cheyenne, number is neutralized in the inflection of animate obviative nominals, as illustrated for Menominee in Table 5.

The number syncretism is nonaccidental. It occurs across multiple exponents (i.e., on both noun and demonstrative inflection) and multiple paradigms (i.e., nominal inflection, independent and conjunct verb agreement). The syncretism could have arisen from regular sound change in Cree, but not in the other languages (Bloomfield 1946:94). The question, then, is why this number syncretism is such a common innovation. It is worth noting that, as was the case for the obviation syncretism, verb agreement can occasionally provide evidence that animate obviatives continue to be subject to a covert number contrast. This is the case in the East Cree conjunct dubitative, which, as shown in (9), uses the plural marker *-waa* to distinguish 3′SG and 3′PL (Junker and MacKenzie 2011–2014).

(9) a. 3SG nepaa-**k**-we
sleep-3-DUB
'if s/he is sleeping'

b. 3PL nepaa-**waa**-**k**-wen-**ich**
sleep-**PL**-**3**-DUB-**3PL**
'if they are sleeping'

c. 3′SG nepaa-**yi-k**-wen-**h**
sleep-**OBV-3**-DUB-**3′**
'if s/he [obv] is sleeping'

d. 3′PL nepaa-**yi-waa-k**-wen-**h**
sleep-**OBV-PL-3**-DUB-**3′**
'if they [obv] are sleeping'

Because the number contrast emerges in verb agreement, we cannot say that animate obviatives are inherently numberless. Instead, the absence of a number contrast in the inflection of animate obviative nominals is simply another syncretism. We have thus observed two different syncretisms for animate nouns: the Blackfoot-type pattern in Table 3, in which obviation is neutralized on animate plural nouns, and the Menominee-type pattern in Table 5, in which number is neutralized on animate obviative nouns. The latter pattern is much more widespread.

We now turn to syncretisms that neutralize animacy. The first pattern is one in which animacy is neutralized in the inflection of proximate singular nouns. Put more concretely, this is the common pattern in which 3SG and 0SG are both -Ø. This occurs in Menominee, Ojibwe, Cree, Mi'gmaq, Maliseet-Passamaquoddy, Penobscot, Delaware, Massachusett, and Cheyenne, and is illustrated by the Oji-Cree paradigm in Table 6.

Unlike the obviation and number syncretisms discussed above, this syncretism is clearly accidental, arising from deletion of final short vowels (*-*a* 3SG, *-*i* 0SG). As such, it does not affect multiple exponents: although the 3SG and 0SG peripheral suffixes merge, the 3SG and 0SG demonstratives typically remain distinct, as in the Oji-Cree forms in (10) (Todd 1971).

TABLE 6. Oji-Cree

<table>
<tr><th></th><th colspan="2">ANIMATE</th><th colspan="2">INANIMATE</th></tr>
<tr><th></th><th>PROX</th><th>OBV</th><th>PROX</th><th>OBV</th></tr>
<tr><td>SG</td><td>-Ø</td><td rowspan="2">-an</td><td>-Ø</td><td>-iniw</td></tr>
<tr><td>PL</td><td>-ak</td><td colspan="2">-an</td></tr>
</table>

TABLE 7. Blackfoot

	ANIMATE		INANIMATE	
	PROX	OBV	PROX	OBV
SG	*-wa*	*-yi*		
PL	*-iksi*		*-istsi*	

(10)

	3SG	0SG
near	wahawe	ohowe
distant	ahawe	ihiwe

Blackfoot also has an animacy syncretism, but in this case, the same suffix *-yi* is used for animate obviative singular as well as inanimate (proximate and obviative) singular. This is illustrated in Table 7 and exemplified in (11) below.

(11) a. Omi sááhkomaapiyi ííksspitaayináyi.
om-yi saahkomaapi-yi iik-sspitaa-yini-ayi
DEM-OBV boy-OBV INTNS-be.tall.AI-OBV-3SG.PRN
'That boy (obv) is tall.'

b. Omi náápioyisi ííksspiiwa.
om-yi naapioyis-yi iik-sspii-wa
DEM-INAN house-INAN INTNS-be.tall.II-3
'That house is tall.'

Like the other animacy syncretism, Blackfoot's animacy syncretism appears to be accidental. It is confined to the nominal paradigm only, is limited to a single exponent, and does not target a morphosyntactic class. In general, then, there is no evidence for nonaccidental animacy syncretisms in Algonquian.

The two final syncretism patterns that we discuss are those that cross-cut nominal categories. First, in the inflection of Proto-Algonquian and most Central and Eastern languages (but not Miami-Illinois and Massachusett), inanimate plural and animate obviative singular forms are syncretic, as illustrated for Proto-Algonquian in Table 8.

This syncretism is clearly nonaccidental, since, as Wolfart (1973:14) has observed, it occurs across multiple exponents. In Plains Cree, for example, the 3′/0PL

TABLE 8. Proto-Algonquian

	ANIMATE		INANIMATE	
	PROX	OBV	PROX	OBV
SG	**-a*	**-ali*	**-i*	
PL	*-aki*	**-ahi*	**-ali*	

TABLE 9. Miami-Illinois

	ANIMATE		INANIMATE	
	PROX	OBV	PROX	OBV
SG	*-a*	*-ali*	*-i*	
PL	*-aki*	*-ahi*	*-a*	

syncretism affects the nominal peripheral suffix *-a(h)* (3′/0PL), the demonstrative *ôhi* 'this' (3′/0PL), and the question word *tâniwêhâ* 'where is' (3′/0PL). Unlike other nonaccidental syncretisms in Algonquian, however, the 3′SG/0PL syncretism does not target a coherent morphosyntactic class and does not involve adjacent cells in the paradigm. In the typological literature, this is referred to as a "polarity syncretism" (Baerman et al. 2005), and nonaccidental examples of these syncretisms are said to be rare (Baerman et al. 2005:105–107).

What are the implications of this pervasive pattern of syncretism? One possible analysis, proposed by Piriyawiboon (2007) for Ojibwe, is that 3′SG and 0PL are in fact the same category: a personless nominal with indeterminate number. A problem for this analysis is that the 3′SG/0PL syncretism, although pervasive, is not universal: it is not found in Miami-Illinois, Massachusett, or the Plains languages. Any analysis that completely erases the 0PL/3′SG distinction will not be applicable to these languages. Since the function of obviation in Miami-Illinois appears to be quite parallel to that in Ojibwe, it seems undesirable to posit such a fundamental difference between the two languages. Moreover, despite their inflectional syncretism, 3′SG and 0PL nouns co-occur with different verb classes (AI and II, respectively), which clearly rules out an analysis in which they are grammatically identical.[7] The 3′SG/0PL syncretism thus remains unexplained.

Interestingly, a different pattern of polarity syncretism is found in Miami-Illinois. In this language, the 0PL suffix changed from the PA pattern (syncretic with

OBVIATIVE singular *-ali*) to being syncretic with PROXIMATE singular *-a*, as shown in Table 9.

The fact that Miami-Illinois retains obviative singular *-ali* from PA indicates that shift of the inanimate plural suffix from **-ali* to *-a* cannot be due to regular sound change. Rather, the system seems to have switched from one polarity syncretism to another. The reason for this change remains unexplained.

Generalizations

Having surveyed the range of syncretisms across Algonquian, we now point to some generalizations. In particular, we saw that nonaccidental syncretisms involving neutralization of obviation and number contrasts are common, but those involving neutralization of animacy contrasts are unattested. In the inanimate subparadigm, obviation syncretisms are widely attested, and in the animate subparadigm, there are two different patterns: one in which obviation is neutralized (with plural nouns in Blackfoot, for example) and one in which number is neutralized (with obviative nouns in Menominee, for example). We also saw two types of polarity syncretisms: the widely attested pattern in which inanimate plural is syncretic with animate obviative singular and the Miami-Illinois innovation in which inanimate plural is syncretic with animate proximate singular. In short, while syncretisms are pervasive across Algonquian nominal paradigms, the range of variation is constrained. This provides a valuable test for any potential analytical framework for Algonquian nominal features: only these syncretisms should follow naturally, and only the attested variation should follow naturally.

As we look toward developing an analysis of Algonquian nominal features, we note that interactions between features can be taken to reveal dependency relations among the features (Aihkenvald and Dixon 1998; Aalberse and Don 2011; Baerman et al. 2005). Our survey of syncretisms sheds light on these interactions in Algonquian. The nonaccidental syncretisms that we have observed are consistent with respect to which features can condition the neutralization of which other features. The pattern, summarized in Table 10, is as follows: the neutralization of obviation can be conditioned by either number or animacy; the neutralization of number can be conditioned by obviation; and the neutralization of animacy does not occur at all.

The pattern in Table 10 suggests the dependency relation in (12).

TABLE 10. Neutralization Patterns in Nonaccidental Syncretisms

SYNCRETISM	CONTEXT FOR NEUTRALIZATION
obviation	number, animacy
number	obviation
animacy	— (all accidental)

(12) Obviation, Number >> Animacy

Moreover, in terms of pan-Algonquian variation, we have observed that in some languages (Menominee, Ojibwe, Cree, Delaware, Massachusett, Cheyenne), number is neutralized in the context of obviation, suggesting a dependency relation like that in (13a), whereas in other languages (Blackfoot, Mi'gmaq), obviation is neutralized in the context of number, suggesting a dependency relation like that in (13b).

(13) a. Number >> Obviation >> Animacy

b. Obviation >> Number >> Animacy

Conclusion

This pan-Algonquian survey of syncretisms in nominal inflection has enabled us to draw several generalizations about the range of possible and impossible patterns and has given us a window on the dependency relations that hold between nominal features. These results, we suggest, can help to guide the way toward a deeper analysis of nominal features in Algonquian.

Appendices: Survey of Nominal Paradigms

The following paradigms show the forms of the nominal peripheral suffix in each language. The paradigms are presented in a regularized orthography, with č, š for alveopalatals, ʔ for glottal stop, and ə for schwa.

APPENDIX 1. Proto-Algonquian (Bloomfield 1946)

<table>
<tr><th></th><th>3</th><th>3′</th><th>0</th><th>0′</th></tr>
<tr><td>SG</td><td>-a</td><td>-ali</td><td colspan="2">-i</td></tr>
<tr><td>PL</td><td>-aki</td><td>-ahi</td><td colspan="2">-ali</td></tr>
</table>

APPENDIX 2. Central Languages

<table>
<tr><th>LANGUAGE</th><th></th><th>3</th><th>3′</th><th>0</th><th>0′</th></tr>
<tr><td rowspan="2">Shawnee (Andrews 1994)</td><td>SG</td><td>-a</td><td>-ali</td><td colspan="2">-i</td></tr>
<tr><td>PL</td><td>-aki</td><td>-hi</td><td colspan="2">-ali</td></tr>
<tr><td rowspan="2">Miami-Illinois (Costa 2003)</td><td>SG</td><td>-a</td><td>-ali</td><td colspan="2">-i</td></tr>
<tr><td>PL</td><td>-aki</td><td>-ahi</td><td colspan="2">-a</td></tr>
<tr><td rowspan="2">Meskwaki, Kickapoo (Goddard 1994; Voorhis 1967)</td><td>SG</td><td>-a</td><td>-ani</td><td colspan="2">-i</td></tr>
<tr><td>PL</td><td>-aki</td><td>-ahi</td><td colspan="2">-ani</td></tr>
<tr><td rowspan="2">Menominee (Bloomfield 1962)</td><td>SG</td><td>-Ø</td><td rowspan="2">-an</td><td colspan="2">-Ø</td></tr>
<tr><td>PL</td><td>-ak</td><td colspan="2">-an</td></tr>
<tr><td rowspan="2">Nishnaabemwin (Valentine 2001)</td><td>SG</td><td>-Ø</td><td rowspan="2">-an</td><td colspan="2">-Ø</td></tr>
<tr><td>PL</td><td>-ag</td><td colspan="2">-an</td></tr>
<tr><td rowspan="2">Oji-Cree, Deer Lake[1] (Todd 1971)</td><td>SG</td><td>-Ø</td><td rowspan="2">-an</td><td>-Ø</td><td>-iniw</td></tr>
<tr><td>PL</td><td>-ak</td><td colspan="2">-an</td></tr>
<tr><td rowspan="2">Oji-Cree, Round Lake (Rogers 1964)</td><td>SG</td><td>-Ø</td><td>-an</td><td>-Ø</td><td>-ini</td></tr>
<tr><td>PL</td><td>-ak</td><td>-a</td><td>-an</td><td>-an/-ini</td></tr>
<tr><td rowspan="2">Potawatomi (Hockett 1966)</td><td>SG</td><td>-Ø</td><td rowspan="2">-ən</td><td colspan="2">-Ø</td></tr>
<tr><td>PL</td><td>-ək</td><td colspan="2">-ən</td></tr>
<tr><td rowspan="2">Plains Cree (Wolfart 1973, morphophonemic)</td><td>SG</td><td>-a</td><td rowspan="2">-ah</td><td colspan="2">-i</td></tr>
<tr><td>PL</td><td>-ak</td><td colspan="2">-ah</td></tr>
<tr><td rowspan="2">Plains Cree (Okimāsis 2004, phonemic)</td><td>SG</td><td>-Ø</td><td rowspan="2">-a</td><td colspan="2">-Ø</td></tr>
<tr><td>PL</td><td>-ak</td><td colspan="2">-a</td></tr>
<tr><td rowspan="2">Moose Cree (Ellis 1971)</td><td>SG</td><td>-Ø</td><td rowspan="2">-a(h)</td><td>-Ø</td><td>-iliw</td></tr>
<tr><td>PL</td><td>-ak</td><td colspan="2">-a(h)</td></tr>
<tr><td rowspan="2">Southern East Cree (Junker 2000–14)</td><td>SG</td><td>-Ø</td><td rowspan="2">-h</td><td>-Ø</td><td>-iyuu</td></tr>
<tr><td>PL</td><td>-ač</td><td colspan="2">-h</td></tr>
<tr><td rowspan="2">Innu (Drapeau 2014)</td><td>SG</td><td>-Ø</td><td rowspan="2">-a</td><td>-Ø</td><td>-iǹu</td></tr>
<tr><td>PL</td><td>-at</td><td colspan="2">-a</td></tr>
</table>

1. Vestiges of PA 3s *-*a* and 0s *-*i* are found on monosyllabic stems in Ojibwe and Oji-Cree, but the number of such stems is small and there are also animate nouns that end in -*i* (e.g., *inini* 'man') (Valentine 2001:178). Synchronically, we feel that there is no justification for positing an underlying 3s -*a* and 0s -*i* on all Ojibwe nouns. We have thus amended the paradigms from Oji-Cree to show the 3s and 0s suffixes as -Ø in place of the -*a* and -*i* given by the original authors.

APPENDIX 3. Eastern Languages

<table>
<tr><th>LANGUAGE</th><th></th><th>3</th><th>3′</th><th>0</th><th>0′</th></tr>
<tr><td rowspan="2">Maliseet-Passamaquoddy (Francis and Leavitt 2008)</td><td>SG</td><td>-Ø</td><td>-ol</td><td colspan="2">-Ø</td></tr>
<tr><td>PL</td><td>-ok</td><td>-Ø[1]</td><td colspan="2">-ol</td></tr>
<tr><td rowspan="2">Penobscot (Voorhis 1979)</td><td>SG</td><td>-Ø</td><td>-al</td><td colspan="2">-Ø</td></tr>
<tr><td>PL</td><td>-ak</td><td>-a</td><td colspan="2">-al</td></tr>
<tr><td rowspan="2">Delaware (Goddard 1979)</td><td>SG</td><td>-Ø</td><td rowspan="2">-al</td><td colspan="2">-Ø</td></tr>
<tr><td>PL</td><td>-ak</td><td colspan="2">-al</td></tr>
<tr><td rowspan="2">Massachusett (Goddard and Bragdon 1988)</td><td>SG</td><td>-Ø</td><td rowspan="2">-ah</td><td colspan="2">-Ø</td></tr>
<tr><td>PL</td><td>-ak</td><td colspan="2">-aš</td></tr>
<tr><td rowspan="2">Mi'gmaq (Proulx 1978)</td><td>SG</td><td>-Ø</td><td>-l</td><td colspan="2">-Ø</td></tr>
<tr><td>PL</td><td>-k</td><td>-Ø[2]</td><td colspan="2">-l</td></tr>
<tr><td rowspan="2">Mi'gmaq (some stem types) (Proulx 1978)</td><td>SG</td><td>-Ø</td><td>-l</td><td colspan="2">-Ø</td></tr>
<tr><td>PL</td><td colspan="2">-k</td><td colspan="2">-l</td></tr>
<tr><td rowspan="2">Listuguj Mi'gmaq (Manyakina 2012)</td><td>SG</td><td>-Ø</td><td>-l</td><td colspan="2">-Ø</td></tr>
<tr><td>PL</td><td colspan="2">-g</td><td colspan="2">-l</td></tr>
</table>

1. The Maliseet-Passamaquoddy 3′p suffix -Ø is distinguished from the 3s/0s suffix -Ø by morphophonemic effects.
2. The Mi'gmaq 3′p suffix -Ø is distinguished from the 3s/0s suffix -Ø by morphophonemic effects.

APPENDIX 4. Plains Languages

<table>
<tr><th>LANGUAGE</th><th></th><th>3</th><th>3′</th><th>0</th><th>0′</th></tr>
<tr><td rowspan="2">Blackfoot (Frantz 2009; Bliss 2013)</td><td>SG</td><td>-wa</td><td colspan="3">-yi</td></tr>
<tr><td>PL</td><td colspan="2">-iksi</td><td colspan="2">-istsi</td></tr>
<tr><td rowspan="2">Cheyenne (Goddard 2000)</td><td>SG</td><td>-e</td><td rowspan="2">-o</td><td colspan="2">-e</td></tr>
<tr><td>PL</td><td>-o</td><td colspan="2">-ote</td></tr>
<tr><td rowspan="2">Arapaho (Cowell and Moss 2008)</td><td>SG</td><td>-Ø</td><td>-Ø[1]</td><td colspan="2">(-i)[2]</td></tr>
<tr><td>PL</td><td>-oʔ</td><td>-o</td><td colspan="2">-o</td></tr>
</table>

1. A stem-final consonant is retained after 3′s -Ø but not after 3s -Ø.
2. Inanimate singular -i is not pronounced but has morphophonemic effects.

NOTES

1. We are grateful to David Pentland, Conor Quinn, Sonja Thoma, Martina Wiltschko, the audience at the Forty-Sixth Algonquian Conference, and two anonymous reviewers for helpful discussion and suggestions. This work was supported by a SSHRC postdoctoral fellowship (#756-2013-0189) awarded to the first author.
2. Abbreviations are as follows: 0 = inanimate, 1, 2, 3 = first, second, third person, DEM = demonstrative, DIR = direct, DUB = dubitative, IMPF = imperfective, INAN = inanimate, INTNS = intensifier, PL = plural, PRN = pronoun, PROX = proximate, PVB = preverb, OBV = obviative, SG = singular, TI = transitive inanimate.
3. We thank an anonymous reviewer for pointing out the earlier Arapaho data.
4. It could in fact be the case that inanimate obviative verb agreement may have existed in some of these languages as well, with the relevant verb forms never having been documented due to their infrequent occurrence (David Pentland, personal communication, 2014).
5. Blackfoot also neutralizes animate obviative singular with inanimate. We return to this below.
6. An anonymous reviewer indicates that this pattern occurs for most noun stems in Gros Ventre as well.
7. We thank Ives Goddard (personal communication, 2014) for pointing this out.

REFERENCES

Aalberse, Suzanne, and Jan Don. 2011. Person and number syncretisms in Dutch. *Morphology* 21:327–350.

Aihkenvald, Alexandra Y., and Robert M. W. Dixon. 1998. Dependencies between grammatical systems. *Language* 74:56–80.

Andrews, Kenneth. 1994. Shawnee grammar. PhD thesis, University of South Carolina.

Baerman, Matthew, Dunstan Brown, and Greville G. Corbett. 2005. *The syntax-morphology interface: A study of syncretism.* Cambridge: Cambridge University Press.

Bliss, Heather. 2013. The Blackfoot configurationality conspiracy: Parallels and differences in clausal and nominal structures. PhD diss., University of British Columbia.

Bloomfield, Leonard. 1946. Algonquian. In *Linguistic structures of Native America*, ed. Harry Hoijer et al., 85–129. New York: Viking Fund Publications in Anthropology 6.

———. 1962. *The Menomini language*, ed. Charles F. Hockett. New Haven, CT: Yale University Press.

Caha, Pavel. 2009. The nanosyntax of case. PhD thesis, University of Tromsø.

Clarke, Sandra. 1982. *North-West River (Sheshâtshît) Montagnais: A grammatical sketch*. Ottawa, ON: National Museum of Man Mercury Series, Canadian Ethnology Service Paper 80.

Costa, David J. 2003. *The Miami-Illinois language*. Lincoln: University of Nebraska Press.

Cowell, Andrew, and Alonzo Moss Sr. 2008. *The Arapaho language*. Boulder: University Press of Colorado.

Cowell, Andrew, Alonzo Moss Sr., and William J. C'Hair. 2014. *Arapaho stories, songs, and prayers: A bilingual anthology*. Norman: University of Oklahoma Press.

Drapeau, Lynn. 2014. *Grammaire de la langue innue*. Montreal: Presses de l'Université du Québec.

Ellis, C. Douglas. 1971. Cree verb paradigms. *International Journal of American Linguistics* 37:76–95.

Francis, David A., and Robert M. Leavitt. 2008. *Peskotomuhkati Wolastoqewi Latuwewakon: A Passamaquoddy-Maliseet dictionary*. Orono: University of Maine Press; Fredericton, NB: Goose Lane Editions.

Frantz, Donald G. 2009. *Blackfoot grammar*. 2nd ed. Toronto: University of Toronto Press.

Goddard, Ives. 1979. *Delaware verbal morphology: a descriptive and comparative study*. New York: Garland.

———. 1994. *Leonard Bloomfield's Fox lexicon: Critical edition*. Algonquian and Iroquoian Linguistics Memoir 12. Winnipeg.

———. 2000. The historical origins of Cheyenne inflections. In *Papers of the Thirty-First Algonquian Conference*, ed. John D. Nichols, 77–129. Winnipeg: University of Manitoba.

Goddard, Ives, and Kathleen J. Bragdon. 1988. *Native writings in Massachusett*. American Philosophical Society Memoirs 185. Philadelphia.

Hockett, Charles F. 1966. What Algonquian is really like. *International Journal of American Linguistics* 32:59–73.

Jakobson, Roman. 1962. Beitrag zur allgemeinen Kasuslehre: Gesamtbedeutungen der russischen Kasus. In *Selected writings*, Vol. 2, 23–71. The Hague: Mouton.

Joseph, Brian. 1980. Locatives and obviation in Cree. *International Journal of American Linguistics* 46:168–169.

Junker, Marie-Odile, ed. 2000–2014. *The interactive East Cree reference grammar*. http://www.eastcree.org/cree/en/grammar.

Junker, Marie-Odile, and Marguerite MacKenzie. 2011–2014. *East Cree (Southern Dialect) verb conjugation*. 3rd ed. http://verbs.eastcree.org.

Manyakina, Yuliya. 2012. An analysis of obviation in Mi'gmaq. BA Honours thesis, Concordia University.

Okimāsis, Jean. 2004. *Cree: Language of the plains*. Regina, SK: Canadian Plains Research Centre.

Pentland, David H. 1996. Verbs of precipitation in Algonquian. In *nikotwâsik iskwâhtêm, pâskihtêpayih! Studies in honour of H. C. Wolfart*, ed. John D. Nichols and Arden C. Ogg, 338–353. Winnipeg: Algonquian and Iroquoian Linguistics.

Piriyawiboon, Nattaya. 2007. Algonquian obviation reanalysis. In *Proceedings of the 2007 annual conference of the Canadian Linguistic Association*, ed. by Milica Radišić. Saskatoon: University of Saskatchewan.

Proulx, Paul. 1978. Micmac inflection. PhD thesis, Cornell University.

Rhodes, Richard A. 1976. The morphosyntax of the Central Ojibwa verb. PhD thesis, University of Michigan.

Rogers, Jean H. 1964. Survey of Round Lake Ojibwa phonology and morphology. In *Contributions to Anthropology 1961–62*, part 2, 92–154. National Museum of Canada Bulletin 194, Ottawa.

Todd, Evelyn M. 1971. A grammar of the Ojibwe language: The Severn dialect. PhD thesis, University of North Carolina.

Valentine, J. Randolph. 2001. *Nishnaabemwin reference grammar*. Toronto: University of Toronto Press.

Voorhis, Paul. 1967. Kickapoo grammar. PhD thesis, Yale University.

———. 1979. *Grammatical notes on the Penobscot language from Frank Speck's Penobscot Transformer Tales*. Winnipeg: University of Manitoba Anthropology Papers 24.

Wolfart, H. C. 1973. Plains Cree: A grammatical study. *Transactions of the American Philosophical Society*, vol. 63, part 5:1–90.

———. 1978. How many obviatives: Sense and reference in a Cree verb paradigm. In *Linguistic studies of native Canada*, ed. Eung-Do Cook and Jonathan Kaye, 255–272. Vancouver: UBC Press.

Two Idiomatic Verbs of Speaking in North East Cree

Vincent Collette

In this paper, I explore the syntax and semantics of two verbs of speaking in North East Cree, *âyimwâuhîwâw* (II) and *âyimwâuhîkuw* (AI).[1] In spite of extensive lexicographic work done on East Cree in the last decade (Bobbish-Salt 2012), these words, which are very common in certain contexts, went unmentioned. They are attested only in Vaillancourt's *Dictionnaire français-cri* (1992). Drawing insights from Rhodes' analysis of Ojibwe verbs of speaking (1986), I show that these verbs are idiomatic relative to their morphemic composition and semantics. Both are built on a root *âyim-* 'difficult', but they share the meaning 'to speak (about a sensitive matter)'. That being said, the pragmatics of their use provides the link to their semantic past, since they are often used of speaking in formal contexts that entail a certain level of psychological and emotional difficulty.

Overview of Verb Classes in North East Cree

East Cree is an Algonquian language belonging to the Cree-Innu-Naskapi-Atikamekw continuum (often called the Cree-Montagnais-Naskapi continuum). It consists of a chain of dialects expanding from the Rockies to the Atlantic Ocean in

Canada. North East Cree (NEC) is spoken in four communities along the east coast of James Bay and southeast coast of Hudson Bay—that is, Eastmain, Wemindji, Chisasibi, and Whapmagoostui, although the last may be more akin to Western Naskapi spoken in Kawawachikamach. (In this paper I have kept the orthography used by the Cree School Board and the various Cree authors cited here, except for long and tensed vowels such as <aa>, which I have replaced by <â>.)

The NEC verb is inflected for PERSON/NUMBER, OBVIATION, DIRECTION, and ASPECT, which indicates also temporal reference, TENSE, and MOOD, which also marks the source of knowledge in some contexts. Verbal lexemes can occur with up to four distinct stems, which are distinguished in TRANSITIVITY and in agreement with the notional absolutive in ANIMACY (subject of intransitive verbs or objects of transitive ones). This morphosyntactic distinction is realized through the morpheme, or morphemic complex, at the end of the stem, generally called the FINAL in Algonquian linguistics (underlined in the examples below).

(1) a. Transitive Animate (TA)
mâkupit-âw 'S/he ties it (animate) up.'

b. Transitive Inanimate (TI)
mâkupitim-w 'S/he ties it (inanimate) up.'

c. Animate Intransitive (AI)
mâkupisi-w 'She/he/it (animate) is tied up.'

d. Inanimate Intransitive (II)
mâkupitâ-w 'It (inanimate) is tied up.'

However, this simple presentation of lexemic possibilities belies the fact that, due to semantic infelicities, most lexemes lack one or more of the four agreement forms. For instance, the lexeme 'see' has no simple II form since the ability to see is a property of animates.

(2) a. TA: wâpim-âw 'S/he sees him/her/it.'

b. TI: wâpihtim-w 'S/he sees it.'

c. AI: wâpi-w 'S/he sees/can see.'

d. II: ———

To coerce the corresponding II verb 'it sees, has the faculty of seeing' for example, in order to describe this capacity on a robot, the impersonal inanimate subject suffix -L*mikin* is added to the corresponding AI stem *wâpi-* yielding *wâpîmikin-Ø* 'it sees' (II) (L indicates lengthening of the preceding vowel).

The verbs of speaking that are the focus of this paper contain two derivational suffixes that require some discussion. They are the AI/II antipassive *-îwâ* and the so-called AI inverse *-iku*. The derivational antipassive suffix *-îwâ* is added directly on a TA causative stem (*-h*) as in (3c). Its function is to lower the valency of the stem, indicating that an animate subject is doing something to an unspecified object. (In East Cree the short and lax vowel /ɪ/ is phonetically lengthened by a preceding aspirate /h/ and spelled as < î >.)

(3) a. nipâw 'S/he sleeps' (AI)

b. nipâ-h-â-w
sleep-CAUS.TA-3/3'-SG
'S/he puts her/him to sleep' (TA)

c. nipâh-îwâ-w
sleep-ATP.AI/II-3, 0SG
'S/he/it puts one to sleep' (AI/II antipassive)

'Inverse' AI verbs are a small class of derived verbs built with *-iku*, a suffix historically akin to the TA inverse *-ik* (PA <**-ekw*>). These AI verbs are obtained by adding *-iku* directly on a stem (4c) or to a causative TA stem.

(4) a. uchipitim^{w} 'S/he pulls it' (TI)

b. n-uchipit-ik-w
1-pull-TA.INV.1/3-SG
'S/he (3) pulls me (TA)

c. n-uchipit-iku-n
1-pull-AI+O-SG
'I have cramps' (AI+OBJECT)

However, even if the labeling 'AI inverse' could seem justified on historical, morphological, and semantic grounds—since, after all, the grammatical animate subject of *nuchipitikun* is the experiencer of something (i.e., the cramps causing the pain) that is outside his/her control—it is nevertheless problematic because this suffix is a true derivational element. The resulting derived verb is a morphologically intransitive verb with a syntactic object, like *ayâw* 's/he has it' (these are often labeled AI+O(BJECT) or TI2 in the literature). As seen in the next section, a syntax-orientated labeling of this type of derived verbs avoids many potential obstacles to our understanding of the syntax and the semantic framing of the two verbs under study.

Problems in the Morphological Analysis of Some Derived Verbs of Speaking

In this section, I examine the basic verbs of speaking in NEC and address some issues concerning the morphology of two derived verbs of speaking. In NEC the following initials and roots are found in the most common verbs of speaking:

(A) *yî-* 'to say'[2]

AI *yîw*	'S/he says.'
II *yînâniwiw*	'It is said.' (derived II)

(B) *it-* 'to say it to him/her'

TA *itâw*	'S/he says it to him/her.'
AI *itâkiniwiw*	'It is said about him/her.' (derived AI passive)

(C) *ayim-* 'to speak, to talk'

AI *ayimiw*	'S/he speaks.' [jɪmu:]
AI *ayimihâw*	'S/he prays.' (lit. 's/he makes it speak')
TA *ayimihâw*	'S/he talks, speaks to him/her.' [jɪmha:ʊ]

(Di) *âyim-* 'difficult'+*-um* 'to speak about someone' (TA) / *-utim* 'to speak about something' (TI)
TA *âyimumâw* 'S/he talks, speaks about him/her.'
TI *âyimutim*ʷ 'S/he talks, speaks about it.'

The most important difference between these verbs of speaking is that they each activate different "semantic frames." For Johnson and Fillmore (2000:56), frame semantics "characterizes the semantic and syntactic properties of predicating words by relating them to semantic frames . . . which are schematic representations of situations involving various participants, props and other conceptual roles." The COMMERCIAL TRANSACTION FRAME, for instance, implies a buyer, a seller, goods, and money. Put differently, predicate words are like encyclopedic units that trigger a set of obligatory or optional features (or FRAME ELEMENTS) in terms of semantic roles, grammatical arguments and discourse structure. Whether or not these features are realized syntactically or morphologically is a property of the verbal lexeme. In sum, to know a word necessitates the understanding of its semantic frame(s). Let us now turn to the BASIC COMMUNICATION FRAME. It requires a speaker, an addressee, and a topic, or subject matter under discussion. While the semantic frame of *âyimumâw* 's/he talks, speaks about him/her' (TA) obligatorily requires a speaker and a topic, both of which map as animate arguments, marked on the verb, the addressee is optional. On the other hand, the semantic frame of *itâw* 's/he says to him/her' (TA) is different since here both the speaker and the addressee are obligatory (again as arguments they are realized through verbal inflection). However, while being also obligatory, the thing said is realized as a clausal complement. Moreover, the verbs in A and B above can license a quote, and are often used as a lexical means to express the source of knowledge (hearsay), while the verbs in C and D cannot do so. With these important linguistic distinctions in mind, we can now turn to the topic of this paper.

As mentioned earlier, the derived verbs of speaking under study are built on the root *âyim-* 'difficult'. The morphological analysis is as follows:

(Dii) *âyim-* 'difficult' + *-wâ* 'speech'

AI+O *âyim-wâ-u-h-îku-w*

difficult-speech-/u/-CAUSATIVE-AI+O-3SG

'S/he talks (publicly) about something.'

II *âyim-wâ-u-h-îwâ-w*

difficult-speech-/u/-CAUSATIVE-ATP.II-0SG

'It is talked about (publicly).'

As can be seen in (Dii) there is a mismatch between the meaning of these verbs in synchrony and the expected meaning that results from the addition of the individual components. This is a problem of lexical pragmatics that I deal with in the last section of this paper. In what follows, I digress on their morphology and derivational history.

First, the meaning of the initial *âyim-* is 'difficult', as can be found in *âyimin* 'it is difficult' (II). Second, the short vowel /u/ is a postvocalic variant of the causative *-h* as is required, for instance, in *tâchikwâ-w* 's/he yells' (AI); *tâchikwâ-uh-âw* 's/he makes him/her yell' (TA). I have set up the initial form for the historical derivations as *âyimwâuh- 'to speak in a difficult way'. The important point here is that the meaning of the causative suffix *-h* is not palpable synchronically as can be seen with *pîchishkwâ-w* 's/he talks a lot, gossips' (AI) > *pîchishkwâuh*îkuw 's/he gossips about people' (AI+O). Dixon (2012:284–286) notes that in some languages of the world it is quite common for causative markers not to express causation but either an increase in valency (e.g., *wîchi-w* 's/he lives there' (AI) > *wîchih*âw 's/he helps him/her' (TA)) or a more completely affected patient or even a greater effort on the part of the agent. As we will see later, the latter case fits the lexical pragmatics of the derived verbs of speaking under study. Table 1 summarizes the derivational history of the stem under consideration (the asterisk indicates that the form or the meaning is not attested synchronically; I also compare the NEC forms with those of South East Cree [SEC], a neighboring subdialect.)

As shown in Table 1, the meanings of *âyimwâuhîkuw* (AI+O) and *âyimwâuhîwâw* (II) are idiomatic since there is a considerable discrepancy between the expected compositional meanings ('difficult' + 'speech') and the attested synchronic meanings of these two verbs of speaking ('to speak (publicly) about something'). Even though I have included the form *âyimwâ-* 'to afflict by speech' in Table 1, the source for the derived verbs *âyimwâuhîwâw* and *âyimwâuhîkuw* seems to be the morphemic

TABLE 1. Historical Derivation of NEC/SEC Idiomatic Verbs of Speaking

NEC	SEC	GLOSSES
*âyimwâ-	*âyimwe-	*NEC 'to afflict by speech'[1]; SEC 'to sneeze' (AI)[2]
*[âyim-wâ-u-h] difficult-speech-/u/-CAUS	*[âyim-we-u-h] difficult-speech-/u/-CAUS	*'to speak in a difficult way'
[âyimwâuh]-îku- INITIAL-AI+O-	[âyimweuh]-îku- INITIAL-AI+O-	'to speak (publicly) about a given topic' (AI+OBJECT)
[âyimwâuh]-îwâ- INITIAL-ANTIPASSIVE.II-	[âyimweuh]-îwe- INITIAL-ANTIPASSIVE.II-	'to say something about people (in a public venue)'; 'to be spoken of (publicly)' (*AI, II)

1. To the best of my knowledge, this AI verb is not attested in East Cree, but some historical grammars of Cree and Ojibwe have it. For Plains Cree, Lacombe lists *ayimwew* 'Il médit'; *konata ayimwew* 'Il calomnie' (1874:327), as does Watkins: *Ayimwâo* 'He is troublesome in speaking' (1865:197). The oldest mention is in Fabvre (1693:32), *Arim8an* 'Est8rdir le m(on)de de paroles'. *Âyimwâhâw* 's/he speaks about him/her' (TA) is listed by Vaillancourt (1992:295) only.

2. Even though the initials *âyiyimu-* and *âyim-* were retained in NEC, their phonetic similitude seems to be the source of some spelling problems, as seen when comparing *âyiyimuw* 's/he sneezes' (AI) and *âyimuhâw* 's/he makes him, her sneeze' (TA) (Bobbish-Salt et al., 2012). According to Kevin Brousseau (personal communication 2014), the original stem *âyiyimu-* 'to sneeze' was confounded—due to phonetic similarity—with the initial *âyim-* 'difficult' in SEC. This could explain why SEC speakers recognize the NEC derived verbs of speaking but do not often use the equivalents in their subdialect.

complex *âyimwâuh-* 'to speak in a difficult way' and not the shorter form that is less appropriate semantically. My working hypothesis is that the synchronic meaning of these verbs has shifted from a narrow ('to speak in a difficult way') to a more general and attenuated meaning ('to speak about something'), the latter being the translation offered by my consultants. Interestingly, data on the contextual use of these verbs provide the key to an intermediate stage of development ('to speak publicly about something'). In the next section, I analyze the semantic frames of these derived verbs of speaking.

Semantic Frames of âyimwâuhîkuw (AI) and âyimwâuhîwâw (II)

As mentioned earlier, frame semantics encompasses the mapping between grammatical arguments, semantic roles, and discourse structure. Recall that the particularity of the semantic frame of the verbs in set (Di) is that they do not require an addressee, while the speaker and the topic under discussion are verbal arguments expressed morphologically. Despite Vaillancourt's (1992:296) translation of *âyimwâuhîkuw* as 'one talks about him (with an animate object)', the verbs in (Di) as well as *âyimwâuhîkuw* (AI) have a grammatical object that maps directly as the topic of the discussion, a notion defined by Trask (1993:279) as "that element of a sentence which is presented as already existing in the discourse and which the rest of the sentence (the comment) is in some sense 'about'." The syntactic object is either an EXPLICIT TOPIC expressed by an anaphoric inanimate noun phrase (5) or a subordinate clause (9),[3] or an IMPLICIT TOPIC left unexpressed but disambiguated by the discourse context (12). In many cases the discourse topic/object is implicitly referred to with the relative preverb *îshi-* 'thus, in such a way' (6).

(5) Âwik^{w} mâk an aschiy-Ø, iyâyimwâuh-îku-y-ân.
it.is.that COOR DEM.SG land.NI-0SG IC.talk.about.it-AI+O-/y/-1SG
'It is this land that I am talking about.' (RAD-10-2013b-15:10, man, 70's) (VC)

(6) Âkutâ ây, chi-niniskum-iti-nâ-wâw châkwân-h
ok HES 2-thank.TA-1>2-SG-(2)PL thing.NI-0PL

â-îshi-âyimwâuh-îku-y-âk^{w} ûtih.
CPL-thus-talk.about.it-AI+O-/y/-2PL here
'Ok uh, I thank you all for what you have discussed about here (a public meeting).' (GWR-406a-13:15, man, 70s) (VC)

The morphosyntax and semantics of *âyimwâuhîwâw* (II) is more complex since usually AI antipassives in *-iwâ* are derived from TA verbs and require a prototypical animate object (ex. *minihîwâw* 's/he serves drinks (to people)'), while inanimate intransitive antipassives in *-ichâ* are derived from TI verbs and require an inanimate object (ex. *tipihîchâw* 's/he pays (for something)'). However, in NEC many antipassives can be AI and II depending on the gender of the subject. Thus, the AI version of *âyimwâuhîwâw* should normally mean 's/he speaks publicly about people'. My database does not contain any examples of this antipassive verb used as an AI, but only as an II verb meaning roughly 'it says something about people (in a public venue)'. In many cases, speakers have extended it in order to indicate that 'something is spoken of (publicly)' as we will see later.

In terms of frame semantics *âyimwâuhîwâw* necessitates a referential speaker and an inanimate subject mapped directly as the discourse topic that can be explicitly marked or implicitly understood from the context. It does not necessitate an addressee. In (7), for instance, the implicit subject/topic of the two first verbs is the dismantlement of the *Eeyou Istchee Commission in Energy and Sustainable Development*, which was mentioned earlier in the discourse.

(7)	[. . .] âkâ	nâshtiyich	châ-âyimwâuh-îwâ-ch. [. . .]	Châkwân	wâhch
	CJ.NEG	not.at.all	CJ.PROS-talk.about.it-ATP.II-0SG	why	IC.SOURCE

âkâ	châ-âyimwâuh-îwâ-ch?	Û	wîyi	iyâyimwâuh-îku-y-ihk^{w}.
CJ.NEG	CJ.PROS-talk.about.it-ATP.II-0SG	DEM.SG	EMP	IC.talk.about.it-AI+O-/y/-21

'[. . .] It (the Eeyou Istchee Commission) will not be discussed any further. Why isn't it under discussion? That thing (i.e., the issue concerning the land and water) we are referring to.' (RAD-2013b-4:20, 5:17, man, 70s) (VC)

In the next section, I provide examples that show that these verbs can also be used without the grammatical object/topic (AI+O) or subject/topic (II). Now that we have analyzed some of the differences in the mapping between grammatical relations, semantic roles, and the discourse structure of the derived verbs of speaking under study, we can turn to their lexical pragmatics in order to shed some light on the semantic past of these verbs.

The Range of Focus of *âyimwâuhîkuw* (AI) and *âyimwâuhîwâw* (II)

According to Wilson and Carston (2007:1) the field of lexical pragmatics concentrates on the fact that "the meaning of words are frequently pragmatically adjusted and fine-tuned in context, so that their contribution to the proposition expressed is different from their lexically encoded sense." As Rhodes puts it:

> There is an important distinction between the class of referents a given form can label, its lexical semantics, and the class of referents that it is normally used to label, its lexical pragmatics. Put another way, the distinction is between the potential *range of reference* of a form and its more restricted *ranges of focus* within that range of reference. . . . The basic problem in the study of exotic languages is to understand in the meaning of morphologically complex forms the balance between the contribution of the semantics of the component morphemes and the contribution of pragmatics and extension. (1986:8)

In the previous section I have set up the synchronic meaning of *âyimwâuhîkuw* (AI+O) as 's/he speaks (publicly) about something' and *âyimwâuhîwâw* (II) as 'it says something about people (in a public venue)'. The latter usually means 'it is spoken of'. Keeping in mind that for Rhodes (1986:1, footnote 2) the term 'referent' denotes primarily mental representations, the above meanings constitute the range of reference of these two verbs. They are general enough to explain every occurrence of these verbs in my corpus. However, since verbs of speaking often obey very subtle cultural conventions, they may express a specific content that is used almost exclusively in a given context: this constitutes one of the ranges of focus of a word. In this section, I will try show that *âyimwâuhîkuw* (AI+O) and *âyimwâuhîwâw* (II) are both used to refer to informal (general use) or formal (restricted use) speech events.

In order to circumscribe the ranges of focus of these derived verbs of speaking, I will use Dell Hymes' (1974:54–60) classic S.P.E.A.K.I.N.G. model for the analysis of speech in context. According to Fasold's (1990:44) refinement of the model, the 'situation' includes the *setting* (the physical circumstances of a communicative event) and the *scene* (the psychological or cultural setting of a communicative event), while the 'end' comprises the *outcome* (the cultural purpose of an event) and the *goal* (the purpose of the speaker).

First, my corpus indicates that these two verbs of speaking are often used in formal physical *settings* (e.g., community meetings, political assemblies, formal interviews) and in specific *psychological scenes* (e.g., open microphone discussions, question periods of a band meeting). The identification of the scene will prove crucial to my analysis since it encompasses the dimension of formality.

Second, in terms of *goal*, the type of discussions within which these verbs are used is often motivated by issues which imply a higher level of affective or socio-psychological sensitivity (e.g., personal concerns; local, regional, financial or political issues) than casual talk. I have arranged my data in three groups which concord with the psychological scenes (degrees of formality) and goals.

The first range of focus encompasses the general or psychologically neutral use of *âyimwâuhîkuw* 's/he talks (publicly) about something'. The following examples show that it can be used in public meetings but not exclusively, and within a specific psychological scene (8, political speech) or a more casual context like storytelling (9). In terms of goal, the explicit topic/object need not refer to a personal or community issue.

(8)

Mîn	kutik-Ø	an	châkwân-Ø,	Team	Concept	approach
more	other.NI-0SG	DEM.SG	thing.NI-0SG	team	concept	approach

kâ-y-âyimwâuh-îku-t	ây,	Robert.
CJ.REL-y-talk.about.it-AI+O-3SG	HES	Robert

'And there is one more thing, the Team Concept approach which, uh, Robert has mentioned.' (RAD-10-2013i-22:56, man, 40s) (VC)

(9)

Â âyimwâh-îku-t	mâkwâch	kâuschinîchu-wi-t,	an-iyû
CPL talk.about.it-AI+O-3	while	CJ.PERF be.young-AI-3	DEM-0'SG

ninâhkû	kâ	chî	ishi	tut-âkiniwi-yi-ch	châkwâ-yû . . .
different	CJ	PERF	thus	do.it-PASSIVE.AI-OBV-0(')SG	thing.NI-0'SG

'She talked about when she was young and of the different things that were done [. . .]' (Anonymous 1995b:83) (VC)

The verb *âyimwâuhîwâw* (II) can also be used in a general and psychologically neutral sense. In (10) for instance, the topic/subject under discussion does not imply any specific end. It is simply informative.

(10)

[. . .]	ayiyimwâuh-iwâ-ch	iyiyiw	kischihun-Ø	kiya
	IC.talk.about.it-ATP.II-0SG	Cree	knowledge.NI-0SG	and

ka-mayupi-t-wâw	iyiyu-ch
CJ.PART-well.being.AI-3-PL	Cree.NA-3PL

'there will be (public) discussions about traditional (Cree) knowledge and the wellbeing of the Cree people' (Anonymous 1995a:19)

The second range of focus illustrates a more specific use of *âyimwâuhîkuw*. While the setting and the scene are not relevant to understand the range of focus in the following examples, the difference in end (outcome+goal) is crucial since the explicit topic/object clearly refers to sensitive issues, be it personal (11), or of local or regional interest (12–13). A more appropriate English translation of this verb would be 's/he addresses, discusses an issue'.

(11) Ây apishîsh ni-chî âyimwâh-îku-n an an-iyâyiw [. . .]. Nîyân
HES little 1-ABL talk.about.it-AI+O-SG DEM.SG DEM-0'SG us.13

kiyâ, nâshtâ mâkushkâ-ku-y-âhch âwik^{w} û châkwân-Ø,
EMP really put.pressure-AI+O-/y/-13 it.is.that DEM.SG thing.NI-0.SG

âwikun aniyâyiw kâ-îshi âyimwâh-îku-t.
that.which DEM.0'SG CJ.REL-thus talk.about.it-AI+O-3SG
'I can talk about it a little bit. [. . .] As for us, we were worried (it puts pressure on us) by what she talked about.' (GWR-406a-31:33, woman, 70s) (VC)

(12) Chi-chischâyihtâ-nâwâ-chchâ û châkwân-Ø
2-know.it.ti-PL-DUB DEM.SG thing.NI-0SG

kâ-y-âyimwâh-îku-y-âk^{w}.
CJ.REL-y-talk.about-AI+O-/y/-2PL
'You guys (addressing politicians) probably remember the issue you were discussing.' (RAD-10-2013b-5:44, man, 70s) (VC)

(13) Kiyipwâ châshtinâsh châ-wî itâyimi-y-âk^{w} û châkwân-Ø
EMP for.sure CJ.PROS-VOL feel.thus.AI-y-2PL DEM.SG thing.NI-0SG

âshi âyimwâh-îku-y-ân.
IC.thus talk.about.it-AI+O-/y/-1SG
'And for sure you (pl.) will feel in a certain way regarding the issue I am discussing here. [i.e., the undrinkable water flowing in the river]'. (RAD-10-2013f-10:16, man, 70s) (VC)

As expected, *âyimwâuhîwâw* (II) can be also used to indicate that the topic/subject of the discussion is a sensitive issue as indicated by example (14) which is an excerpt taken from a narrative about the frightening presence of a cannibal around a summer campsite. The existence of the cannibal is previously mentioned and constitutes the explicit topic/subject of the conjunct verb *iyâyimwâuhîwâyichâ*.

(14) [. . .] an aka̅ chi-ki mûshihtâ-htâ-nânû utih â ihta-y-ihk^{w}.
DEM.SG CJ.NEG 2-PROS feel.AI-IRR-21 here CPL be.AI-/y/-21

Iyâyimwâuh-îwâ-yi-ch-â kîpwâ.
IC.talk.about.it-ATP.II-OBV-0(')SG-SUBJ EMP
'We never felt it before in our camp, so everyone began to talk about it.'
(Petagumskum 2000:10) (VC)

Finally, in the third range of focus we find the most specific uses of *âyimwâuhîkuw* and *âyimwâuhîwâw*. Examples (15–17) show how Cree politicians employ *âyimwâuhîwâw* to refer to formal communicative events (i.e., in formal discussions or negotiations); in these examples, it is best translated as 'it is formally (and publicly) assessed'.

(15) kutich-Ø châkwân-Ø shâsh âyimwâuh-îwâ-w.
other.NI-0SG thing.NI-0SG already talk.about.it-ATP.II-0SG
'Discussions are under way.' ('Another issue is now being assessed, discussed publicly.' (VC)) (Moses 2005:3)

(16) An mâk châkwân nîshtim châ âyimwâuh-îwâ-ch iskutik
DEM.SG COOR thing.NI-0SG first CJ.PROS talk.about-ATP.II-0SG when

ayimih-îtu-nâniwi-ch âukw wîyi îyiyiw-Ø châ chîpimipiyihtwâ-su-ch
talk-RECIP-INDEF.II-0SG that.is EMP Cree.NA-3SG CJ.PROSconduct-REFL.AI-3PL

aniyû châkwâyiw châ ihtut-ikiniwî-kupinâ kiyâh aniyû
DEM.0'SG thing.NI-0SG CJ.PROS do.it-PASSIVE.II-DUB.PRET and DEM.0'SG

châ wîchih-îku-ch îyiyiu-ch (. . .)
CJ.PROS help-AI+O-3PL Cree.NA-3PL
'The first thing to be dealt with in these discussions is to find a way for the Cree Nation to assume the responsibilities for delivering certain programs and services to the Crees' (Moses 2005:3) '

(17) Châk mâk, chi-chîh tipâskunichâ-nâniw uhchi âh nûtâhtikwâ-niwi-ch
finally COOR 2-PERF bring.to.court.TI-21 source CPL logging-INDEF.II-0SG

kiyâh mâk mîn chîh âyimwâuh-îwâ-ch wâpimâkushtû-sîpî
and COOR again PERF talk.about.it-ATP.II-0SG Whapmagoostui-river

chishchinâch mîn chi-pih pîhtikitâ-nâniw tipâskunichâukimiku-hc.
surely again 2-should bring.it.in.TI2-21 court.NI-LOC

'In the end, we were in court for forestry issues and if Great Whale [a project by the Quebec government to dam Great Whale River in 1986] had been proposed again we would have probably gone back to the court to stop it.' (Moses 2005:5)

As can be seen in (18) NEC speakers have extended the meaning of the two verbs of speaking under study and may now use them to indicate that 's/he is testifying (in court)' (AI+O) or that 'there is a court hearing' (II).

(18) Ây kâ-âti âyimwâh-îku-ch kiyâ James Bay Agreement,
HES CJ.PERF-begin talk.about.it-AI+O-3PL EMP James Bay Agreement,

kâ âti chihchipiyi-ch 71 days âyimwâh-îwâ-t ay, an
CJ.PERF begin start.II-0SG 71 days talk.about.it-ATP.II-0SG, HESDEM.SG

kiyâ hearings [. . .]
EMP hearings

'Euh, when they began testifying for the James Bay Agreement, when the 71 days court hearings began [. . .].' (VC) (RAD-10-2013i-, man, 40s)

Here, the semantic frames for these extended uses are different from the one presented earlier. When the non-basic verbs of speaking, such as in (18), are used to refer to highly formal communicative events, they call for a sub-frame of the communication frame called the FRAME OF EVIDENCE (or STATEMENT), and are similar to the English verbs *claim* and *assert* (Johnson and Fillmore 2000:59–60). More specifically, the semantic frame of *âyimwâuhîkuw* (AI+O) implies a relation between a speaker and a message, or a formally communicated proposition which stands as an illocutionary act. It does imply a referential hearer but the topic (which maps as the subject or the object) is unmarked and left implicit. In its extended sense *âyimwâuhîwâw* (II) is not a genuine verb of speaking but a label for a highly formal speech event implying a given physical/psychological situation and end.

In this section, I have documented the lexical pragmatics of the two idiomatic verbs of speaking under study. The data show that these verbs are mostly used to describe the kind of formal speaking that happens during public consultations or band meetings (second and third ranges of focus), where the level of intellectual difficulty is much higher than during casual conversations in informal settings, although it can also be used as such (first range of focus).

Verbs of Speaking and East Cree Conversational Codes of Ethics

After having analyzed the semantic frames and the lexical pragmatics of these two verbs of speaking under study, I can now return to the difficult question of their idiomaticity. I have shown that in terms of semantic shift, the ranges of focus of these verbs provides solid evidence to my initial claim that we are dealing here with a case of semantic attenuation and widening which can be represented as such: *'to speak in a difficult way' > 'to speak about something publicly' ~ 'to testify' > 'to talk about something'.[4] The question here is what motivates this shift?

As a traditionally small-scale and non-stratified society, the cultural features of East Cree conversation are characterized, on one hand, by a high respect for the personal freedom of the individual to act as s/he sees fit, and on the other hand, by a reticence for open contradiction or personal conflict (Salisbury 1986:30). Darnell has formulated the following conversational principles for Plains Cree, but her principles seem to apply, to a certain extent, to East Cree as well.

> Each individual has the right to his or her opinion and should not contradict directly . . . (Darnell 1991:92, Principle 5)
>
> Because it is so important not to offend other persons by disagreement, it is good to avoid confrontation . . . The individual who is unhappy need not say something that he or she will regret, and the relationship can be repaired when consensus is ideally reached. (Darnell 1991:92, Principle 6)
>
> After someone has spoken, particularly the formal monologic speech of an elder or medicine man, that speaking becomes a text open to exegesis. People will discuss, often disagreeing, the meaning of a message. . . . Public business meetings also set up conditions for exegesis. (Darnell 1991:97, Principle 25)

These conversational codes of ethics put into light the fact that an act of speaking can be potentially harmful to both the speaker and the hearer or audience, and that personal independence, kinship ties and protection of others' face make it difficult to directly challenge someone, or to speak about a conflictual situation that concerns someone present in the scene, and even more so in public situations where spoken words are open to exegesis and scrutiny. These codes of ethics are palpable when one examines the lexical pragmatics of these verbs. I have tried to show that the second and third ranges of focus shed light on the idiomaticity (i.e. non-compositionality) and semantic past of these verbs of speaking precisely because their usage in these specific contexts implicitly calls to mind the aforementioned tension between the need to publicly address some sensitive or psychologically difficult topics (i.e., practical, political or societal matters) and the cultural traits of personal independence and avoidance of conflict.

Since the verbs of speaking under study are used almost exclusively in North East Cree communities[5] which were heavily affected by the partial flooding of their traditional homeland, I speculate that in the sociopolitical context that followed the announcement by Premier Robert Bourassa to build hydroelectric infrastructures in northern Quebec in 1972, the meaning of these verbs of speaking may have started to shift in order to fit new political parameters and needs as well as alien and formal communicative events like band meetings, public debates and court hearings.

Conclusion

The aim of this paper was to describe the semantics, syntax, and the lexical pragmatics of two idiomatic verbs of speaking in North East Cree. I have shown that the meaning of *âyimwâuhîkuw* (AI+O) and *âyimwâuhîwâw* (II) are idiomatic since there is a mismatch between the expected compositional and synchronic meanings of these verbs. The hypothesis was that when the meaning of the morphemic complex *âyimwâuh-* started shifting from 'to speak in a difficult way' to 'to speak publicly about something, to testify' (semantic attenuation) and then to 'to speak about something' (semantic widening), the meaning of both *âyimwâuhîkuw* (AI+O) and *âyimwâuhîwâw* (II) evolved. To verify this hypothesis I analyzed their lexical pragmatics and found that both of these verbs have extended ranges of focus since they are used: a) as general verbs of speaking with a rather neutral sense in terms of situation and end; b) as verbs of speaking with a narrow meaning related to a higher degree of formality (scene) and with personal, political or societal ends pertaining to a given issue; and c) as specific verbs referring to highly formal communicative situations (testimony, court hearings) which entails definite communicative ends. The last two ranges of focus shed light on the important connection between the meaning of the root *âyim-* 'difficult' and the higher level of psychological difficulty implied in formal communicative situations (*-wâ* 'speech)' like political speeches, band meetings, court hearings, etc. I hope that the description and analysis proposed here will prove insightful for a more complete study of the numerous verbs of speaking in East Cree.

NOTES

1. The abbreviations used in this paper are: ABL = abilitative, AI = animate intransitive, ATP = antipassive, CAUS = causative, CJ = conjunct order, COOR = coordinator, CPL = complementizer, DEM = demonstrative, DIR = direct, DUB = dubitative, EMP = emphatic, GWR = Great-Whales-River (Whapmagoostui), HES = hesitation, IC = initial change, II = inanimate intransitive, IMPERS = impersonal inanimate subject, INCL = inclusive, INDEF = inanimate indefinite, INV = inverse, IRR = irrealis, NA = animate noun, NEG = negative, NI = inanimate noun, OBV = obviative, PART = participial, PERF = perfective, PL = plural, PROS = prospective, RAD = recorded radio broadcast, RECIP = reciprocal, REFL = reflexive, REL = relative conjunct clause, SG = singular, SUBJ = subjunctive, TA = transitive animate, TI = transitive inanimate, VC = author's translation, VOL = volition preverb, 1 = first person, 2 = second person, 3 = animate third person, 3' = animate third person obviative, 13 = exclusive plural, 21 = inclusive plural, 0'SG = inanimate obviative singular.
2. The transcription of these verbs is supported by the initial change of the vowel in the conjunct order: *yîw* > *yât* as in *Tân yât?* 'What is s/he saying?'; *Tân yâyin?* 'What are you saying?' Despite the phonetic surface similarity of *ayim-* 'speak' and *âyim-* 'difficult' the form of initial change of the latter is /â/ > /iyâ/ (e.g., *Tân iyâyimwâuhîkuyin* 'What are you talking about?') indicating that the first segment is /a:/ and not /a/. This confirms that we are dealing with two different roots.
3. My sources of data for the documentation of these two verbs of speaking are published children's stories, published political discourses translated from English, and speeches given by politicians and nonpoliticians at local meetings or at the Cree Government Information Sessions held in Val d'Or (Quebec) in October 2013. Some of the speeches, which were broadcast on CBC Northern Quebec, are available at http://new.livestream.com/accounts/5888244/events/2505688.

4. A similar semantic shift can be observed in Romance languages. Classical Latin *causari* 'plead, dispute, bring to court', led to 'debate, argue in order to gain time' (attenuation); the Modern French verb *causer* 'to chat' (widening and attenuation), is a development from the earlier idea of a 'lengthy discussion'. http://www.cnrtl.fr/etymologie/causer.
5. The verbs of speaking under study do have South East Cree counterparts (*âyimweuhîkuw*, *âyimweuhîwew*) but they are seldom used, except by translators.

REFERENCES

Anonymous. 1995a. Minutes of the Eeyou Istchee Commission. Conference held in Chisasibi, April 17–19, 1995.

Anonymous. 1995b. Âti sîkunîkuhch/Signs of Spring (Cree Y East Northern Dialect). Markham, ON: Fitzhenry and Whiteside/Ministry of Indian Affairs.

Bobbish-Salt, Luci, Alice Duff, Marie-Odile Junker, and Marguerite MacKenzie (eds.). 2004, 2012. *Eastern James Bay Cree dictionary (Northern Dialect)*. Chisasibi, QE: Cree School Board.

Darnell, Regna. 1991. Thirty-nine postulates of Plains Cree conversation. In *Papers of the twenty-second Algonquian conference*, ed. William Cowan, 89–102. Ottawa: Carleton University Press.

Dixon, Robert M. W. 2012. *Basic linguistic theory*. Vol. 3. Cambridge: Cambridge University Press.

Fabvre, Bonaventure. [before 1695] 1970. *Racines montagnaises*. Québec: Université Laval, Centre d'Études Nordiques.

Fasold, Ralph. 1990. *Sociolinguistics of language*. London: Blackwell.

Hymes, Dell. 1974. *Foundations of sociolinguistics: An ethnographic approach*. Philadelphia: University of Pennsylvania Press.

Johnson, Christopher, and Charles Fillmore. 2000. The FrameNet tagset for frame- semantic and syntactic coding of predicate-argument structure. In *Proceedings of the first North American chapter of the Association for Computational Linguistics Conference*, 56–62. Seattle.

Lacombe, Albert. 1874. *Dictionnaire de la langue des Cris*. Montréal: C.-O. Beauchemin et Valois.

Moses, Ted. 2005. *Chishâuchimâhkân kiyâh nâkânipishtihk Doctor Ted Moses / Message from the Grand Chief/Chairman, Doctor Ted Moses*. IGCCEI/CRA Annual Report of 2004–2005.

Petagumskum, John, Sr. 2000. Kâ utishiwât mâyâtishîuwâkin. *Nation*, April 7, 2000.

Rhodes, Richard. 1986. The semantics of the Ojibwa verbs of speaking. In *International Journal of American Linguistics* 52.1: 1–19.

Salisbury, Richard. 1986. *A homeland for the Cree, regional development in James Bay 1971–1981.* Montreal/Kingston: McGill-Queens' University Press.

Trask, Robert Lawrence. 1993. *A dictionary of grammatical terms in linguistics.* London: Routledge.

Vaillancourt, Louis-Philippe. 1992. *Dictionnaire français-cri.* Québec: Presses de l'Université du Québec.

Watkins, E. A., Rev. 1865. *A dictionary of the Cree Language, as spoken by the Indians of the Hudson's Bay Company territories.* London: Society for Promoting Christian Knowledge.

Wilson, Deirdre, and Robyn Carston. 2007. *A Unitary Approach to Lexical Pragmatics: Relevance, Inference and Ad Hoc Concepts.* http://www.phon.ucl.ac.uk/home/robyn/pdf.

Obviation and Information Structure in Meskwaki

Amy Dahlstrom

The Algonquian phenomenon of OBVIATION is a discourse-based opposition within third person. Unmarked PROXIMATE forms are used for the third person most central to the discourse; more peripheral third persons are referred to with marked OBVIATIVE forms. In Meskwaki, for animate gender, obviation can be observed in noun and demonstrative inflection and in verb agreement, while for inanimate gender, obviation is covert, visible only in intransitive subject agreement. The examples below illustrate proximate and obviative marking, with noun and demonstrative inflection in boldface and the verb agreement underlined.

(1) a·kwi wi·to·hkawa·čini i·tepi wi·ha·niči owi·wani i·na neniwa

a·kwi	wi·to·hkaw-a·čini	i·tepi	wi·h-a·-niči	ow-i·w-**ani**
not	allow-3>3'/NEG	there	FUT-go.thither-3'/AOR	his-wife-OBV

i·n-**a**	neniw-**a**
that-SG	man-SG

'That man (prox) doesn't allow his wife (obv) to go there.' (Goddard 2006:71)[1]

(2) mo·hči no·sa ne·tamwa mi·ša·mi we·nekwi·kani·mikateniki,

mo·hči	n-o·s-a	ne·t-amwa	mi·ša·m-i
even	my-father-SG	see-3>0/IND	sacred.pack-INAN.SG

IC-onekwi·kani-·mikateniki
IC-have.wings-0'/PART/0
'Even my father (prox) saw the sacred pack (obv) which had wings.'
(Dahlstrom 2003b:46)

In (1) the subject *i·na neniwa* 'that man' is proximate, evident from the use of unmarked third-person singular suffixes on the demonstrative and noun, and the object *owi·wani* 'his wife' is obviative, bearing the obviative suffix *–ani*. The underlined verb inflection likewise indicates that the subject of 'allow' is proximate and the object is obviative and that the subject of 'go thither' is obviative. In (2) the inanimate object *mi·ša·mi* 'sacred pack' does not have overt obviative morphology on the noun itself, but the verb agreement on 'have wings' reflects the obviative status of the inanimate noun.

In an effort to sharpen the characterization of proximate status, some Algonquianists have proposed that proximate can be equated with the information structure relation of TOPIC. Wolvengrey has a particularly clear statement: "I would argue that using a term like 'topic' and equating the proximate with the more prototypically topical third person referent is exactly the function conveyed by this Algonquian phenomenon" (Wolvengrey 2011:14).

A similar claim is made by Junker (2004:345): "Algonquian languages have a way to grammatically encode (non)topicality, a phenomenon traditionally called 'obviation'." Russell (1996:379) suggests that obviative marks the absence of topic: "It may well be that the proximate . . . merely functions as the unmarked member in opposition to the obviative category, which might positively mark non-topicality."

In the present paper, however, I argue that although topics are often proximate, proximate status cannot be equated with the information structure relation of topic. I will first make explicit what I mean by the terms TOPIC and FOCUS before turning to evidence against equating proximate with topic.

Information Structure Definitions

I assume the constructional framework for information structure developed by Lambrecht (1994, 2000, 2001).[2] Some basic assumptions of this approach are listed in (3):

(3) a. PRAGMATIC PRESUPPOSITION: The set of propositions lexico-grammatically evoked in a sentence that the speaker assumes the hearer already knows or believes or is ready to take for granted at the time the sentence is uttered.

b. PRAGMATIC ASSERTION: The proposition expressed by a sentence that the speaker expects the hearer to know or believe or take for granted as a result of hearing the utterance.

c. FOCUS: That component of a pragmatically structured proposition whereby the pragmatic assertion differs from the presupposition. The focus component is by definition an unpredictable part of the proposition. (Lambrecht 2001:474)

d. TOPIC: A referent is interpreted as the topic of a proposition if in a given situation the proposition is construed as being about this referent, i.e., as expressing information which is relevant to and which increases the addressee's knowledge of this referent. (Lambrecht 1994:131)

It is important to note at the outset that Lambrecht is not talking about semantics in the narrow sense but rather about a pragmatic level of information structure. Given that, we can recognize that in the midst of connected discourse the speaker and hearer already have mental representations of what has been said earlier. These propositions are what Lambrecht calls the PRAGMATIC PRESUPPOSITION (3a). As a result of the following utterance in the conversation or narrative, another proposition is added to the set of what the addressee knows. This added proposition is what Lambrecht calls the PRAGMATIC ASSERTION (3b). The pragmatic assertion usually contains some part that is already established in the pragmatic presupposition. The remainder, the unpredictable part, is what Lambrecht calls FOCUS (3c). (Lambrecht goes on to propose three basic types of focus constructions, but his typology is beyond the scope of the present paper; see Dahlstrom 2003a for discussion.) (3d) states Lambrecht's definition of TOPIC, which is based on an aboutness relationship between the topic and the following comment.

The relation of topic and the relation of focus are mutually exclusive. If a topic is the starting point for the following comment to be about, it cannot also be the unpredictable element bearing a focus relation to the proposition. The incompatibility of topic and focus will be important when we examine Meskwaki examples below.[3]

Another important point is that the relations of topic and focus are quite different in nature from the discourse statuses of ACTIVATION (also called GIVENNESS) and IDENTIFIABILITY (or DEFINITENESS). Topic and focus are relations to a proposition as defined in (3). Activation and identifiability, on the other hand, are properties of discourse referents in the interlocutors' mind (Lambrecht 1994:160). In particular, activation or givenness is not a sufficient criterion for identifying what is the topic. Likewise, focus need not be inactive or new information. For example, expressions referring to the speaker and addressee are necessarily given information—they are active in the consciousness of the interlocutors.

(4) Who needs a ride to the airport? I do!

The question in (4) presupposes that "x needs a ride to the airport." The answer "I do!" asserts that the value of x is "I". The first person pronoun is active in terms of its discourse status, but functions as focus in this context, in terms of the pragmatic articulation of the utterance's information structure.

Examples of Topic and Focus in Meskwaki

Having established general definitions of topic and focus, let us now look briefly at ways in which Meskwaki encodes these relations. (See Dahlstrom 2003a for more discussion, especially of Lambrecht's typology of focus constructions.) A template that accounts for much of Meskwaki word order (Dahlstrom 1993, 1995) is given in (5):

(5) [$_{S'}$ TOPIC [$_{S}$ NEG FOCUS OBL V {SUBJ, OBJ, OBJ2, COMP}]]

An overt topic, if present, appears at the left edge of the utterance, before a negative element, if present, as in (6), where a new topic is announced with the first person pronoun *ni·na*.

(6) ni·nayo a·kwi kosetawakini kemeso·ta·naki
ni·na=iyo a·kwi kosetaw-akini ke-meso·ta·n-aki **Top Neg V O**
I=of.course not fear-1>3P/NEG your-parent-PL
'As for me, I'm not afraid of your parents.' (Goddard 2006:78)

An element in focus, on the other hand, would appear to the right of a negative element if present. Immediately before the verb is the unmarked position for syntactic oblique arguments expressing location, manner, or measure phrases. All other grammatical relations appear to the right of the verb if not functioning as topic or focus.

Topic

In the template in (5) notice that the topic position is outside the core S consituent, while all other elements are daughters of S. This structural difference between overt topics and other elements has a number of consequences. For example, Meskwaki displays numerous second position enclitics expressing a range of evidential, aspectual, and other notions. (7) illustrates the tendency for a string of enclitics to appear attached to the first phonological word of the clause:

(7) o·sanike·hipimeka·pehe wi·te·mekočini.
o-o·s-ani=ke·hi=ipi=meko=a·pehe IC-wi·te·m-ekočini.
his-father.OBV=and=hrsy=EMPH=always IC-go.with-3'>3/PART/3'
'It was his father, you see, who would always go with him, it's said.'
(Dahlstrom 2003b:11)

When an overt topic is present, however, there are two possible locations for second position enclitics to attach to a host. They may appear after the first phonological word of the topic, after the first phonological word of the comment, or in both the topic and the comment. (8) is an example where both the topic and the comment host enclitics: the first word of the topic is the host for *=ke·hi* 'and, moreover', which often appears on new or shifted topics, while the first word of the comment hosts an emphatic, *=meko*, the hearsay enclitic *=ipi*, and a cliticized form of *i·ni* 'then'.

(8) i·niye·kake·hi ki·h–kočawičiki wi·hča·kiha·wa·či apeno·hahi,
i·niye·ka=ke·hi ki·h–kočawi-čiki wi·h-ča·kih-a·wa·či apeno·h-ahi,
those.ABSENT=and PERF–try-3P/PART/3P FUT-kill.all-3P>3'/AOR child-OBV.PL

waninawemekopi·ni e·hinohinote·wa·či.
waninawe=meko=ipi=i·ni e·h-inoh-inote·-wa·či.
all.directions=EMPH=HRSY=then AOR-REDUP-move.thither-3P/AOR
'As for those aforementioned ones (prox) who had tried to kill all the children (obv), they (prox) then moved away in all directions, it's said.' (Kiyana 1913:250DE)

Recognizing that the comment forms a constituent separate from the topic provides an explanation for the occurrence of the enclitics attaching to *waninawe* 'all directions'. If no left edge of S is posited to occur there, it would be hard to explain why these enclitics occur on the fifth word of the sentence.

Regarding the pragmatic function of topics, once a topic is established with an overt NP in topic position, that topic will often be maintained over several clauses or sentences, with only pronominal reference referring back to the topic in the later clauses. The passage in (9) illustrates an introduced topic sustained over a span of several clauses.

(9) a. o·ni·na oškinawe·he·ha
o·ni=i·na oškinawe·he·h-a
and.then=that young.man.DIM-SG
'And then that young teenage boy,

b. "nahi, natawi–po·ni–mahkate·wi·no," e·hineči e·hina·hpawa·či.
"nahi, natawi–po·ni–mahkate·wi·-no," e·h-in-eči
okay, time.to–stop–fast-2/IMP AOR-say.thus.to-X>3/AOR

e·h-ina·hpawa·-či
AOR-dream.thus-3/AOR
"Okay, it's time for you to stop fasting," he dreamed he was told.

c. “wi·kiya·peki=meko pe·hki ki·hawi,” e·hineči.
“wi·kiya·py-eki=meko pe·hki ke-i·h-awi-Ø,”
house-LOC=EMPH really 2-FUT-be.[there]-2/IND

e·h-in-eči
AOR-say.thus.to-X>3/AOR
“You should be in the main house,” he was told.

d. pye·ya·niči o·sani,
IC-pya·-niči o-o·s-ani,
IC-come-3’/CH.CONJ his-father-OBV
When his father came,

e. e·ha·čimoha·či e·na·hpawa·či.
e·h-a·čimoh-a·či IC-ina·hpawa·-či.
AOR-tell-3>3’/AOR IC-dream.thus-3/PART/OBL
he told him what he had dreamed.’ (Dahlstrom 1996:130)

In (9) the NP *oškinawe·he·ha* ‘that young teenage boy’ is announced in line (a) as a new topic, and the subsequent verbs in lines (b, c, e) are inflected for a third person proximate argument, referring to the boy. In (d) the possessor inflection on ‘his father’ refers to the boy as well. (The elements inside the quotes can be ignored for our purposes here, since the quoted material is a representation of a separate world of discourse.)

In both examples of overt third person topics seen so far (8–9) the topics are proximate. As stated earlier, such convergence of topic and proximate status is common. We will see, however, in a later section that topics are not necessarily proximate.

Focus

Let us now look briefly at focus (Lambrecht’s (1994) ARGUMENT-FOCUS). (10) is an example of contrastive focus:

(10) ki·nawe·na ki·hnepe
ki·na=we·na k-i·h-nep-e **Foc V**
you=rather 2-FUT-die-2/IND
'Rather, you will die.' (Jones 1907:68.16)

(10) presupposes that "x will die." The assertion is that it is the addressee, *ki·na* 'you', who will die. The second person pronoun is therefore expressing focus, since it is the component whereby the assertion differs from the presupposition.

Focus can also be seen with additive expressions, such as *ni·na=ne·hi* 'I too' in (11), with focus particles such as *mo·hči* 'even' in (12) and (2) or *še·ški* 'only', with question word questions, as in (13), and often with indefinite pronouns such as *owiye·ha* 'someone, anyone' in (14) or *ke·ko·hi* 'something'.

(11) nahi, nekwi·hi, ni·nane·hi ne·tama·ne
nahi, nekwi·hi, ni·na=ne·hi ne·t-ama·ne
well son.VOC I=also see-1>0/SUBJUNCT
'Well, son, if I see it too . . .' (Dahlstrom 2003b:34)

(12) a·kwi mo·hči nekoti nesakečini
a·kwi mo·hči nekoti nes-akečini
not even one kill-1P>3/NEG
'We didn't kill even one.' (Dahlstrom 2003b:43)

(13) ke·swiča·hi i·nahi awiwaki?
ke·swi=ča·hi i·nahi awi-waki?
how.many=so there be.[there]-3P/IND
'How many [people] were there?'

(14) a·kwi owiye·hani ki·wi-wi·te·ma·wa·čini.
a·kwi owiye·h-ani ki·wi–wi·te·m-a·wa·čini.
not someone-OBV around–accompany-3P>3'/NEG
'They didn't travel with anyone else.' (Dahlstrom 2015:153)

In the negated examples of (12) and (14) notice that the focus element follows the negative word *a·kwi,* as expected by the template in (5).

Evidence against Equating Proximate with Topic

I now turn to data that shows that we cannot equate proximate status with topic; the following section argues that we also cannot equate proximate status with focus.

Recall that the pragmatic relations of topic and focus are in complementary distribution. If an element is focused, it cannot be a topic. It is easy, however, to find examples of focused elements exhibiting proximate status, as in the question word of (15).

(15) we·ne·hča·h ne·sa·ta neto·kima·mena·nan?
we·ne·h-a=ča·h IC-nes-a·ta ne-okima·m-ena·n-an?
who-SG=SO IC-kill.3>3'/PART/3 1-chief-1P-OBV
'Who (prox) killed our (exclusive) chief (obv)?' (Jones 1907:26.13)

(2), repeated here, is another example of a proximate element functioning as focus: the focus particle *mo·hči* 'even' appears with the proximate third person *no·sa* 'my father'.

(2) mo·hči no·sa ne·tamwa mi·ša·mi we·nekwi·kani·mikateniki,
mo·hči n-o·s-a ne·t-amwa mi·ša·m-i
even my-father-SG see-3>0/IND sacred.pack-INAN.SG

IC-onekwi·kani-·mikateniki
IC-have.wings-0'/PART/0
'Even my father (prox) saw the sacred pack (obv) which had wings.'
(Dahlstrom 2003b:46)

(16) and (17), taken from the same long text about the culture hero Wisahkeha, form a minimal pair with overt topics. In (16) Wisahkeha, referred to by his personal name in proximate form, is an overt topic, followed by the enclitic *=ke·hi* 'and, moreover', which often co-occurs with a new or shifted topic. In (17) the overt topic again refers to the character of Wisahkeha, but here he is identified as the grandson of the character currently proximate, with an obviative NP. The overt topic in (17) likewise displays the enclitic *=ke·hi,* attached to the first phonological word of the topic. The comment about the topic is the same in (16) and (17): Wisahkeha was peacefully sound asleep. The only difference between the

comments in (16) and (17) is the agreement on the verb *nepa·-* 'sleep', proximate in (16) and obviative in (17), agreeing with the overt topics.

(16) wi·sahke·hake·hi wa·natohkameko e·hkehči—nepa·či

wi·sahke·h-a=ke·hi wa·natohka=meko e·h-kehči—nepa·-či

W-SG=and peacefully=EMPH AOR-greatly—sleep-3/AOR

'As for Wi·sahke·ha (prox), he was peacefully sound asleep.' (Kiyana 1913:163)

(17) i·ninike·hi o·šisemani wa·natohkameko e·hkehči–nepa·niči

i·n-ini=ke·hi o-o·šisem-ani

that-OBV=and her-grandchild-OBV

wa·natohka=meko e·h-kehči–nepa·-niči

peacefully=EMPH AOR-greatly–sleep-3'/AOR

'As for her grandson (obv), he was peacefully sound asleep.' (Kiyana 1913:10)

It might be objected that examples like (17) are not strong counterexamples to the claim that topics are always proximate. Since the topic in (17) is a noun possessed by a third person, it is obligatorily marked obviative: it cannot be expressed in the proximate status. However, notice that the speaker/writer of such examples has in fact chosen to identify the topic not with an independent name or description but rather with a kinship term, a relational form: that is, the character of Wisahkeha is identified here with a specific link to the proximate character of the grandmother. Wisahkeha is the topic of both (16) and (17), but the version in (17) reminds the hearer that the grandmother's point of view is still present in the scene. (See the discussion of (21) below for another example of expressed point of view.)

A property of topic constructions in many languages is that an overt topic can be followed by a comment that contains no gap or anaphoric element co-referential to the topic. A well-known example of this from Li and Thompson (1976) is the Japanese example in (18), where the comment is understood as about the announced topic.

(18) sakana wa, tai ga oiishi

fish TOPIC red.snapper SUBJ delicious

'As for fish, red snapper is delicious.' (Japanese; Li and Thompson 1976)

Constructions similar to (18) are also possible with overt topics in Meskwaki. (19) is an example with an obviative topic, 'his wife'. The following quote is understood as being spoken by the wife, even though the wife is not marked as an argument on the quoting verb following the quote.

(19) owi·wani: "kašina·kwa, kaši=ča·h ina·čimowa?" e·hineči.
ow-i·w-ani:
his-wife-OBV

"kašina·kwa, kaši=ča·h ina·čimo-wa?" e·h-in-eči.
well.what.happened? how=so tell.thus-3/IND AOR-say.to-X>3/AOR
'His (prox) wife (obv):
"Well, what happened? What did he say?" he (prox) was asked.' (Dahlstrom 1996:134)

The verb is inflected for an unspecified agent acting on the proximate third person, the woman's husband. Again, such a syntactic structure is possible with overt topics; and here, the topic is obviative.

As stated earlier, most third person topics in Meskwaki narratives enjoy proximate status, though the examples above demonstrate that topics are not obligatorily proximate. Another common pattern is for an overt topic introduced as an obviative NP to shift to proximate status in the immediately following clause. The passage in (20) is an example of this pattern.

(20) a. i·nike·hipi·na o·sani e·ha·nawapwi·hekoči.
i·ni=ke·hi=ipi=i·na o-o·s-ani e·h-a·nawapwi·h-ekoči.
then=and=HRSY=that.ANIM his-father-OBV AOR-fail.to.wait.for-3'>3/AOR
'And then, it's said, that [boy (prox)]'s father (obv) got tired of waiting for him (prox).

b. i·tepi e·ha·či.
i·tepi e·h-a·-či.
there AOR-go.thither-3/AOR
He (prox) went there.

c. e·hanemimeko–a·hkwe·wite·he·či,
e·h-anemi–=meko–a·hkwe·wite·he·-či,
AOR-away–=EMPH–feel.angry-3/AOR
He (prox) went off feeling angry,

d. "ne·wake, ni·hkehči–neškima·wa," e·hina·či owi·wani.

"ne·w-ake,	n-i·h-kehči–neškim-a·wa,"	e·h-in-a·či
see-1>3/SUBJNCT	1-FUT-greatly–scold-1>3/IND	AOR-say.to-3>3'/AOR

ow-i·w-ani.
his-wife-OBV
telling his wife (obv), "When I see him, I'm really going to scold him."'
(Dahlstrom 2003b:18)

In the (a) clause of (20) the new topic is *o·sani* 'his father', an obviative NP. The following clauses (b–d) relate actions of the father, but in those clauses the father is referred to with proximate inflection on the verb. Such a shift in status is another reflection of the frequent co-occurrence of proximate status and topichood, but proximate shifts are not obligatory. For example, the obviative topic seen in (17) is not followed in the narrative by a proximate shift.

The next textual excerpt illustrates a different pattern found in narratives. In (21) the obviative subject of the verbs is a young man who has been fasting. These lines report that the young man's footprints show that he had almost returned to his camp, that he then took off running, and that he was joined by some other creature.

(21) i·ya·hmeko aščiči pye·čihkawe·niči e·howi·kiniči,

i·ya·hi=meko	ašiči	IC-pye·čihkawe·-niči	e·h-owi·ki-niči,
there=EMPH	near	IC-S's.tracks.come-3'/CH.CONJ	AOR-live-3'/PART/OBL

kapo·twe e·hkehči–penowi·hka·šiniči.

kapo·twe	e·h-kehči–penowi·hka·ši-niči.
at.some.point	AOR-greatly–appear.to.go.fast-3'/AOR

kapo·twe e·hpemi–takwihkawe·niči owiye·hanimeko
kapo·twe e·h-pemi–takwihkawe·-niči owiye·h-ani=meko
at.some.point AOR-along–S's.tracks.together.with-3'/AOR someone-OBV=EMPH
'When his (obv) footprints came almost to the place
where he (obv) was camping,
at a certain point it looked like he (obv) took off really fast.
At a certain point his (obv) footprints were joined by the tracks of
some creature (obv).' (Dahlstrom 1996:139)

I would argue that the lines in (21) are about the young man: in other words, that we have here another example of an obviative topic, referred to pronominally by the inflection on the verbs. The young man remains in obviative status, however, without a shift to proximate status comparable to that seen in (20). Instead, the proximate third person during this episode is the young man's father, who has come out to look for his son. Sustaining the young man's obviative status in this episode conveys a particular stylistic effect in the text: we are seeing the action from the point of view of the proximate character.

Evidence against Equating Proximate with Focus

The previous section argued that it is incorrect to equate proximate status with the pragmatic relation of topic. It is also not possible to equate proximate status with the other major pragmatic relation, that of focus. For example, question words are prototypical members of the category of focus elements. It is possible to have a question word like *we·ne·ha* 'who' in an obviative form:

(22) we·ne·haniyo we·wi·hka·ničini no·sa?
we·ne·h-ani=iyo IC-owi·hka·ni-čini n-o·s-a
who.OBV=of.course IC-have.O2.as.friend-3/PART/3' my-father-SG
'Who [obv] did my father have as a friend?' (Kiyana 1913:914)

A further example of a focused element with obviative status was seen above in (14), repeated below:

(14) a·kwi owiye·hani ki·wi-wi·te·ma·wa·čini.

a·kwi	owiye·h-ani	ki·wi–wi·te·m-a·wa·čini.
not	someone-OBV	around–accompany-3P>3'/NEG

'They didn't travel with anyone else.' (Dahlstrom 2015:153)

In other words, the discourse-based opposition of proximate and obviative third persons must be recognized as distinct from the information structural relations of both topic and focus.

Conclusion

I have argued in this paper that topics in Meskwaki are often proximate but need not be: in other words, the definition of proximate cannot be reduced to that of topic, nor to that of focus. The relationship between topic and proximate is similar to the well-known relationship between topic and activation or givenness: topic cannot be defined solely in terms of activation, though topics are frequently active or given information (cf. Lambrecht 1994). Instead, we must recognize that the proximate vs. obviative opposition can be sensitive to a variety of other factors as well, such as empathy, agency, and point of view.

NOTES

1. Abbreviations in examples: 0 = inanimate, 0' = obviative inanimate, 1P = first person exclusive plural, 3P = third plural, 3' = obviative, ABSENT = absentative, ANIM = animate, AOR = aorist conjunct, CH.CONJ = changed conjunct, EMPH = emphatic, FUT = future, HRSY = hearsay, IC = Initial Change, IMP = imperative, INAN = inanimate, IND = independent indicative, LOC= locative, NEG = negative, O2 = second object, OBL = oblique, OBV = obviative, PART = conjunct participle, PL = plural, REDUP = reduplication, S = subject, SG = singular, SUBJNCT = subjunctive, VOC = vocative, X = unspecified subject. '>' separates subject and object in the gloss of transitive verbs. The first line of textual examples presents the Meskwaki sentence without clitic boundaries or morpheme boundaries, following the convention in recent texts edited by Dahlstrom (e.g., Dahlstrom 2015). Examples without a text citation are elicited.
2. See Dahlstrom 2003a for more extensive discussion of Lambrecht's framework.
3. It should be noted, however, that not all approaches to information structure agree

that topic and focus are in complementary distribution. For example, Skopeteas et al. (2006) posit separate dimensions of topic-comment and focus-background in which it is possible for topic and focus to overlap.

REFERENCES

Dahlstrom, Amy. 1993. The syntax of discourse functions in Fox. In *BLS 19 special session on the syntax of Native American languages*, ed. David Peterson, 11–21. Berkeley, CA: Berkeley Linguistics Society.

———. 1995. *Topic, focus, and other word order problems in Algonquian*. The Belcourt Lecture 5, Winnipeg: Voices of Rupert's Land.

———. 1996. Narrative structure of a Fox text. In *nikotwâsik iskwâhtêm, pâskihtêpayih! Studies in Honour of H. C. Wolfart*, ed. John D. Nichols and Arden C. Ogg, 113–162. Winnipeg: Algonquian and Iroquoian Linguistics.

———. 2003a. Focus constructions in Meskwaki (Fox). In *Proceedings of the LFG03 Conference*, ed. Miriam Butt and Tracy Holloway King, 144–163. Stanford, CA: CSLI Publications.

———. 2003b. Warrior powers from an underwater spirit: Cultural and linguistic aspects of an illustrated Meskwaki text. *Anthropological Linguistics* 45:1–56.

———. 2015. Highlighting rhetorical structure through syntactic analysis: An illustrated Meskwaki text by Alfred Kiyana. In *New voices for old words: Algonquian oral literatures*, ed. David J. Costa, 118–197. Lincoln: University of Nebraska Press.

Goddard, Ives. 2006. *The autobiography of a Meskwaki woman*. Winnipeg: Algonquian and Iroquoian Linguistics.

Jones, William. 1907. *Fox texts*. American Ethnological Society Publications 1. Leiden.

Junker, Marie-Odile. 2004. Focus, obviation and word order in East Cree. *Lingua* 114:345–365.

Kiyana, Alfred. 1913. *wisakea osani okyeni osimeani okomeseani*. [Wisahkeha, his father, his mother, his younger brother, his grandmother.] Manuscript 2958-a in National Anthropological Archives, Smithsonian Institution, Washington, DC.

Lambrecht, Knud. 1994. *Information structure and sentence form*. Cambridge: Cambridge University Press.

———. 2000. When subjects behave like objects: An analysis of the merging of S and O in sentence-focus constructions across languages. *Studies in Language* 24:611–682.

———. 2001. A framework for the analysis of cleft constructions. *Linguistics* 39:463–516.

Li, Charles N., and Sandra A. Thompson. 1976. Subject and topic: A new typology of language. In *Subject and topic*, ed. Charles N. Li, 457–489. New York: Academic Press.

Russell, Kevin. 1996. Does obviation mark point of view? In *nikotwâsik iskwâhtêm, pâskihtêpayih! Studies in Honour of H. C. Wolfart*, ed. John D. Nichols and Arden C. Ogg, 367–382. Winnipeg: Algonquian and Iroquoian Linguistics.

Skopeteas, Stavros, Ines Fiedler, Samantha Hellmuth, Anne Schwarz, Ruben Stoel, Gisbert Fanselow, Caroline Féry, and Manfred Krifka. 2006. *Questionnaire on information structure (QUIS): Reference manual.* Interdisciplinary Studies on Information Structure 4. Universitätsverlag Potsdam, Potsdam, Germany.

Wolvengrey, Arok Elessar. 2011. *Semantic and pragmatic functions in Plains Cree syntax.* Utrecht: LOT.

La sémantique de l'accord à longue distance en algonquin

Brandon J. Fry et Éric Mathieu

Abstract

In this paper, we argue that long-distance agreement (LDA) in Algonquin Ojibwe does not express topicality, as is generally claimed in the Algonquian literature, but rather that it correlates with evidentiality and belief ascription. In this sense, LDA resembles, in its semantics, ECM (Exceptional Case Marking) constructions. However, we show that LDA does not bear ECM's syntactic properties.

Dans ce chapitre, nous proposons que l'accord à longue distance (ALD) en algonquin n'exprime pas la topicalité, comme il est généralement proposé dans la littérature pour les langues algonquiennes, mais plutôt l'évidentialité ainsi que l'attribution de croyances. Dans ce sens, l'ALD ressemble, selon nous, dans son aspect sémantique, à une construction ECM (Exceptional Case Marking). Toutefois, nous démontrons que l'ALD ne partage pas avec la construction ECM ses caractéristiques syntaxiques.

L'ALD en algonquin

Comme dans les autres langues algonquiennes (voir Dahlstrom 1991 pour le cri, Rhodes 1994 pour l'odawa, Bruening 2001 et LeSourd 2010 pour le malécite-passamaquoddy, Branigan et MacKenzie 2002 pour l'innu), l'accord à longue distance (ALD) est possible en algonquin lorsqu'un verbe principal s'accorde avec son sujet local et avec un élément appartenant à son complément phrastique.[1] Certains verbes subordonnants peuvent apparaitre sous une forme transitive inanimée (VTI), comme en (1), auquel cas le verbe s'accorde avec le sujet de la proposition principale et prend la proposition subordonnée comme objet, ou bien sous une forme transitive animée (VTA), comme en (2)–(3), où le verbe s'accorde avec son sujet local et avec le sujet de son complément phrastique (2) ou avec son sujet local et avec l'objet de la proposition subordonnée (3).[2]

(1) Ngikendan giibashkizwaadj.
ni-gikendan gii-bashkizw-aad
1-savoir.VTI(IND) PASSÉ-tirer.sur.VTA-2>3(CONJ)
'Je sais que tu as tiré sur lui.' (Lochbihler et Mathieu 2016:23)

(2) Ggikenimin giibashkizwaadj.
gi-gikenim-in gii-bashkizw-aa-d
2-savoir.VTA-DIR.1(IND) PASSÉ-tirer.sur.VTA-2>3(CONJ)
'Je sais que tu as tiré sur lui.' (Lochbihler et Mathieu 2016:23)

(3) Ngikenimaa giibashkizwaadj
ni-gikenim-aa gii-bashkizw-aa-d
1-savoir.VTA-DIR.3(IND) PASSÉ-tirer.sur.VTA-2>3(CONJ)
'Je sais que tu as tiré sur lui.' (Lochbihler et Mathieu 2016:23)

La sémantique de l'ALD est souvent associée à la topicalité (Rhodes 1994; Polinsky et Potsdam 2001; Branigan et MacKenzie 2002; Ritter et Rosen 2005). Dans la tradition algonquienne, une traduction typique de (2) est 'Je sais que, toi, tu as tiré sur lui', une traduction typique de (3) est 'Je sais que, lui, tu as tiré sur lui', alors que l'exemple en (1) ne reçoit pas d'interprétation topique. Il s'agit d'une description tout à fait naturelle, puisqu'après tout l'ALD est facultatif et puisque dans d'autres langues, l'accord facultatif exprime la topicalité (pour les langues bantoues, voir Bresnan et Mchombo 1987 et Corbett 2006). Cependant, tel que discuté par Bruening (2001, 2006) pour le malécite-passamaquoddy et Mathieu et Fry 2014 pour l'ojibwé, l'idée selon laquelle l'ALD exprime la topicalité est problématique. Nous apporterons des arguments en faveur de cette analyse dans la prochaine section.

L'ALD ne correspond pas à la topicalité

Nous offrons quatre arguments contre l'analyse de l'ALD comme expression de topicalité.

Premièrement, l'ALD est possible avec des syntagmes nominaux obviatifs, comme en (4), et selon nous, ceux-ci ne sont pas des topiques. En effet, même s'ils font référence à des éléments qui ont déjà été introduits dans le discours, les obviatifs, contrairement aux proximatifs, ne figurent pas au premier plan; ils ne sont pas le sujet du discours (voir Rhodes 1990, entre autres).[3] Dans ce sens, les obviatifs ne ressemblent pas à des topiques, mais plutôt à des éléments focalisés.

(4) Ogikenimaan kedikedodj noosan.

o-gikenim-aa-n	ke-d-ikedo-dj	n-oos-an
3-savoir.VTA-DIR.3-OBV(IND)	WH.FUT-ÉPEN-dire-3OBV(CONJ)	1-père-OBV

'Elle sait ce que mon père dira.'

Deuxièmement, les mots interrogatifs comme *wegonesh* 'qui' et *aaniin* 'quoi' sont possibles dans les constructions ALD en algonquin (voir aussi Bruening 2001 pour le malécite-passamaquoddy et Branigan et MacKenzie 2002 pour l'innu). Pour illustrer, considérez l'exemple en (5) où *wegonesh* 'qui' détermine l'accord à longue distance du verbe, à la troisième personne du singulier. Le problème est que les mots interrogatifs sont des focus plutôt que des topiques (Chomsky 1977; Brody 1990; Rizzi 1997).[4]

(5) Ngikenmaa wegonesh gaa-zheshemgowang nen kwezhegaasan.

ni-gikenim-aa	wegonesh	gaa-zheshemgow-ang
1-savoir.VTA-DIR.3(IND)	qui	WH.PASSÉ-voler-3.PL(CONJ)

nen	kwezhegaas-an
ces	biscuit-PL

'Je sais qui a volé ces biscuits.'

Troisièmement, l'ALD est possible avec des quantificateurs universels, tel que *gakina awiiya* 'tout le monde' (voir aussi Branigan and MacKenzie 2002 pour l'innu), comme en (6). Les quantificateurs universels sont généralement analysés comme des focus plutôt que des topiques. Par exemple, ils créent un effet d'intervention (Beck 2006) et ils ne sont pas facilement topicalisés (*#Tout le monde, il aime qui?*) (Rizzi 1997).

(6) Ninoondawaag gakina awiiya ge-ji-biizhawaadj.

ni-noondaw-aa-g	gakina	awiiya
1-entendre.VTA-DIR.3-PL(IND)	chaque	personne

ge-ji-biizhawaa-d
à.propos-afin.que-venir.VAI-3(CONJ)
'J'entends tout le monde venir.'

Finalement, le mot 'seulement' se place devant et a sa portée au-dessus du syntagme nominal qui participe à l'ALD (voir aussi Bruening 2001 pour le malécite-passamaquoddy), ce qui indique que l'ALD n'exprime pas la topicalité du syntagme, puisqu'il est généralement admis que l'adverbe 'seulement' exprime le focus (Rooth 1992).

(7) Ngikenimaa gii-bashkizwaadj wiineta.

ni-gikenim-aa	gii-bashkizaw-aa-d	wiin-eta
1-savoir.VTA-DIR.3(IND)	PASSÉ-tirer.sur.VTA-2>3(CONJ)	lui-seulement

'Je sais que tu as tiré seulement sur lui.'

En résumé, les syntagmes nominaux qui peuvent participer à l'ALD ne sont pas facilement analysables comme des topiques. Par conséquent, l'idée selon laquelle l'ALD en algonquin exprime la topicalité est problématique. Dans la prochaine partie de notre article, nous proposons que la contribution sémantique de l'ALD est liée à l'évidentialité et l'attribution de croyances.

L'ALD, l'évidentialité et l'attribution de croyances

Nous proposons, après plusieurs observations faites en travail de terrain, que l'ALD est typique dans des contextes où la source des éléments de preuve et l'attribution des croyances sont pertinentes, notamment dans la présence des verbes de perception et des verbes de connaissance. Cette observation rend l'ALD moins idiosyncratique comme construction, puisque ce sont ces contextes qui caractérisent les constructions ECM (Exceptional Case Marking) que l'on retrouve en anglais et dans d'autres langues (exemples: 'I saw him leave', 'Je l'ai vu partir'). Ainsi, l'ALD et l'ECM forment une classe naturelle de constructions sémantiques. Cependant, si l'ALD ressemble aux constructions ECM d'un point de vue sémantique, la syntaxe de l'ALD diffère de celle de l'ECM (voir aussi Branigan et MacKenzie 2002) : toutes les propositions en ojibwé et en algonquin portent un temps verbal (il n'y a pas d'infinitifs dans les langues algonquiennes), alors que les phrases enchâssées dans les constructions ECM sont à l'infinitif (Johnson 1991; Bowers 1993; Koizumi 1995); le sujet ou l'objet enchâssé peut participer à l'ALD en algonquin alors que seul le sujet peut participer à l'ECM; et l'ECM concerne le cas structural alors que les langues algonquiennes n'ont pas de cas structural (Ritter et Rosen 2005).

Bien que les constructions ALD ne partagent pas, avec les constructions ECM, leurs caractéristiques syntaxiques, ils partagent toutefois leurs traits sémantiques, en particulier l'attribution des croyances. Suivant Moulton (2009) pour l'anglais, nous proposons que la présence de l'ALD algonquin exprime une croyance de ce qui est perçu et l'absence de l'ALD exprime un fait et des inférences, souvent associées aux modaux épistémiques (voir aussi Izvorski 1997:225; Dixon 2003:270-271; et Aikhenvald 2007:213). Par exemple, (8) est un rapport (conduisant à une interprétation *de dicto*) alors que (9) est un jugement du comportement de quelqu'un, une propriété subjective (Borkin 1984) et porte sur un individu (conduisant à une interprétation *de re*).

(8) I see that he's French.

(9) I see him to be French.

L'observation selon laquelle l'ALD en algonquin exprime une croyance en relation avec une perception provient de notre travail de terrain. Selon les locuteurs, (10) a le sens de : 'J'entends dire qu'il arrive' alors que (11) a le sens de : 'Je l'entends arriver (j'entends ses pas)'.

(10) *Marie et moi sommes à une fête. Une rumeur circule qu'un homme célèbre viendra plus tard dans la soirée.*
Ni-noondage ge-ji-biizha-d
1-entendre.VTI(IND) à.propos-afin.que-venir.VAI-3(CONJ)
'J'entends qu'il vient.'

(11) *Je lis tranquillement dans le salon. Tout d'un coup, j'entends des bruits de pas qui s'approchent. Mon ami a une démarche particulière. Je peux dire que ce sont ses pas que j'entends.*
Ni-noondaw-aa ge-ji-biizha-d
1-entendre.VTA-DIR.3(IND) à.propos-afin.que-venir.VAI-3(CONJ)
'Je l'entends venir.'

La même distinction apparait lorsque les verbes de perception visuelle sont employés. (12) exprime une inférence à partir d'un état de faits alors que (13) exprime une expérience perceptuelle.

(12) *Je marche vers le bord de la rivière. Mon ami est assis au bord de la rivière, à bout de souffle, ses vêtements sont tout mouillés.*
N-waabandaan gii-bikobiise-Ø
1-voir.VTI(IND) PASSÉ-tomber.dans.l'eau-3
'Je vois qu'il est tombé dans l'eau.'

(13) *Je marche vers le bord de la rivière. Mon ami se tient debout près de la rivière. Je l'interpelle et lui fais peur, si bien qu'il tombe dans la rivière.*
N-waabam-aa gii-bikobiise- Ø
1-voir.VTA-DIR.3(IND) PASSÉ-tomber.dans.l'eau-3
'Je le vois tomber dans l'eau.'

Puisque les connaissances peuvent être acquises par la perception visuelle, auditoire, tactile, olfactive, etc., il n'est pas surprenant que les verbes de connaissance puissent également participer à l'ALD (la perception est la connaissance, Dancy 1985, et la connaissance constitue une preuve, Williamson 2000). Selon les locuteurs que nous avons consultés, (14) exprime une inférence alors que (15) exprime une source directe de preuve (par exemple une expérience perceptuelle).

(14) *On a dit au locuteur que la personne A a tiré sur la personne B.*
Ni-gikendan gii-bashkizaw-aad
1-savoir.VTI(IND) PASSÉ-tirer.sur.VTA-2>3(CONJ)
'Je sais que tu as tiré sur lui.'

(15) *Le locuteur a vu la personne A tirer sur la personne B.*
Gi-gikenim-in gii-bashkizaw-aad
2-savoir.VTA-DIR.2(IND) PASSÉ-tirer.sur.VTA-2>3(CONJ)
'Je sais que tu as tiré sur lui.'

Même si l'on peut penser a priori que le verbe 'savoir' est, en général, très différent des verbes de perception (dans la mesure où il est automatiquement factif), il en va tout autrement. Notamment, le verbe 'savoir' s'utilise dans les constructions ECM et dans ces contextes il n'est pas factif (Moulton 2009). Considérez les exemples en (16) et (17).

(16) Donna never knew him to lie...so he must not have. (Moulton 2009:202)

(17) #Donna never knew that he lied...so he must not have. (Moulton 2009:202)

En fait, il s'avère que 'savoir' tel qu'il est employé dans d'autres contextes n'est pas nécessairement factif (Chierchia et McConnell 1990; Hazlett 2010, 2012). Par exemple, un locuteur peut énoncer « Quand j'étais petit, je savais que le Père Noël livrerait des cadeaux à chaque année », où la proposition enchâssée est fausse. Dans ce cas, 'savoir' a le sens de 'croire'.

Pour résumer, l'ALD exprime une source directe de preuve et une croyance *de re*. Certaines langues, comme l'anglais, expriment cette notion grammaticale par la présence et l'absence de complémenteurs. D'autres langues expriment cette distinction par l'emploi de complémenteurs différents. C'est le cas du lele, une langue austronésienne (Frajzyngier 1995). En lele, le complémenteur *gō* employé avec des verbes de perception, comme en (18), indique la perception directe alors que l'emploi du complémenteur *ná* avec des verbes de perception, comme en (19), indique la perception indirecte (Frajzyngier 1995:485-488).

(18) ǹ-gòl-dù gō jè wàl-dù kúlbà
1SG-voir-3F COMP PROGR tuer-3F vache
'Je l'ai vu tuer une vache.' (Frajzyngier 1995:485)

(19) ǹ-gòl ná wàl-dí kúlbà
1SG-voir COMP tuer-3M vache
'J'ai vu qu'il a tué une vache.' (Frajzyngier 1995:487)

L'ALD a par conséquent une corrélation directe avec l'évidentialité et l'interprétation *de re*.

L'explication formelle

Lochbihler et Mathieu (2016) proposent que l'ojibwé a deux complémenteurs distincts : l'un s'emploie à l'ordre indépendant et porte des traits φ comme personne, nombre, et animé; l'autre s'emploie à l'ordre conjonctif et porte des traits δ (δ pour *discours*) comme *qu-*, focus, et topique. Cette distinction sert à expliquer une variété de différences entre les ordres indépendant et conjonctif, comme la présence des préfixes personnels sur les verbes à l'ordre indépendant et leur absence à l'ordre conjonctif ainsi que l'apparition du changement initial (analysé comme l'accord-*qu* par Lochbihler et Mathieu 2013) sur les verbes à l'ordre conjonctif et l'absence de ce phénomène à l'ordre indépendant. Puisque les deux complémenteurs portent des traits ininterprétables, les deux sont des têtes phasiques (Chomsky 2007, 2008; Richards 2007), alors leur compléments (ST) ne sont pas visibles aux opérations syntaxiques en dehors de la phase (SC).

Nous proposons que le complémenteur C en algonquin peut porter un trait δ spécial : un trait *de re*, appelé DOX, suivant Moulton (2009). C_{DOX} entraine le déplacement d'un SD vers son spécifieur (voir Polinsky et Potsdam 2001; Branigan et MacKenzie 2002; Fry et Hamilton 2014; Lochbihler et Mathieu 2016), où il devient visible au *v** de la phrase principale, qui s'accorde avec ce SD. Cette construction est représentée en (20).

(20)

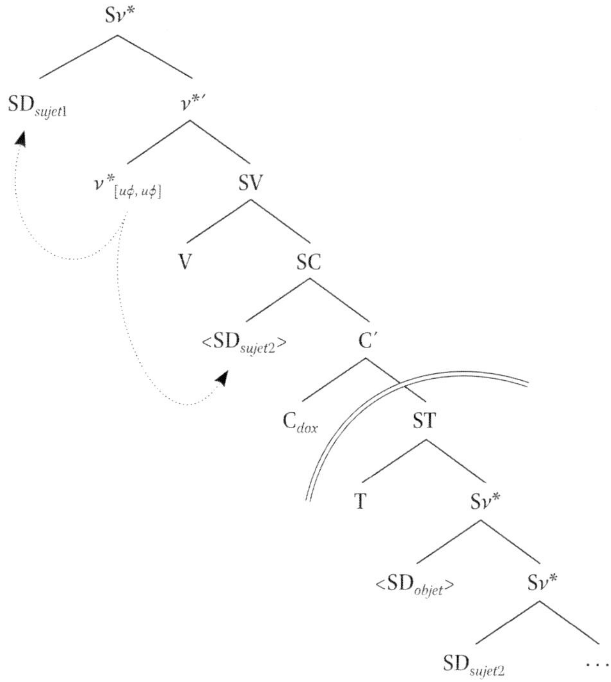

Dans les contextes où l'ALD n'a pas lieu, un complémenteur différent, C_{rapport} est employé. C_{rapport} empêche le déplacement d'un SD vers son spécifieur, alors le *v** de la phrase principale ne peut pas s'accorder avec un SD appartenant à la phrase enchâssée. Cette construction est représentée en (21).

(21)

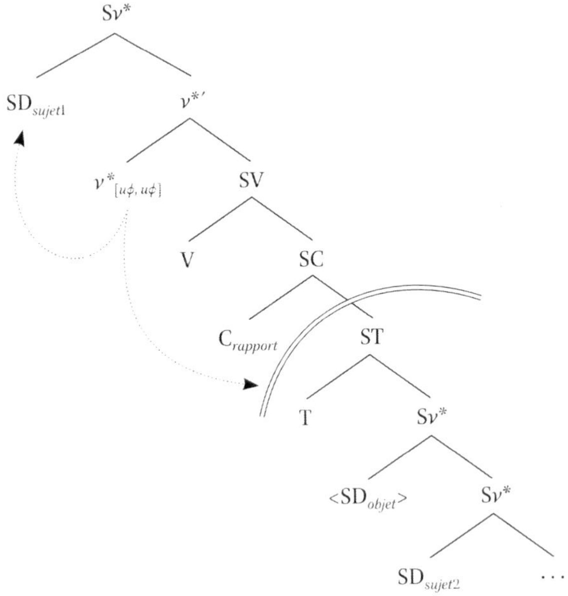

Pour tenir compte de la nature portemanteau des marques d'accord VTA en algonquin, qui indiquent simultanément l'accord avec un sujet et un objet, nous proposons que le *v* en algonquin porte deux traits uφ, l'un qui s'accorde avec le sujet et l'autre avec l'objet: $v^*_{[u\varphi,u\varphi]}$. Suivant Preminger (2011), une dérivation syntaxique n'est pas nécessairement illégitime ('crash') si des traits ininterprétables ne sont pas vérifiés. Si les deux traits uφ de *v** sont vérifiés, alors le verbe apparait dans sa forme VTA. Lorsque le verbe est VTI, alors deux traits sont vérifiés, mais il s'agit du trait associé au sujet du verbe principal et du trait associé à la proposition enchâssée (l'objet du verbe VTI).

Notre proposition est en accord avec d'autres analyses récentes (Moulton 2009, 2010; Kratzer 2013) (et contre la vue traditionnelle de Hintikka 1962) qui proposent que l'attribution des croyances est située dans la périphérie gauche de la phrase et non pas dans la dénotation du verbe surbordonnant. Suivant l'analyse des constructions ECM offerte par Mouton (2009), l'ALD algonquin exprime une croyance *de re* de ce qui a été perçu. C_{DOX} introduit cette composante de croyance *de re* et porte la dénotation en (22).

(22) $[[C_{DOX}]]$ = λP.λs.λx.λw.x croit P de re de s en w. (adapté de Moulton 2010 :8)

Le verbe enchâssant, quant à lui, exprime seulement un évènement. Des dénotations semi-formelles des verbes 'entendre', 'voir', et 'savoir' sont présentées en (23)-(25).

(23) [[noondaw]] = λs.λw.entendre s en w.

(24) [[waabam]] = λs.λw.voir s en w.

(25) [[giken]] = λs.λw.savoir s en w.

Selon Moulton (2010), l'objet de ces verbes n'est pas le sujet de la phrase enchâssée. Par exemple, en (26), le cas n'implique pas que Rodney entend nécessairement un violon.

(26) Rodney hears a violin to be playing . . . but it was really a cello. (Moulton 2010:9)

L'objet de ces verbes est une éventualité : Rodney entend une éventualité et croit de cette éventualité qu'elle consiste en un violon qui joue.

Il est intéressant de noter que Bruening (2006) offre une analyse similaire des constructions ALD en malécite-passamaquoddy. Selon son analyse (Bruening 2006:18), les verbes qui participent dans les constructions ALD expriment une relation triadique entre un individu qui porte une croyance, un objet et une propriété que l'individu attribue à l'objet, comme en (27), alors que les mêmes verbes dans les constructions non ALD expriment une relation dyadique entre un individu qui porte une croyance et une proposition, comme en (28).

(27) [[savoir]] = λP.λx.λy.λw.pour tout w′ compatible avec ce que y sait en w, P(x)(w′).

(28) [[savoir]] = λp.λx.λw.pour tout w′ compatible avec ce que x sait en w, p(w′).

La distinction fondamentale entre l'analyse de Moulton (2009, 2010) et celle de Bruening (2006) concerne la position où réside la croyance : là où Moulton propose que la croyance se situe dans la périphérie gauche de la phrase et que la sémantique du verbe ne change pas selon la construction (ALD ou non ALD), Bruening propose que le même verbe a deux interprétations distinctes. Mais méthodologiquement, une proposition qui emploie l'ambigüité comme stratégie analytique est très difficile à falsifier. Dans une perspective théorique, la variation dans la structure fonctionnelle de la phrase est commune; par exemple, il existe plusieurs variétés de *v** (Folli et Harley 2004) alors que la variation au niveau des catégories lexicales est peu commune. D'ailleurs, on retrouve dans certaines langues différents complémenteurs pour exprimer la distinction de *re/de dicto*. Pour ces raisons, une analyse en accord avec le modèle de Moulton, comme celle présentée dans ce chapitre, est préférable.

Conclusion

Dans cet article, nous avons proposé que la contribution sémantique des constructions ALD en algonquin est reliée à l'évidentialité et l'attribution de croyances. Dans une perspective formelle, le complémenteur de la phrase enchâssée peut introduire une croyance *de re* (C_{DOX}) ou simplement un rapport ($C_{rapport}$). La marque d'accord qui apparait sur le verbe principal est une indication morphologique d'une relation syntaxique entre le *v** de la phrase principale et le SD de la phrase enchâssée qui s'est déplacée pour occuper le spécifieur de C_{DOX} de la phrase enchâssée. Puisque $C_{rapport}$ n'entraine pas le déplacement d'un SD vers son spécifieur, une relation entre le *v** principal et un SD appartenant à la phrase enchâssée ne peut pas être établie.

NOTES

1. La variante d'algonquin que nous étudions dans ce chapitre est parlée dans la communauté de Kitigan Zibi au Québec. Nous aimerions remercier nos locuteurs pour avoir partagé leurs connaissances linguistiques avec nous. Pour des commentaires sur ce travail, nous tenons à remercier Heather Bliss, Phil Branigan, Amy Dahlstrom, Rose-Marie Déchaine, Miloje Despic, Michael David Hamilton, Sarah Murray ainsi que Charlotte Reinholtz. Cette recherche a été financée par le Conseil de recherches en sciences humaines (subvention 410-2011-2417 accordée à Éric Mathieu et bourse d'études supérieures du Canada Joseph-Armand Bombardier accordée à Brandon J. Fry).

   Les abréviations suivantes sont employées dans ce chapitre : 1 = 1ère personne, 2 = 2ième personne, 3 = 3ième personne; X>Y = X est l'argument externe et Y est l'argument interne; comp = complémenteur, conj = ordre conjonctif, dir = direct, épen

= épenthéthique, f = féminin, fut = futur, ind = ordre indépendant, m = masculin, obv = obviatif, pl = pluriel, progr = progressif, sg = singulier, vai = verbe intransitif avec sujet animé, vta = verbe transitif avec objet animé, vti = verbe transitif avec objet inanimé.

2. Les langues algonquiennes varient selon les contraintes qu'elles imposent sur l'ALD : certaines langues permettent l'ALD seulement avec le sujet enchâssé dans le direct et l'inverse, d'autres permettent l'ALD seulement avec le sujet dans le direct et seulement avec l'objet dans l'inverse, et encore d'autres, comme l'algonquin, permettent l'ALD avec le sujet ou l'objet dans le direct et l'inverse. Voir Fry et Hamilton 2014 pour une vue d'ensemble et une analyse théorique de cette variation.
3. Nous ne traitons pas des constructions possessives où le possédé est nécessairement obviatif (Grafstein 1984).
4. Notez que ces mots interrogatifs ne sont pas liés au discours (*D-linked*). En tsez, les mots interrogatifs liés au discours peuvent participer dans les constructions ALD mais les focus ne le peuvent pas (Polinsky et Postdam 2001).

RÉFÉRENCES

Aikhenvald, Alexandra Y. 2007. Information source and evidentiality: What can we conclude? *Revista di Linguistica* 19:209–227.

Beck, Sigrid. 2006. Intervention effects follow from focus interpretation. *Natural Language Semantics* 14:1–56.

Borkin, Anne. 1984. *Form and function.* Norwood, NJ : Ablex Publishers.

Bowers, John. 1993. The syntax of predication. *Linguistic Inquiry* 24:591–656.

Branigan, Phil et Marguerite MacKenzie. 2002. Altruism, A'-movement, and object agreement in Innu-aimûn. *Linguistic Inquiry* 33:385–407.

Bresnan, Joan et Sam A. Mchombo. 1987. Topic, pronoun, and agreement in Chichewa. *Language* 63:741–782.

Brody, Michael. 1990. Some remarks on the focus field in Hungarian. *UCL Working Papers in Linguistics* 2:201–226.

Bruening, Benjamin. 2001. Syntax at the edge: Cross-clausal phenomena and the syntax of Passamaquoddy. Thèse de doctorat, MIT.

Bruening, Benjamin. 2006. Discrepancies between projection and selection: Split coordination and raising to object in Passamaquoddy. Manuscrit, University of Delaware.

Chierchia, Gennaro et Sally McConnell-Ginet. 1990. *Meaning and grammar: An introduction to semantics.* Cambridge : MIT Press.

Chomsky, Noam. 1977. On wh-movement. *Formal syntax*, sous la direction de Peter Culicover,

Thomas Wasow, et Adrian Akmajian, pp. 71–132. New York : Academic Press.

Chomsky, Noam. 2007. Approaching UG from below. *Interfaces + recursion = language?*, sous la direction de Uli Sauerland et Hans-Martin Gärtner, pp. 1-29. New York : Mouton de Gruyter.

Chomsky, Noam. 2008. On phases. *Foundational issues in linguistic theory: Essays in honor of Jean-Roger Vergnaud*, sous la direction de Robert Freidin, Carlos P. Otero, et Maria Luisa Zubizarreta, pp. 133-166. Cambridge : MIT Press.

Corbett, Greville. 2006. *Agreement.* Cambridge : Cambridge University Press.

Dahlstrom, Amy. 1991. *Plains Cree morphosyntax.* New York : Garland.

Dancy, Jonathan. 1985. *An introduction to contemporary epistemology.* Oxford : Blackwell.

Dixon, Robert M. W. 2003. Evidentiality in Jarawara. *Studies in evidentiality*, sous la direction de Alexandra Y. Aikhenvald et Robert M. W. Dixon, pp. 165–187. Amsterdam : John Benjamins.

Folli, Raffaella and Heidi Harley. 2004. Flavors of v: Consuming results in Italian and English. *Aspectual Inquiries*, ed. By Roumyana Slabakova and Paula Kempchinsky, 95–120. Dordrecht: Kluwer

Frajzyngier, Zygmunt. 1995. A functional theory of complementizers. *Modality in grammar and discourse*, sous la direction de Joan Bybee et Suzanne Fleischman, pp. 473–502. Amsterdam et Philadelphie : John Benjamins Publishing Company.

Fry, Brandon J. et Michael David Hamilton. 2014. Long-distance agreement in Algonquian: Accounting for syntactic variation. Manuscrit, Université d'Ottawa et McGill University.

Grafstein, Ann. 1984. Argument structure and syntax in a non-configurational language. Thèse de doctorat, McGill University.

Hazlett, Allan. 2010. The myth of factive verbs. *Philosophy and Phenomenological Research* 80:497–522.

Hazlett, Allan. 2012. Factive presupposition and the truth condition and knowledge. *Acta Analytica* 27:461–478.

Hintikka, Jaakko. 1962. *Knowledge and belief.* Ithaca, NY : Cornell University Press.

Izvorski, Roumyana. 1997. The present perfect as an epistemic modal. *Proceedings of SALT VII*, sous la direction de Aaron Lewis, pp. 222–239. Ithaca, NY : Cornell University.

Johnson, Kyle. 1991. Object positions. *Natural Language and Linguistic Theory* 9:577–636.

Koizumi, Masatoshi. 1995. Phrase structure in minimalist syntax. Thèse de doctorat, MIT.

Kratzer, Angelica. 2013. Modality and the semantics of embedding. Communication présentée au Amsterdam Colloquium, Amsterdam.

LeSourd, Phillip S. 2010. On Raising to Object in Maliseet-Passamaquoddy. *Proceedings of WSCLA 14: The Workshop on Structure and Constituency in the Languages of the Americas.*

University of British Columbia Working Papers in Linguistics 26, sous la direction de Heather Bliss et Amelia Reis Silva, pp. 171-182. Vancouver : Department of Linguistics, University of British Columbia.

Lochbihler, Bethany, et Éric Mathieu. 2013. Wh-agreement in Ojibwe Relative Clauses: Evidence for CP Structure. *Canadian Journal of Linguistics* 58: 293-318.

Lochbihler, Bethany, et Éric Mathieu. 2016. Clause typing and feature inheritance of discourse features. *Syntax* 19 (4): 354–391.

Mathieu, Éric, et Brandon J. Fry. 2014. Long-distance agreement in Ojibwe and de re belief. Manuscrit, Université d'Ottawa.

Moulton, Keir. 2009. Natural selection and the syntax of clausal complementation. Thèse de doctorat, University of Massachussetts - Amherst.

Moulton, Keir. 2010. The meaning of ECM. Communication présentée au TOM Semantics Workshop 6, McGill University.

Polinsky, Maria, et Eric Potsdam. 2001. Long-distance agreement and topic in Tsez. *Natural Language and Linguistic Theory* 19:583–646.

Preminger, Omer. 2011. Agreement as a fallible operation. Thèse de doctorat, MIT.

Rhodes, Richard Alan. 1990. Obviation, inversion, and topic rank in Ojibwa. *Proceedings of the Sixteenth Annual Meeting of the Berkeley Linguistics Society: Special session on general topics in American Indian linguistics*, pp. 101–115. Berkeley : Berkeley Linguistics Society.

Rhodes, Richard Alan. 1994. Agency, inversion, and thematic alignment in Ojibwe. *Proceedings of the Berkeley Linguistics Society*, sous la direction de Susanne Dolbey, Andy Gahl, et Christopher Johnson, pp. 431–446. Berkeley : Berkeley Linguistics Society.

Richards, Marc D. 2007. On feature inheritance: an argument from the Phase Impenetrability Condition. *Linguistic Inquiry* 38:563–572.

Ritter, Elizabeth, et Sara Thomas Rosen. 2005. Agreement without A-positions: Another look at Algonquian. *Linguistic Inquiry* 36:648–660.

Rizzi, Luigi. 1997. The fine structure of the left periphery. *Elements of grammar*, sous la direction de Liliane Haegeman, pp. 281–337. Kluwer Academic Publishers.

Rooth, Mats. 1992. A theory of focus interpretation. Natural Language Semantics 1, 75–116.

Williamson, Timothy. 2000. *Knowledge and its limits.* Oxford : Oxford University Press.

Agi nenadi iboni medgakiwiyattini: Understanding the Individual in Meshkwaki Culture through History

Erik D. Gooding

Agi nenadi iboni medgakiwiyattini 'They will never stop being Meshkwaki'.[1] The *Meshkwaki:haki* ('People of the Red Earth'), or Meshkwaki, are a Central Algonquian American Indian group. Referred to initially by outsiders as the 'Fox', today the US government recognizes them officially as the Sac and Fox of the Mississippi River in Iowa, while they use their term for themselves, Meshkwaki (or Meskwaki in English). The Meshkwaki are most closely related to the *Asa:kiwa* (Sauk, 'People Emerging from the Ocean') and *Kikapo:wa* (Kickapoo, 'Stands Here and There').[2] These three, probably along with the Mascouten, speak related dialects of the same language referred to as Sauk-Fox-Kickapoo.[3]

The Meshkwaki have resided in multiple locations.[4] Beginning in Quebec, they followed a series of southerly then primarily westward movements into the American Northeast, then into Ohio, Michigan, Wisconsin, Illinois, and finally Iowa. During these movements they encountered and interacted with a variety of other native groups (Dakota, Illinois, Iroquois, Iowa, Shawnee, and others) and later Europeans (British and French). These interactions were at times peaceful and beneficial to all parties, and at other times were combative and caused great trauma. The most notable of these traumatic interactions were with the French. Two periods of warfare with the French in the eighteenth century decimated the

Meshkwaki population, and additional conflicts with other native groups over time greatly impacted their culture. Late in the eighteenth century the Meshkwaki moved into Iowa, where they resided when the US government removed them to a reservation in Kansas. Shortly after their arrival, those who were removed began to return to Iowa to meet up with those who remained, eventually acquiring 80 acres of land in east-central Iowa in 1857. Today the Meshkwaki Settlement has expanded to over 8,000 acres and is home to 1,400 Meshkwaki.

Meshkwaki people, both individually and in groups, strive to endure.[5] They are burdened with two ultimate responsibilities that will ensure their survival, one to the world of the *maneto:wa* ('spirit') and one to this world. First, they must please the *maneto:wa*, thus ensuring the continuance of the world. This is accomplished through a series of prescribed formal and informal solitary actions or group rituals. Second, they must contribute to the group in some way, thus aiding in the survival of the Meshkwaki in this world. To be Meshkwaki, one must participate in the Meshkwaki way of life and do something that benefits the people.

The Meshkwaki were created from the red earth. The Creator and the *maneto:wa* then gifted the Meshkwaki their way of life and their culture—a series of institutions and mechanisms (structures) and symbols. These structures, which themselves have symbolic dimensions, and symbols explicitly and tacitly guide and explicate Meshkwaki life.[6] These structures form, cross cut, and integrate the various domains of Meshkwaki culture. Individuals belong to, participate in, and contribute to these structures in the form of specific social statuses (positions) with accompanying social roles (actions/behaviors). Three types of structures exist in Meshkwaki society: gender-based, kinship-based, and voluntary.[7] Meshkwaki have both ascribed and achieved forms of statuses, and individuals assume multiple statuses as needed within and between these three types of social structures. This paper discusses these structures and the statuses/roles of the individuals within them.

Gender-Based Structures

The first structure type is gender-based. Meshkwaki gender is a cultural construction with considerations to biological sex. Meshkwaki recognize two biological sexes that form the starting point for the construction of gender, which is primarily based on the actions/behaviors of an individual. Sexuality is another dimension of individuality, but does not factor into the cultural construction of gender.[8]

Meshkwaki culture recognizes two gender continua, *Ge* and *Neniwa*.[9] *Ge* represents a 'female' continuum with four stages:

1. *Idge:se:a* 'girl'
2. *Askigea* 'single woman'
3. *Onabemita* 'married woman'
4. *Metemo:ka* 'old woman/post-menopausal woman'

Each of these stages is marked by a publicly recognized event. A female child is born into the first stage, *Idge:se:a*. She is in this stage until she has *ashkikwe:wiweni*, her first menstruation, and undergoes the women's puberty ceremony, the *sakatti-yiya*. After this ceremony she enters into the second stage, *Askigea*, in which she is classified as a single woman. At marriage she enters into the third stage, *Onabemita*, where she remains until she begins menopause. Following menopause she enters into the fourth and final stage of *Metemo:ka*.

Neniwa, the male continuum, also has four stages:

1. *Gi:yese:ha* 'boy'
2. *Odkinawe:a* 'young man'
3. *Neniwiwa* 'man'
4. *Padito:ha* 'old man'

The male continuum differs from the female continuum in that the markers for each stage are not as clearly defined. A male is born into the first stage of *Gi:yese:ha*. As he grows older a series of small actions may occur that begin his transition to the second stage of *Odkinawe:a*. These actions can be subtle and private, or public. They reflect the changing responsibility over the child, transitioning from his female relatives to his male relatives, and the change in his participation in corresponding activities. Upon the completion of an appropriate activity or activities, either religious- or warfare-based, a *Odkinawe:a* can be recognized as a *Neniwiwa*.[10] He will remain a *Neniwiwa* until he attains the status of an elder, in which he is classified as a *Padito:ha*.[11]

In addition to the four stages in each of the gender continua is a fifth aspect, a biological opposite individual that assumes the actions/behaviors of the other continuum. These are *E:e:igewa* and *E:e:neniwa*. The first, *E:e:igewa* 'acts like a woman', is a biological male who assumes the actions/behaviors of a female. This form was first documented by Catlin (1841:243) in his painting *Dance to the Berdashe*, which was based on a sketch drawn at a Meshkwaki village in 1835. The second, *E:e:neniwa* 'acts like a man', is a biological female who acts like a man. This form is historically undocumented by outsiders, yet was and is known among Meshkwaki consultants. Historically, both of these additional gender forms were valued.

Individuals of both continua are expected to contribute to the continuance of the Meshkwaki through participation in gender-based structures. The primary gender-based structure is occupations. These are temporary or permanent social statuses, both achieved and ascribed, with accompanying roles (action/behaviors) that are determined by an individual's gender. Historic social statuses were gender-based, while contemporary Meshkwaki social statuses tend to be less biased except for those few remaining ascribed social statuses. These social statuses include occupations and activities related to a variety of cultural domains, including those associated with subsistence (hunter, gatherer, gardener, cook, farmer, etc.), politics (*Okima:wa* 'chief, leader', *Tebowe:neni:a* 'Councilman', *Ashka:pe:wa* 'village crier', *Ne:nawito:waki* 'village police', *Me:ya:wosa:ta* 'leader of a war party', etc.), religion (clan leader, *Mami:di:a* 'ceremonial attendant', ceremonial singer, etc.), and economics (*Wi:htwiya:a* 'silversmith', 'bead worker', etc.). Age also factors into gendered participation. For example, a *Metemo:ka* 'post-menopausal woman' can grow tobacco, something that a younger woman is forbidden to do.

Kinship-Based Structures

The second type of structure is kinship-based. Meshkwaki kinship has been described as the Omaha type. Individuals are simultaneously members of a series of kinship-based structures and assume a variety of statuses within these structures based on the two types of Meshkwaki 'love', *ketebanenwa* 'love of relative' and *kemenwenamenwi* 'romantic love'. Kinship-based structures derived from these two concepts of love include clan, lineage, family, household, and dual division.[12]

The first structure is the clan, *mi:so:ni* 'clan, name'. Meshkwaki clans are patrilineal groups, formerly exogamous, with naming and religious functions. Individuals are named according to the eponym of the clan, from a stock of clan-owned names. Clans also own sacred bundles and hold a variety of occasional and calendrical ceremonies.

Today there are seven acknowledged clans: Bear, Eagle, Fox,[13] Swan, Thunder,

Water (Fish), and Wolf, which vary in size and ceremonial activity. Meskwaki individuals often equate clan with family, both today and historically. Some current consultants who are older, fluent Meshkwaki speakers have difficulty separating the concepts of family and clan, and the account from the 1650s in which a Meshkwaki individual identified himself as 'Fox', not Meshkwaki, illustrates this dilemma. Meshkwaki clans also appear to have been the defining feature of their villages in the 1670s (Goddard 1975).

In addition to responsibilities to one's own clan, an individual may have responsibilities to other clans. These can be through adoption(s), marriage, and/or clan reciprocity.

The second structure within kinship is lineage. Lineages are also patrilineal groupings that are component groups of clans. Lineages are named after forms of the clan eponym. The following is a list of active clans with possible lineages based on Callendar (1962:27) and recent fieldwork:[14]

- Bear: Brown Bear, Black Bear, Grizzly Bear
- Eagle: Eagles, Hawks
- Fox: Black Fox, Red Fox (also War Chiefs, Kindly Chiefs)
- Swan: Swan, Goose, Duck
- Thunder: High Thunder, Low Thunder
- Water (Fish): Bass, Sturgeon, Ringed Perch
- Wolf: Black Wolf, White Wolf, Coyote

Formerly, lineages played a number of important roles in Meshkwaki culture, including assigning ascribed statuses (Peace Chief, War Chief, Intermediary Chief, clan chiefs, etc.), regulating secondary marriages (levirate and sororate) and influencing polygyny (sororal extended to lineage), determining burial groupings, owning secondary bundles and being responsible for related ceremonies, possible village groupings, and possible winter camping and hunting groupings.[15] The lineage system is in decline; individuals recognize few today. Clan has become the primary large kinship unit. Today lineages are differentiated in the Meshkwaki language by the term *wittisomattiki* ('the ones you are named with' or 'clan family') combined with the term for the lineage eponym.[16]

The third structure is the family. This structure consists of an individual's bilateral family and affinal relatives along with individuals with whom one had children and their families. These are people with whom an individual may interact concerning family-related matters, such as the training of children, possible winter camping and hunting groupings, ceremonial commitments, as well as financial/economic responsibilities. This structure also includes a relationship between a woman and her stepchildren's mother, and a man and his stepchildren's father, who share responsibility in caring for the children. Adoption also introduces another family unit.

The fourth structure is the household, *nekotikamiki*. This is the living together/economic unit of the Meshkwaki. In the past when the Meshkwaki followed a seasonal round, this unit would have resided in a *o:te:wenika:ni* 'summer house' in a village during the summer season and in a *wi:kiya:pi* 'wickiup' during the fall/winter/spring seasons. A household during the summer typically would have consisted of an extended family (preference to a matrilocal extended family) while a winter household would have consisted of the smaller nuclear family. Either a male or female can head a household; when a couple-unit is dissolved, the initiator of the split leaves the unit, and the children stay with the remaining parent.

The fifth and final kinship-based structure is the dual division. The Meshkwaki were split into two divisions, *ki:dko:ha* and *to:ka:na*, based on birth order.[17] Children were alternatively assigned to a division based on their father's division. The first child was assigned to the division opposite of the father; the second child was assigned to the father's division, and so forth. Dual divisions were/are used to organize ceremonial groupings, game play, and warfare/police groupings.[18]

Voluntary Structures

This final structure type is comprised of temporary or permanent groupings that are not primarily gender- or kinship-based and are typically voluntary in nature. These include social/religious/warfare-based societies/committees, political factions, residence, and modern occupations.

The first voluntary structure is the social society/committee, which is a social-based group. Examples of this type include participation in groupings such as baseball teams, the Meshkwaki band, the Boy Scouts, the Meskwaki Food Sovereignty Initiative, school clubs, and powwow committees.

The second voluntary structure is based on participation in religious societies. These are religious groupings that cross cut the clans. These include groups of individuals who have been blessed by the same spirit.[19]

The third voluntary structure is based on participation in warfare/military societies. These range from temporary raiding parties, temporary hunting groups, participation in the American military, to membership in the Meshkwaki Robert Morgan VFW Post.

The fourth voluntary structure is based on a chosen political faction. Political factions have been observed among Meshkwaki since their early interactions with the French and British. Today there is still lingering factionalism, particularly relating to *Paditoniga*'s chieftainship and his decisions, as well as factions based on more recent disputes.

The fifth voluntary structure is based on residency. Historically over the course of a year the Meshkwaki would have followed a seasonal round, residing in a summer village, a winter camp, hunting camps, trapping camps, and maple sugar camps. While these decisions may have been influenced by kinship, other factors such as politics and economics may have been a factor in choosing where an individual or group resided.

The sixth and final voluntary structure is based on modern occupations. Historic occupations as noted above were gender-based; however, modern occupations are personal choice. Meshkwaki individuals today can choose an occupation within the constraints of American society.

Summary and Conclusions

Meshkwaki history is replete with periods of warfare, both offensive and defensive, against other native groups as well as European powers. Population loss from warfare as well as epidemics, combined with forced and voluntary migrations, greatly impacted Meshkwaki society. Throughout these tumultuous times, the Meshkwaki, as individuals and as a group, were obligated to continue their responsibilities to ensure the survival of this world and of the Meshkwaki people.

What enables the Meshkwaki to fulfill their obligations is their participation in a variety of social statuses and/or by participating in solidary or group rituals in gender-based, kinship-based, and/or voluntary structures. These structures allow for any Meshkwaki, individually or in groups, to contribute to their survival. They can undertake a kinship status, or assume an occupation, or participate in a religious ritual. These three types of structures cross cut and integrate Meshkwaki culture, providing individuals the opportunity to contribute in any cultural domain. And as long as they continue to contribute they will never stop being Meshkwaki. *Agi nenadi iboni medgakiwiyattini.*

NOTES

1. Meshkwaki terms follow the official tribal orthography. For a discussion of the spelling and pronunciation of Meshkwaki and various orthographies, see Goddard and Thomason (2014:1–2). For overviews of the Meshkwaki language in general, see Bloomfield (1925, 1927), Goddard and Thomason (2014), and Voorhis (1971).
2. All terms, including names of other groups, are given from the Meshkwaki perspective.
3. See Goddard (1972) for his discussion on the position of the Mascouten.
4. For general overviews of Meshkwaki culture and history, see Callendar (1978), Joffe (1940), Jones (1939), and Tax (1955).
5. Information presented in this paper is based on two periods of fieldwork with the Meshkwaki people. The first was undertaken as a student intern during the Art of the Red Earth People exhibit at the University of Iowa Museum of Art during the 1987–1988 school year. During this time I interviewed tribal elders/members on aspects of the exhibition and general questions concerning Meshkwaki culture. The second period is from 2002 to the present. During this period I have interacted with Meshkwaki people individually and in groups during fieldwork as well as during my summer field schools held annually at the Meshkwaki Settlement. I have sought out and worked with members of the seven active Meshkwaki clans (Bear, Eagle, Fish, Fox, Swan, Thunder, and Wolf) as well as members of the Historic Preservation Department, Language Preservation Department, the Meskwaki Cultural Center and Museum, and the Language and Culture Department at the Meskwaki Settlement School. I would like to thank all the individuals who assisted with any aspect of this research, and I respect their wishes to remain anonymous.
6. The symbolic dimensions of Meshkwaki culture are beyond the scope of this study.
7. These categories are not mutually exclusive; some structures have aspects of multiple types.
8. Meshkwaki recognize both heterosexual and homosexual behaviors as options for sexual activity.
9. The identification and classification of these two categories grew out of initial fieldwork with several elder females on the *sakattiyiya* (women's puberty ceremony). From those conversations I then sought out Meshkwaki individuals from both genders and from a range of ages. What is presented here is a consensus understanding derived from

fieldwork from over 20 Meshkwaki speakers. Several individuals did point out other interesting terms, such as *bedige* 'divorced woman', that most did not consider a part of these continua.

10. These activities could include but are not limited to first animal kill, vision questing, fasting, where the child sleeps in the summerhouse, and sitting with men during ceremonies.
11. In addition to these stages, Meshkwaki recognize other types of individuals; these include women who have had children, divorced individuals (*pedega:ha*), men and women who are in mourning, generic elders (*kekyeaki*), and generic young people (*eskikiaki*). While these categories are important to Meshkwaki people, they can be viewed as aspects of the systems discussed here.
12. There is the possibility of another kinship-based structure, one based on moieties. Evidence suggests that the Meshkwaki may have had moieties during the 1600s. French sources refer to two extractions, the Terre-Rouge "Red Earths" and the Renards "Foxes" (Bacqueville de la Potherie 1911–1912:360).
13. The Fox clan is also known as the War Chiefs.
14. Callendar (1962) considers a Fish phratry that was comprised of the Bass, Swan, and *Kenwamewok* ('Tailed Water Animal Clan'). He also noted that the *Kenwamewok* clan consisted of three lineages, Beaver, Muskrat, and Underwater Panther.
15. A contemporary consultant noted that lineages may have had other responsibilities, but that they were probably "long lost due to unfortunate times."
16. This term, *wittisomattiki*, is also used in identifying clan membership, combining the term with the clan eponym instead of the lineage eponym.
17. The term *to:ka:na* was reportedly borrowed from Ioway, from their *Tukana* 'Kit Fox' society. The original term was *odkada*.
18. In contemporary times the *to:ka:na*/*ki:dko:ha* are used in other ways; for example, at the Meshkwaki Settlement School the dual divisions are asked to indicate their division by wearing their division colors (white = *ki:dko:ha*, black = *to:ka:na*) during school events.
19. It should also be noted that there are religious groups among the Meshkwaki that are not Meshkwaki in origin; these groups are outside the scope of this study.

REFERENCES

Bacqueville de la Potherie, Claude C. Le Roy. 1911–1912. History of savage peoples who are allies of New France. In *Indian tribes of the upper Mississippi Valley and region of the Great Lakes*, ed. Emma H. Blair, 11–136, 273–372. Cleveland: Arthur H. Clark.

Bloomfield, Leonard. 1925. Notes on the Fox language [Part 1]. *International Journal of American Linguistics* 3:219–232.

———. 1927. Notes on the Fox language [Part 2]. *International Journal of American Linguistics* 4:181–219.

Catlin, George. 1841. *Letters and notes on the customs and manners of the North American Indians*, 2 vols. New York: Wiley and Putnam.

Callendar, Charles. 1962. *Social organization of the Central Algonkian Indians*. Milwaukee Public Museum Publications in Anthropology No. 7.

———. 1978. Fox. In *Handbook of North American Indians, Northeast*, Vol 15, ed. Bruce Trigger, 636–647. Washington, DC: Smithsonian Institution.

Goddard, Ives. 1972. Historical and philological evidence regarding the identification of the Mascouten. *Ethnohistory* 19:123–134.

———. 1975. Fox social organization 1650–1850. In *Papers of the sixth Algonquian Conference*, ed. William Cowan, 128–140. National Museum of Man, Mercury Series, Canadian Ethnology Service Paper 23. Ottawa.

Goddard, Ives, and Lucy Thomason. 2014. *A Meskwaki-English and English-Meskwaki Dictionary, Based on early twentieth-century writings by native speakers*. Petoskey, MI: Mundart Press.

Joffe, Nancy F. 1940. The Fox of Iowa. In *Acculturation in seven American Indian tribes*, ed. Ralph Linton, 249–331. New York: Appleton-Century.

Jones, William. 1939. *Ethnography of the Fox Indians*. Ed. Margaret Fischer. Smithsonian Institution, Bureau of American Ethnology Bulletin 125. Washington, DC.

Tax, Sol. 1955. The social organization of the Fox Indians. In *Social organization of North American tribes*, ed. Fred Eggan, 243–282. Chicago: University of Chicago Press.

Voorhis, Paul H. 1971. New notes on the Mesquakie (Fox) language. *International Journal of American Linguistics* 37:63–75.

Ditransitives and Possessor Raising in Mi'gmaq

Michael David Hamilton

A comparison between ditransitives and "possessor raising" (PR) constructions in Mi'gmaq (Eastern Algonquian) presents an interesting puzzle.[1] The inflection on ditransitives and PR is identical, as shown in (1a) and (1b), respectively.

(1) a. Ditransitive (benefactive)
elugw-**atm-u-i-t-l**
fix-**DFLT-APPL-1OBJ-3-OBV**
'S/he fixes the net (AN) for me.'

b. PR
ges-**atm-u-i-t-l** 'nt-gij-l
love-**DFLT-APPL-1OBJ-3-OBV** 1POSS-mother-OBV
'S/he loves my mother.'

Since both appear with the same sequence of inflection following the verb root, the simplest analysis would be to assume that both constructions have the same underlying syntactic structure. However, there are several asymmetries between these constructions, the most significant being that while the goal Determiner Phrase (DP) in ditransitives can be the primary internal argument in passives and reflexives, the possessor DP in PR cannot. The puzzle is how to derive the surface similarity yet underlying structural asymmetry between these constructions.

I propose that these asymmetries show us that PR differs from ditransitives in two important respects: the base-generated position of the primary internal argument, and the feature specification of the probe (Lochbihler and Mathieu, 2016), which triggers agreement with the primary internal argument. In ditransitives, I propose that the goal DP is base-generated in Spec-Applicative Phrase (ApplP) and agreement with Voice is triggered by a person feature probe (φ-probe), as in (2a). In PR, I propose that the possessor DP is base-generated in Spec-DP of the possessive DP and agreement with Voice is triggered with a discourse-feature probe (δ-probe; Miyagawa 2010), as in (2b).

(2) Ditransitives vs. PR

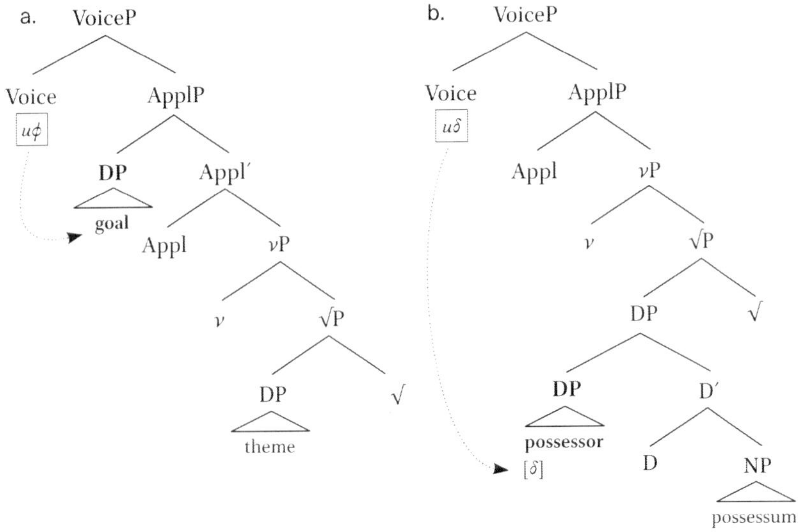

I use syntactic diagnostics to argue that goal DPs are structurally higher than theme DPs in ditransitives, and motivate a "high" applicative (ApplP) (Pylkkänen 2002, 2008) structure. After this, I present several asymmetries that call into question the feasibility of a possessor dative analysis of PR in which the underlying structure parallels that of ditransitives. Instead, I propose a PR analysis in which the possessor DP is base-generated internal to the possessive DP and undergoes movement to Spec-ApplP. Finally, I conclude and discuss potential areas of support for the PR analysis presented.

Ditransitives

In this section, I provide an analysis of ditransitives based on morphosyntactic and syntactic evidence that shows that the goal DP is structurally higher than the theme DP, and that the structure involves a "high" Applicative Phrase (ApplP) (Pylkkänen 2002, 2008). This lays the foundation for a comparison with PR forms.

Transitives and Agreement

The majority of three-place predicates in Mi'gmaq are derived via the inclusion of an applicative morpheme (*-u/w*) and a goal DP that acts as the primary internal argument (Dryer 1986) for agreement. In ditransitives, inflection inside of the applicative morpheme mirrors that on transitive verbs with an animate subject and inanimate object (VTI), while inflection outside resembles that of a transitive verb with animate subject and object (VTA). The similarity with both VTIs and VTAs can be seen by comparing the ditransitive form in (3b) with the VTI and VTA forms in (3a) and (3c), respectively.

(3) a. VTI
elugw-**at**-g
fix-**DFLT**-3
'S/he fixes it (IN).'

b. Ditransitive
elugw-**atm**-u-**i-t-l**
fix-**DFLT**-APPL-**1OBJ-3-OBV**
'S/he fixes it (AN) for her/him.'

c. VTA
elugw-al-**a-t-l**
fix-AN-**3OBJ/DIR-3-OBV**
'S/he fixes it (AN).'

Beginning with a comparison of the ditransitive with the VTI form, notice that both have the same verb root (*elugw* 'fix') and default transitive verb final (*-at(m)*).[2] However, while the VTI verb indexes the third person subject (*-g*), in ditransitives after the applicative morpheme (*-u*), there is a third person object-marking VTA theme sign (*-i*) that indexes the goal DP.[3] The theme sign is followed by a third person subject marker (*-t*) and an obviative clitic (*-l*), both of which index the theme DP. The sequence of inflectional morphemes after the applicative morpheme in the ditransitive form is identical to the VTA form in (3c), except that it has a theme sign that indexes the third person theme DP (*-a*). Therefore, while the theme sign in VTAs indexes the theme DP, in ditransitives it is the goal DP that the theme sign indexes, not the theme DP.

Following Hamilton (2017), I assume the underlying structure of the verbal domain and derivation of the agreement for the VTA form in (3c) as in (4). I further assume that the appearance of an agreement affix is the result of an AGREE relation between a functional head and a DP (Chomsky 2000). A functional head with unvalued features (*u*F) probes downward in its c-command domain for a DP with the relevant interpretable features and enters into an agree relationship with an appropriate goal DP. As a result, the *u*Fs on the functional head are valued correspondingly.

(4) Verbal domain: VTA (3c)

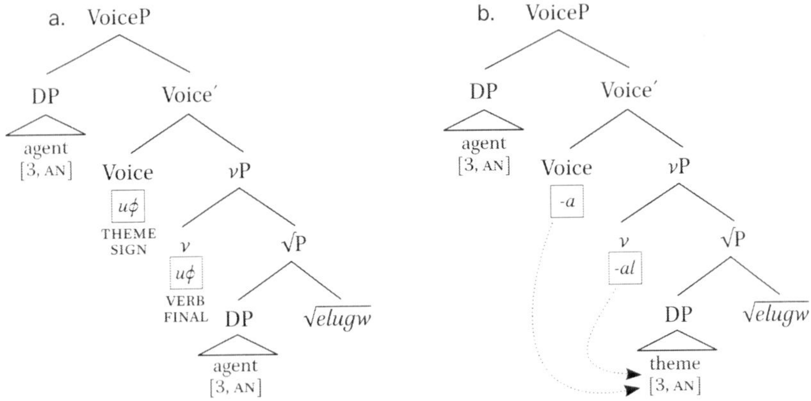

This transitive structure will form the basis for the analysis of ditransitives. In order to determine the underlying structure of ditransitives, we need evidence to determine the structural relation between the goal DP and the theme DP, as well as where ApplP attaches. In the next subsection, I present syntactic diagnostics to show that goal DPs are structurally higher than theme DPs. In the following subsection, I present arguments from the Mirror Principle (Baker 1985) and Pylkkänen (2002, 2008) to argue for a high ApplP.

Goal DPs Are Higher Than Theme DPs

I propose that in ditransitives, goal DPs are higher than theme DPs (e.g., see Branigan and MacKenzie 1999; Bruening 2001; and Lochbihler 2012 for similar proposals in other Algonquian languages). Following the representation above for transitives and a probe-goal account of AGREE, verbal agreement provides supporting evidence for this proposal. The fact that the goal DP is indexed as the primary internal argument supports this proposal, as the goal DP is structurally higher and thus a more local goal for φ-agreement with Voice. We saw that the first person goal DP, not the third person theme DP, was indexed as the primary internal argument in (3b). This results in the appearance of the first person object theme sign (*-i*). If we keep the theme DP constant and vary the goal DP, the theme sign covaries with it. A second person plural goal DP in (5a) and third person goal DP in (5b) result in corresponding changes in the theme signs, *-ugsi* and *-a*. This confirms that the goal DP is indexed on the theme sign and is the primary internal argument.[4]

(5) a. Second person goal
elugw-atm-(u)-**ugsi**-oq-l
fix-DFLT-APPL-**3>SAPPL**-3-OBV
'S/he fixes it (AN) for you-all.'

b. Third person goal
elugw-atm-u-**a**-t-l
fix-DFLT-APPL-**3OBJ**-3-OBV
'S/he fixes it (AN) for her/him.'

Additional evidence for the goal DP being structurally higher than the theme DP comes from passives and reflexives.[5] In ditransitives, the goal DP but not the theme DP can be the primary internal argument for passives and reflexives. The first person plural goal DP, not the third person singular theme DP, is indexed as the primary internal argument on the theme sign (*-ugsi*) in the passive form in (6a). On the reflexive form in (6b), the first person subject DP and goal DP is indexed as the person suffix (*-eg*). These forms support the proposal that goal DPs are more accessible for φ-probes on Voice, since a φ-probe would be involved in the agreement that surfaces on these forms regardless of whether any subsequent movement occurs.

(6) a. Passive
elugw-atm-(u)-ugsi-**eg**-p a'pi-l
fix-DFLT-APPL-3>SAPPL-**2PL**-PST NET-obv
'A/the net (AN) was fixed for us.' (Lit: 'We were fixed a/the net(AN).')

b. Reflexive
elugw-atm-(u)-asi-**eg**-p a'pi-l
fix-DFLT-APPL-REFL-**2PL**-PST net-OBV
'We fixed a/the net (AN) for ourselves.'

The fact that in ditransitives the goal DP and not the theme DP is indexed as the primary argument on a variety of forms, including passives and reflexives, supports an analysis where the goal DP is structurally higher than the theme DP. In the next subsection, I argue for a high ApplP analysis of ditransitives.

High Applicative Phrase

Pylkkänen (2002, 2008) proposes that there are two kinds of Applicative Phrases: a "high" ApplP and a "low" ApplP. High ApplP attaches above the verb root and adds an additional argument that modifies the event. Low ApplP is a complement to the verb root, and the additional argument stands in a particular relationship to the direct object, such as possession. Although Bruening (2001) and Lochbihler (2012) both argue that the goal DP is structurally higher than the theme DP, they differ in whether they posit the goal DP in a high (Bruening 2001) or low (Lochbihler 2012) ApplP. If we assume the Mirror Principle (Baker 1985), ditransitives in Mi'gmaq have high applicatives, since the applicative head appears between the verb final, mapped to v, and the theme sign, mapped to Voice, as in (7):

(7) Ditransitive (3b)

√*verb-*	-*v*^{0}	-Appl^{0}	-Voice^{0}	-T^{0}	-clitic
elugw- fix-	-atm -DFLT	-u -APPL	-i -1.OBJ	-t -3	-l OBV

'S/he fixes it (AN) for me'

In addition, Mi'gmaq ditransitives pass two diagnostics for high ApplPs suggested in Pylkkänen (2002, 2008). The first diagnostic involves the ability to add an applicative to an intransitive verb.[6] The form in (8b) shows an intransitive verb with an animate subject (VAI) *amalgat* 'S/he dances'. An applicative argument can be added to this verb to specify a benefactee for the dancing (i.e., *amalgowatl* 'S/he dances for her/him'). Notice that after the applicative morpheme (-*w*), the verb has the same transitive inflection seen in typical VTA verbs, which indicates that the added argument is being indexed as an internal argument on the verb.

(8) a. Intransitive (VAI)
amalga-t
dance-3
'S/he dances.'

b. Benefactive (VTA)
amalgo-w-a-t-l
dance-APPL-3OBJ-3-OBV
'S/he dances for her/him.'

The second diagnostic involves the ability to add an applicative to a static verb, which does not lead to change of possession (Pylkkänen 2002). Since low applicatives are interpreted as denoting a relation, such as possession, the ability to add an applicative without resulting in a possession relation is an argument against positing a low applicative in the syntactic structure. Assuming that the verb root *genn-* 'hold' in (9a) is a static verb root in Mi'gmaq, as in English, the ability to add an applicative argument in (9b) is evidence against positing a low applicative in this form. Note that the ditransitive in (9b) has the typical inflectional characteristics of other ditransitives, e.g., the default verb final (-*atm*), the applicative morpheme (-*u*), and the first person object theme sign (-*i*).

(9) a. VTA
genn-a-t-l
hold-3OBJ-3-OBV
'S/he holds her/him/it (AN).'

b. Ditransitive
genn-m-<u>u</u>-i-t-l
hold-DFLT-<u>APPL</u>-**3OBJ**-3-OBV
'S/he holds her/him/it (AN) for me.'

As a result of this evidence for the goal DP being structurally higher than the theme DP and for a high ApplP, I propose the representation for ditransitives in (10). The goal DP is base-generated in Spec-ApplP and is thus structurally closer for φ-agreement with Voice for the theme sign, and ultimately T for the person suffix.

(10) Ditransitive

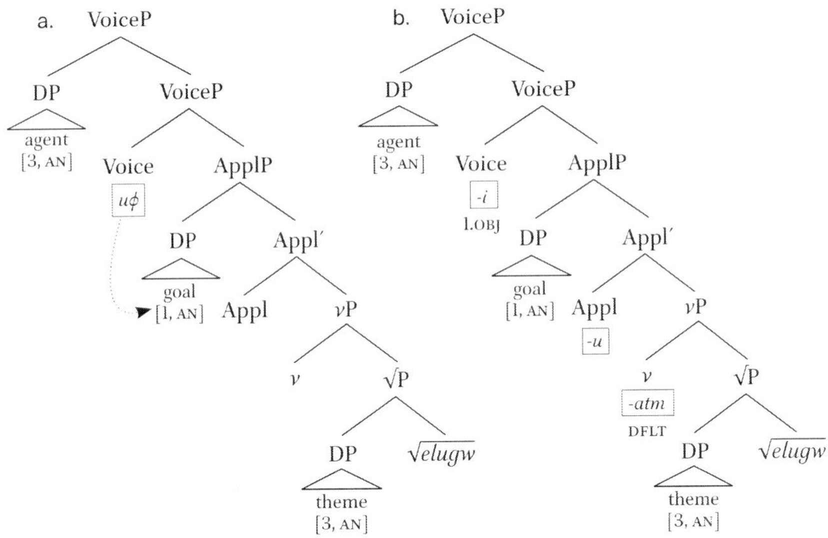

In the next section, I compare PR forms with ditransitives. I argue that although PR forms are superficially similar, they cannot have an underlying syntactic representation that is identical to that of ditransitives.

Possessor Raising

Possessor Dative Account

PR is a construction in which the possessor DP, rather than the entire possessive DP, is the primary internal argument. In non-PR forms, as in (11a), the entire possessive DP (*'ntgijl* 'my mother') is the internal argument, as shown by the third person object theme sign (*-a*) on the verb. In the PR form in (11b), the first person possessor DP, not the third person possessive DP, is indexed on the verb, as shown by the first person object theme sign (*-i*). On the surface, the verbal inflection in PR (11b) is identical to that in ditransitives (11c), with the possessor DP, in parallel with the goal DP, being the primary internal argument. In addition to having the possessor DP and goal DP indexed on the theme sign, they both have the default verb final (*-atm*) and applicative morpheme (*-u*).

(11) a. Non-PR
ges-al-**a**-t-l **'nt-gij-l**
love-AN-**3OBJ/DIR**-3-OBV **1POSS-mother-OBV**
'S/he loves **my mother**.'

b. PR
ges-atm-u-**i**-t-l **'nt**-gij-l
love-DFLT-APPL-**1OBJ**-3-OBV **1POSS**-mother-OBV
'S/he loves **my** mother.'

c. Ditransitive
elugw-atm-u-**i**-t-l a'pi-l
fix-DFLT-APPL-**1OBJ**-3-OBV net-OBV
'S/he fixes the net (AN) **for me**.'

This surface parallel suggests an analysis where PR has the same underlying syntactic structure as ditransitives. Under a possessor dative analysis (e.g., Deal 2013), the possessor DP would be base-generated outside the possessive DP in Spec-ApplP, in parallel with the goal DP in ditransitives, as in (12). As such, the possessor DP would bind a possessor anaphor inside the possessive DP (Guéron 1985). Under this analysis we expect the possessor DP to be parallel to the goal DP syntactically, in triggering the same agreement patterns and undergoing the same kind of movement, and semantically, in receiving an AFFECTEE theta role (Deal 2013).

(12) Ditransitives and PR

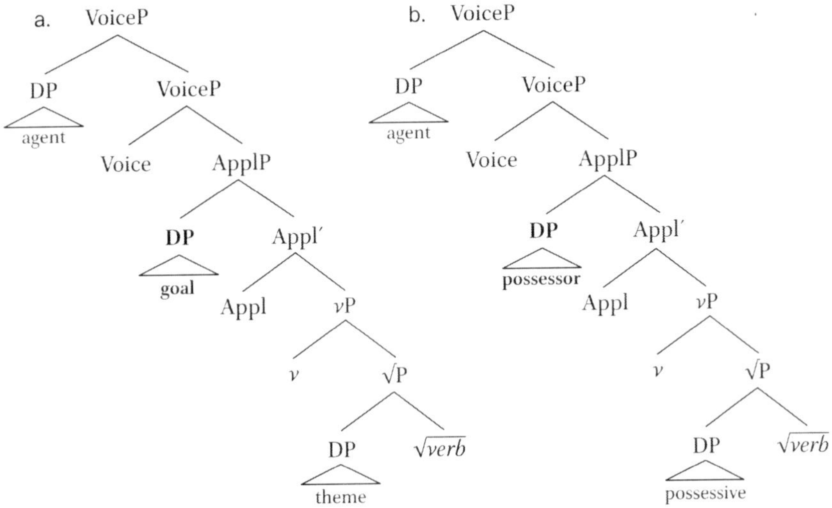

Asymmetries

Although this analysis is initially appealing, there are three asymmetries between PR and ditransitives that need to be accounted for if they are underlyingly identical: the optional and discourse-related characterization of PR, the lack of evidence for an AFFECTEE theta role for the possessor DP, and the inability for the possessor DP to be the primary internal argument for passives and reflexives.

First, while benefactives are mandatory when a goal DP is present, PR is optional. The non-PR form in (13a) is a typical VTA form, in that the verb indexes the entire possessive DP as the primary internal argument and appears without an Appl. The PR form in (13b) is similar to a ditransitive form, in that the verb indexes the possessor DP as the primary internal argument and an Appl appears. Importantly, PR is discourse-driven, and speakers report that the possessor DP is interpreted as being topical when used.

(13) a. Non-PR

ges-al-a-t-l **'nt-gij-l**

love-AN-3OBJ/DIR-3-OBV **1POSS-mother-OBV**

'S/he loves **my mother.**'

b. PR

ges-**atm**-u-**i**-t-l **'nt**-gij-l

love-**DFLT**-APPL-**1OBJ**-3-OBV **1POSS**-mother-OBV

'S/he loves **my** mother.'

Thus, topicality of the possessor DP seems to condition the presence of PR and an ApplP. This is different from ditransitives, which always have an Appl.

Second, if the possessor DP is base-generated in Spec-ApplP, it is predicted to have an AFFECTEE theta role; however, there is no clear evidence to support this. Deal (2013) suggests that possessor affectedness theta roles are limited to possessor DPs that have an inalienable possessum, are goals of eventive verbs, and are animate possessors. In Mi'gmaq, PR can appear with possessums that are inalienable, e.g., *gij*- 'mother' in (14a), and alienable, e.g., *tepaqan* 'car' in (14b). In addition, PR can appear with stative verbs, as with *ges*- 'like/love' in (1b), (13b), and (14a).

(14) a. PR: Inalienable possessum

ges-atm-u-i-t-l **'nt-gij-l**

love-DFLT-APPL-1OBJ-3-OBV **1POSS-mother-OBV**

'S/he loves **my mother.**'

b. PR: Alienable possessum

welap-tm-u-i-t **'n**-tepaqan

like-DFLT-APPL-1OBJ-3 **1POSS**-car

'S/he likes (the look of) **my car.**'

Although possessor DPs in PR must be animate, this is not a surprising occurrence as possessor DPs in Mi'gmaq, and Algonquian languages in general, must always be animate. In fact, absentative DPs are animate and possible in PR, but it is an open question if they can receive an AFFECTEE theta role in any meaningful way in examples such as (15).

(15) PR: Absentative possessor

gnasgm-u-a-t-l **Piel-oq** ugt-atlai'-m-l
wear.DFLT-APPL-3OBJ/DIR-3-OBV **PETER-ABSEN** 3POSS-shirt-POSS-OBV
'S/he is wearing **Peter (deceased)**'s shirt.'

The final and most important asymmetry is that while goal DPs can be the primary internal argument in passives and reflexives, the possessor DP in PR cannot. Earlier examples of ditransitives in (6a) and (6b) are repeated below as (16a) and (17a), and paired with grammatical PR counterparts in (16b) and (17b), respectively, which are both ungrammatical. In both ditransitive examples in (16a) and (17a), the first person goal DP is the primary internal object and is indexed on the verb with a fusional third person subject and first person plural object suffix (*-ugsi*). However, in both PR examples in (16b) and (17b), it is not possible for the first person plural possessor DP to be the primary internal argument in the same way as the goal DP in the ditransitive examples. Typically, the entire possessive DP can be the primary internal argument for passives and reflexives, as shown in the VTA counterpart examples in (16c) and (17c). Both forms have a fusional third person past morpheme (*-p*) showing that the entire possessive DP is the internal argument. However, note that since these are both in VTA form, neither includes an applicative suffix.

(16) Passive

a. Ditransitive

elugw-atm-(u)-ugsi-**eg**-p a'pi -l
fix-DFLT-APPL-3>SAPPL/PASS-**1PL**-PST net-OBV
'A/the net(AN) was fixed for us.' (Lit: 'We were fixed a/the net(AN).')

b. PR

*ges-atm-(u)-ugsi-**eg**-p **'nt**-gij-inen
love-DFLT-APPL-3>SAPPL/PASS-**1PL**-PST **1POSS**-mother-1PL
intended: '**Our** mother was loved.'

c. Non-PR (VTA)

ges-al-u't-'p **'nt-gij-inen**
love-AN-3PASS-PST **1POSS-mother-1PL**
'**Our mother** was loved.'

(17) Reflexive

a. Ditransitive

elugw-atm-(u)-asi-**eg** a'pi -l

fix-DFLT-APPL-REFL-**1PL** net-OBV

'**We** are fixing a/the net(AN) **for ourselves.**'

b. PR

*ges-atm-(u)-asi-**eg** '**nt**-gij-inen

love-DFLT-APPL-REFL-**1PL** **1POSS**-mother-1PL

intended: '**We** love **our** mother.'

c. Non-PR (VTA)

ges-al-si-p **'nt-gij-inen**

love-AN-REFL-3PST **1POSS-mother-1PL**

'**Our mother** loves herself.'

In sum, it appears that the parallel predicted by a possessor dative account between possessor DPs and goal DPs is tenuous. PR itself is optional and has discourse effects, while the possessor DPs cannot participate in passives and reflexives and lack evidence for receiving an AFFECTEE theta role. Thus a representative analysis of PR must account for the surface similarity of ditransitives on the one hand and these asymmetries on the other.

In the next subsection, I propose a classic PR analysis (e.g., Aissen 1987) in order to account for these asymmetries. I account for surface similarities by expanding on the conjecture that discourse (δ) features can drive agreement and movement in the clausal domain (Miyagawa 2010; Lochbihler and Mathieu, 2016).

Possessor Raising Account

I take the asymmetries presented in the last subsection to indicate that a possessor dative analysis makes incorrect predictions regarding parallels between the possessor DP in PR with the goal DP in ditransitives. These asymmetries are unexpected if goal DPs in ditransitives and possessor DPs in PR are base-generated in the same structural position, Spec-ApplP. As such, I propose that while PR does share the same underlying high ApplP structure as ditransitives, one source of these asymmetries can be explained if the possessor DP is base-generated internal to the possessive DP rather than in Spec-ApplP. The second source of variation is that PR is driven by δ-probe rather than φ-probe since probing needs to occur past the possessive DP itself. A comparison of the base-generated structure in ditransitives and PR is shown in (18).

(18) Ditransitive vs. PR

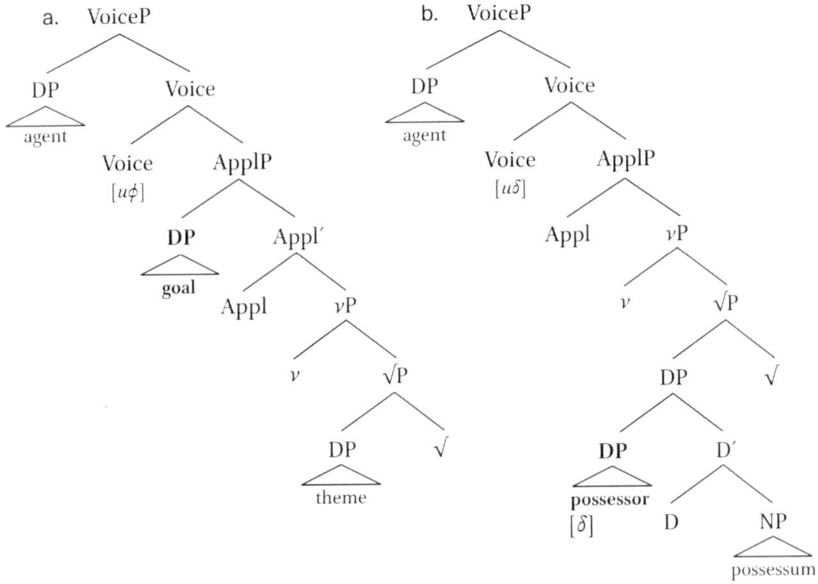

If the possessor DP is base-generated internal to the possessive DP, then the possessor DP is not the structurally highest internal argument. The entire possessive DP is the structurally highest internal argument. This explains why the entire possessive DP, not simply the possessor DP itself, can be the primary internal argument for passives and reflexives. It also explains why the possessor DP seems to lack an AFFECTEE theta role. Given the locality considerations on agreement in the verbal domain, a φ-probe will simply target the structurally highest DP for AGREE, which will always be the entire possessive DP since the possessor DP is base-generated internally. This means that when PR does occur and the possessor DP is the primary internal argument, AGREE cannot be driven by unvalued φ-features. It must be driven by unvalued δ-features, such as TOPIC. This would allow probing of the δ-marked possessor DP past the δ-less possessive DP.[7] This accounts for the optional and discourse-related nature of PR and the incompatibility with φ-driven probes in passives and reflexives.

The remaining piece of the puzzle is the surface similarity between PR and ditransitives. Miyagawa (2010) proposes that δ-features, in addition to φ-features, can drive agreement and movement in the clausal domain, and that the distribution of δ and φ features between C and T is subject to variation. If we assume that Voice has δ features, we can understand why the possessor DP undergoes agreement with Voice.

Therefore in the trees in (19) that show their differing base-generated structures, ditransitives and PR differ in two respects: the goal DP is base-generated in Spec-ApplP in ditransitives, while the possessor DP is base-generated in Spec-DP of the possessive DP in PR; and Voice and Appl have uφ in ditransitives but uδ in PR. As in the VTA forms in (4), I assume that the feature specification of Appl matches Voice in order for Appl to AGREE with the applied argument in each: the goal DP in the ditransitive, and the possessor DP in PR.[8] The ditransitive (19a) and PR (19b) trees would be identical if not for these two differences.

(19) Base-generated positions: Ditransitive vs. PR

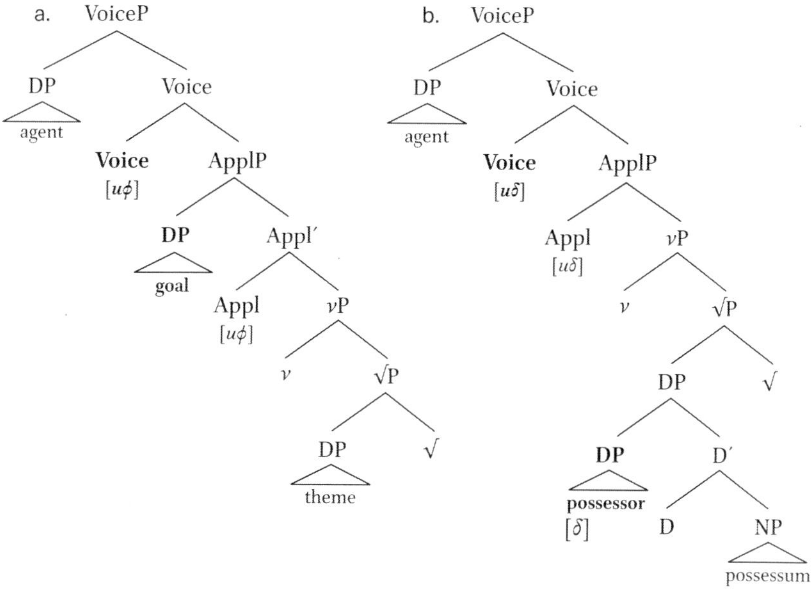

The difference between AGREE in ditransitives and PR is shown in (20). In ditransitives, the uφ-probe on Voice AGREEs with the goal DP since it is the structurally closest DP to this probe. This results in theme sign marking of the goal DP on Voice. In PR, the uδ-probe on Voice AGREEs with the possessor DP, since it is marked with a δ-feature. This results in theme sign marking with the possessor DP on Voice. In both cases, v does not have a probe and appears with default agreement, the default verb final (*-atm*). As a result, we get both forms appearing with the default verb final, applicative morpheme (*-u*), and object agreement with the goal DP and possessor DP, respectively. Thus the ability for both φ and δ to trigger agreement on Voice is attributed as the cause of the surface appearance of symmetry between the goal DP in ditransitives and the possessor DP in PR.[9]

(20) Agree: Ditransitives vs. PR

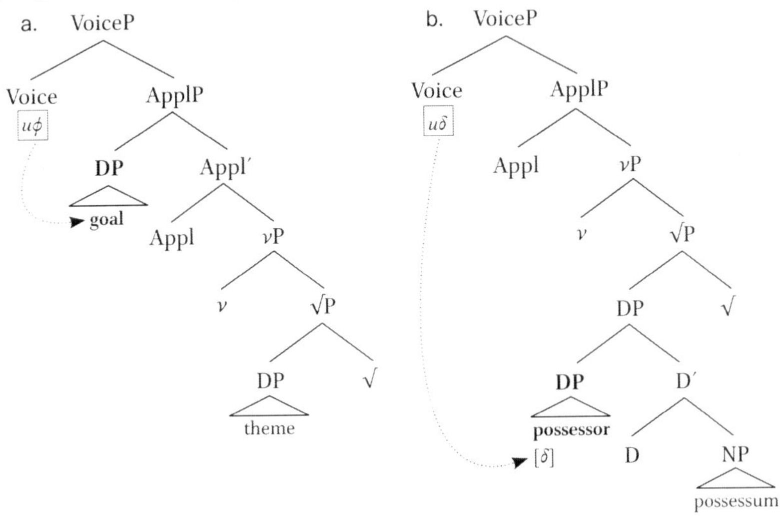

This results in a classic PR analysis, as has been proposed in Aissen (1987) for Tzotzil. Extended to the verbal domain is an account of agreement and movement motivated by discourse (δ) related movement (Miyagawa 2010). This was originally proposed for the clausal domain and has since been argued to be particularly relevant for Algonquian languages as well (Lochbihler and Mathieu, 2016). With this analysis, we can account for the asymmetries between possessor DPs and goal DPs, while still accounting for the surface similarities between PR and ditransitives.

Conclusion

In this paper I have proposed a solution to a puzzle regarding the surface similarity yet underlying asymmetries between derived ditransitives and PR in Mi'gmaq. First, I presented an account of ditransitives in which the goal DP is structurally higher than the theme DP, which results in it being indexed by the verb as the primary internal argument. I proposed that the goal DP is base-generated in the specifier of a high Applicative Phrase. I compared ditransitives with PR forms in which the possessor DP is indexed as the primary internal argument and has identical verbal inflection as ditransitives. Although these constructions have a similar underlying syntactic structure, I propose that possessor DPs are actually base-generated internal to the possessive DP, not in Spec-ApplP as goal DPs are in ditransitives. This explains why possessor DPs do not appear to have an AFFECTEE theta role and are not local enough to be a potential target for a uφ probe present in passives and reflexives. In addition, I proposed that PR is driven by discourse-feature agreement, which explains its optionality, its discourse-sensitive nature, and why it can undergo AGREE when it is not the structurally highest argument.

If this proposal is on the right track, we should find other instances of discourse-driven movement in both the verbal and clausal domain. In Hamilton (2015) I propose that flexible word order in Mi'gmaq is related to discourse movement in the clausal domain and presents experimental evidence that shows that the manipulation of word order is one strategy used by Mi'gmaq speakers to mark focus, a prominent discourse feature. Regarding the search for verb internal δ-driven movement and agreement, Long-Distance Agreement (LDA) forms, in which the matrix verb displays agreement with a constituent from its clausal complement, are particularly relevant in this respect. In LDA forms with embedded interrogatives that involve long-distance *wh*-movement in Mi'gmaq, the matrix Voice shows agreement with the *wh*-phrase on its way to matrix Spec-CP, which is plausibly driven by a δ-feature. As such, the analysis of PR developed here has promising analogues in other constructions.

NOTES

1. I would like to thank Janine Metallic, Mary Ann Metallic, and Janice Vicaire for sharing their knowledge of Mi'gmaq. I would like to thank Amy Rose Deal, Benjamin Bruening, Jonathan Bobaljik, and Lisa DeMena Travis for feedback at various stages of this project;

my supervisors: Jessica Coon, Michael Wagner, and Alan Bale; and the participants of the Mi'gmaq Research Group, LingTea, Forty-Sixth Algonquian Conference, NELS 45, and 2015 LSA annual meeting. Abbreviations: 1 = first person, 2 = second person, 3 = animate third person singular proximate (discourse salient), ABSENT = absentative, AN = animate, APPL = applicative, DFLT = default, DIR = direct, IN = inanimate, NEG = negation, OBJ = object, OBV = obviative, PASS = passive, PL = plural, POSS = possessive, PST = past, REFL = reflexive, SAP = speech act participant (first and/or second person), SG = singular, VAI = intransitive verb with an animate subject, VTA = transitive verb with both animate subject and object, VTI = transitive verb with animate subject and inanimate object, X>Y = X agent, Y patient.

2. Following Bruening (2001) and Quinn (2006), I gloss *-at(m)* as a default morpheme since it appears when the internal argument has no φ-features, such as with inanimate DPs and CPs. While the verb final in the VTA indexes an animate internal argument, *-al* in (3c), the one that appears in ditransitives displays the same default form as the VTI, *-atm* in (3a) and (3b). All derived three-place predicates appear with this default verb final.
3. I use the term "theme sign" throughout to refer to the suffix that appears after the verb final in VTAs. Although I generally follow an object marking analysis of this suffix, I use the term "theme sign" here for convenience.
4. Although omitted for space considerations, agreement on T is another argument for goals being structurally higher than themes. The appearance of the second person plural suffix (*-oq*) in (5a) is the result of an omnivorous number (Nevins 2011) effect related to the φ-probe on T. Only the subject and the structurally highest internal argument are accessible for agreement with T (Coon and Bale 2013; Hamilton 2017). This is another instance in ditransitives in which agreement is only possible with goals and not themes.
5. Passive constructions are also typically analyzed as unspecified actor constructions (Dryer 1996; Déchaine and Reinholtz 1998; Ritter and Rosen 2005; Lochbihler 2012; Oxford 2014). Regardless of the ultimate analysis of these forms, their usefulness as a diagnostic remains the same. In ditransitives, the goal DP but not the theme DP can be an internal argument for passives. Whether these forms involve movement or simply agreement, they support the fact that the goal DP is more accessible for φ-probes on Voice, as a φ-probe would be involved whether or not movement occurs. A similar story holds for whether a movement-based account of reflexives (e.g., Hornstein 1999) is pursued.
6. Pylkkänen (2002, 2008) argues that unergatives but not unaccusatives can be applicativized. Although I do not have independent evidence that *amalga-* 'dance' is unergative or unaccusative, it is certainly intransitive. Thus the ability to be

applicativized may be a test for unergative verbs in Mi'gmaq.

7. Under the assumption that the DP is a phase, and the possessor DP is in Spec-DP, it should be visible to a higher probe even under the strictest definition of locality, i.e., the strict Phase Impenetrability Condition (Chomsky 2000).
8. Note that if this is the case, then we would need to minimally assume probing under m-command (Aoun and Sportiche 1981), so Appl could AGREE with the goal DP in its specifier. Since overt agreement is not visible on Appl, another possible analysis is that Appl could simply have uφ in both cases and AGREE with the secondary internal argument in each: the theme DP in ditransitives and the possessive DP in PR. We could make sense of this as licensing the secondary argument. Finally, Appl could have no feature specification at all, but this would leave unexplained why ApplP was base-generated in PR forms, since ApplP would have no specific role.
9. Although not shown here, the goal DP and possessor DP must move to Spec-VoiceP in order to be in a local relationship for further agreement with T. This accounts for the ability of the subject and goal DP, or possessor DP, to be marked on T. See note 4.

REFERENCES

Aissen, Judith. 1987. *Tzotzil clause structure*. Vol. 7. Springer Science and Business Media.

Aoun, Youssouf, and Dominique Sportiche. 1981. On the formal theory of government. *Glow Newsletter Amsterdam* 6:52–53.

Baker, Mark. 1985. The mirror principle and morphosyntactic explanation. *Linguistic Inquiry* 16.3:373–415.

Branigan, Phil, and Marguerite MacKenzie. 1999. Binding relations and the nature of "'pro" in Innu-Aimun. In *NELS 29: Proceedings of the North East Linguistic Society*, ed. Nancy Hall, Masako Hirotani, and Pius Tamanji, 475–486. Amherst, MA: Graduate Linguistic Student Association.

Bruening, Benjamin. 2001. Syntax at the edge: Cross-clausal phenomena and the syntax of Passamaquoddy. PhD thesis, Massachusetts Institute of Technology.

Chomsky, Noam. 2000. Minimalist inquiries: The framework. In *Step by step: Essays on minimalist syntax in honor of Howard Lasnik*, ed. Roger Martin, David Michaels, and Juan Uriagereka, 89–15. Cambridge, MA: MIT Press.

Coon, Jessica, and Alan Bale. 2013. The inseparability of person and number in Mi'gmaq. Presented at Features in Phonology, Morphology, Syntax, and Semantics, University of Tromsø, CASTL, Norway.

Deal, Amy Rose. 2013. Possessor raising. *Linguistic Inquiry* 44.3: 391–432.

Déchaine, Rose Marie, and Charlotte Reinholtz. 1998. Direct/inverse as case-licensing. Paper read at *WSCLA* 3: The Workshop on Structure and Constituency in the Languages of the Americas, Saskatchewan Federated Indian College.

Dryer, Matthew S. 1986. Primary objects, secondary objects, and antidative. *Language* 62: 808–845.

———. 1996. Passive vs. indefinite actor construction in Plains Cree. In *Papers of the twenty-seventh Algonquian Conference*, ed. David H. Pentland, 54-79. Winnipeg: University of Manitoba.

Guéron, Jacqueline. 1985. Inalienable possession, pro-inclusion and lexical chains. *Grammatical representation*, eds. Richard Kayne, Jacqueline Guéron, Hans-Georg Obenauer, and Jean-Yves Pollock, 43–86. Dordrecht: Foris.

Hamilton, Michael David. 2015. *The syntax of Mi'gmaq: A configurational account*. PhD thesis, McGill University.

———. 2017. Multiple instances of agreement in Mi'gmaq verbs. In *Papers of the forty-fifth Algonquian Conference*, ed. Monica Macaulay, Margaret Noodin, and J. Randolph Valentine. East Lansing: Michigan State University Press.

Hornstein, Norbert. 1999. Movement and control. *Linguistic Inquiry* 30.1: 69–96.

Lochbihler, Bethany. 2012. Aspects of argument licensing. PhD thesis, McGill University.

Lochbihler, Bethany, and Éric Mathieu. 2016. Clause typing and feature inheritance of discourse features. *Syntax* 19(4):354–391.

Miyagawa, Shirgeru. 2010. *Why agree? why move: Unifying agreement-based and discourse configurational languages*. Cambridge, MA: MIT Press.

Nevins, Andrew. 2011. Multiple agree with clitics: Person complementarity vs. omnivorous number. *Natural Language and Linguistic Theory* 29.4: 939–971.

Oxford, William R. 2014. Microparameters of agreement: A diachronic perspective of Algonquian verb inflection. PhD thesis, University of Toronto.

Pylkkänen, Liina. 2002. Introducing arguments. PhD thesis, Massachusetts Institute of Technology.

———. 2008. *Introducing arguments*. Vol. 49. Cambridge, MA: MIT Press.

Quinn, Conor M. 2006. Referential-access dependency in Penobscot. PhD thesis, Harvard University.

Ritter, Elizabeth, and Sara Thomas Rosen. 2005. Agreement without A-positions: Another look at Algonquian. *Linguistic Inquiry* 36.4: 648–660.

The Syntax of Medial Incorporation and Concrete Finals in Menominee

Meredith Johnson and Bryan Rosen

This paper investigates the structure of Menominee verb stems by examining the placement of medials.[1] In the traditional Algonquianist literature, verb stems have been analyzed as containing three components: INITIAL, MEDIAL, and FINAL. The composition of finals is described as having two subtypes: ABSTRACT and CONCRETE. While abstract finals are often treated as monomorphemic, concrete finals are considered either monomorphemic or bimorphemic. When a concrete final is bimorphemic, the two subcomponents have been referred to as a "prefinal" and an "abstract final."

Johnson and Rosen (2017) argue that Menominee abstract and concrete finals are syntactically identical: both instantiate *v*, as shown in (1a). This contradicts previous analyses that assign different statuses to abstract and concrete finals. For example, Slavin (2012) argues that abstract finals are *v* and concrete finals are a Root-*v* combination (in Algonquianist terminology, a prefinal + abstract final). Both the traditional template (e.g., Bloomfield 1962; Goddard 1990) and Slavin's (2012) structures are presented in (1b, c).

(1) a. Our proposal: [Root/XP v $_{stem}$]

b. Traditional template: [Initial (Medial) Abstract final $_{stem}$] OR
[Initial (Medial) [Prefinal Abstract final $_{final}$] $_{stem}$]

c. Slavin (2012): [Root v $_{stem}$] OR [[XP] Root v] $_{stem}$]

In this paper, we further develop our analysis of Menominee finals by providing a thorough examination of verb stems with medials. We discuss and analyze two medial constructions in Menominee. In OBJECT INCORPORATION structures, the medial corresponds to the logical object of the initial. With MODIFIER-MEDIAL INCORPORATION, the medial is modified by the initial. While abstract finals are more common with both medial constructions, concrete finals are also possible with object incorporation and modifier-medial constructions. The two medial constructions are exemplified in (2) with concrete finals.[2]

(2) a. pūhkikatāēhsen [object incorporation]

pōhkw-	e	-kātāē-	-hNenāē	-w
break-	EPEN	-leg-	-lie/lay/fall.AI	-3

'He/she/it falls and breaks his/her/its leg.'

b. sēpekatāēqtaw [modifier-medial]

sēp-	e	-kātāē-	-qtā	-w
long/slow-	EPEN	-leg-	-body.movement/activity.AI	-3

'He/she/it moves with stiff legs.'

We argue that evidence for a homogenous syntactic analysis of finals can be found in the fact that both abstract and concrete finals can occur with medials in these constructions. It is unclear how a heterogeneous approach to finals would account for the placement of medials, as incorporation would need to target two different positions depending on the type of final present.

The paper is organized as follows. The next section reviews Johnson and Rosen's (2017) analysis of Menominee finals. The following section discusses examples of medial incorporation in Menominee. After that, we provide an analysis of Menominee medials and claim that both abstract and concrete finals that occur with medials instantiate v. The last section concludes the paper.

Johnson and Rosen (2017): Finals Are *v*

In this section, we provide background on our analysis of Menominee finals, as presented in Johnson and Rosen (2017). Finals in Algonquian languages are traditionally classified as one of two types: ABSTRACT, which are purely categorizing elements, and CONCRETE,[3] which add some lexical information in addition to categorizing a verb. In Johnson and Rosen (2017), we argue for a homogeneous analysis of Menominee finals. That is, both abstract and concrete finals are instances of "little *v*"; see (3).

(3) a. b.

Our analyses of the example in (4a) with an abstract final and the example in (4b) with a concrete final are shown in (5a, b), respectively. We treat the initial *maeyaw-* 'straight' as a Root in both instances.

(4) a. meyāwa̅e̅w

maeyaw-	-a̅e̅	-w
straight-	-AI	-3

'He/she/it goes in the lead, acts as a leader.'

b. meyāwehsen

maeyaw-	e	hN-	e	-na̅e̅	-w
straight-	EPEN	lie/lay/fall	EPEN	-AI	-3

'He/she/it falls, lands, lies straight.'

(5)

Our analysis is contra previous analyses that assign different statuses to the two final types. Some traditional analyses (e.g., Bloomfield 1962; Goddard 1990) propose that concrete finals can be broken into two pieces—a prefinal and an abstract final—while others refer to finals as "more abstract" or "more concrete" (Wolfart 1973). This is illustrated in (6) (repeated from (1)).

(6) Traditional template:

a. [Initial Abstract final $_{\text{stem}}$]

b. [Initial [Prefinal Abstract final $_{\text{final}}$] $_{\text{stem}}$]

On the theoretical side, Slavin (2012) argues that there are two types of verb stems in Ojicree. We focus on Slavin's work because it provides a more comprehensive formal analysis than the previous theoretical literature. A "simple stem" is formed by concatenating a Root and *v*, as in (7a). In "complex stems," an *a*P merges in the specifier of *v*P to realize an initial, and the concrete final is composed of a Root and *v*; see (7b).[4]

(7)

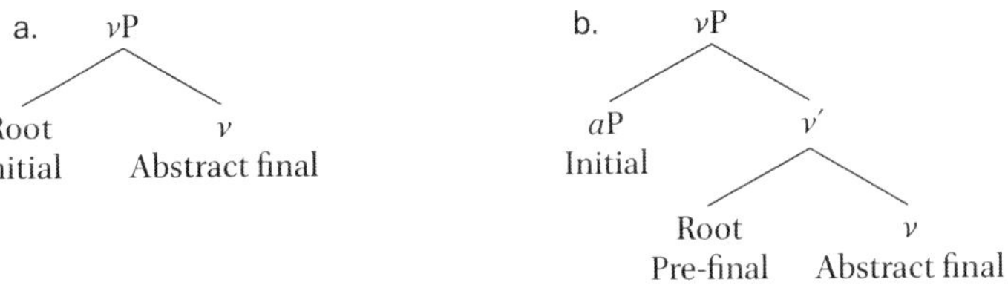

However, we argued that a heterogeneous analysis of the two final types is on the wrong track for several reasons. In particular, we showed that the placement of medials is problematic for analyses that make a syntactic distinction between the two final types. The presence of medials before abstract and concrete finals instead favors a homogenous account. Under Slavin's analysis, the medial would have to target two different positions depending on the type of final present. For examples with an abstract final, the medial would need to move between the Root and *v* to derive the correct ordering. For examples with concrete finals, the medial does not target a position between the Root and *v*. Instead, the medial would need to move between the *a*P and *v*′ to achieve the attested morpheme order of INITIAL–MEDIAL–PREFINAL–ABSTRACT FINAL. The placement of medials in each verb stem type is depicted in (8).

(8)

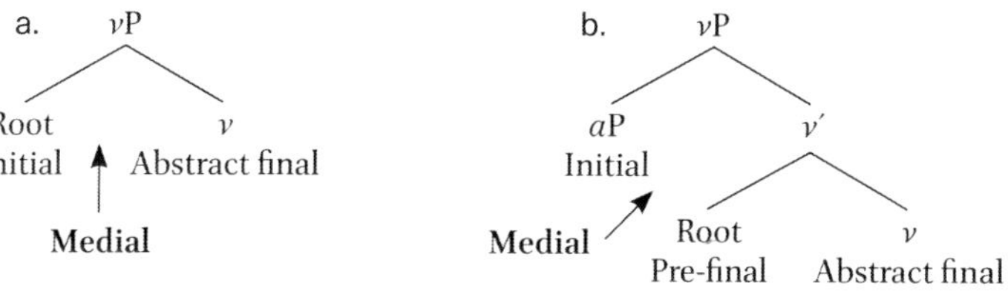

In what follows, we expand on our previous argument in favor of a homogenous analysis of abstract and concrete finals by looking at the position of medials in multiple incorporation structures in Menominee. We provide new empirical evidence that medials in Menominee are different than what has been reported for other Algonquian languages, including Ojicree.

Medials in Menominee

In this section, we discuss two different medial constructions in Menominee that we term "object incorporation" and "modifier-medial incorporation." In object incorporation constructions, the medial corresponds to the direct object of the initial. In modifier-medial incorporation structures, the initial serves as a modifier of the medial. The first two subsections show that each medial construction is possible with both abstract finals and (a subset of) concrete finals. The third subsection discusses the shape of the medial when it combines with abstract versus concrete finals.

Object Incorporation

In Menominee, object incorporation is possible with several medials. In (9) and (10), each medial corresponds to the object of the initial. The examples in (9) contain abstract finals, while the examples in (10) illustrate object incorporation with concrete finals. For example, (9a) shows that the medial *-askw-* behaves as the argument of the initial *mōn-* 'dig'.

(9) a. mōnaskow

mōn-	**-askw-**	-e/ae	-w
dig-	-grass/herb	-AI	-3

'He/she digs up weeds.'

b. nīmesa̅e̅hpow

nīm-	e	**-saehpw-**	-e/ae	-w
take.along-	EPEN	-tobacco-	-AI	-3

'He/she takes tobacco with him/her.'

c. nōceqsakow

nōt-	e	**-qsaskw-**	-e/ae	-w
guard-	EPEN	-muskrat-	-AI	-3

'He/she hunts muskrats.'

d. mana̅e̅hnaew

maN-	e	**-aehN-**	-a̅e̅	-w
gather-	EPEN	-wood/board-	-AI	-3

'He/she picks up sticks, gathers, makes firewood.'

e. kesēqnena̅e̅hciw

kaeseqN-	e	**-naehcy-**	-a̅e̅	-w
hot/warm-	EPEN	-finger/hand-	-AI	-3

'He/she washes his/her hands.'

(10) a. pēhtaehkīqtaw

pēht-	**-aehkī-**	-qtā	-w
inside.something	face/head/hair	body.movement/activity.AI	-3

'He/she/it sticks his/her/its head in.'

b. pūhkikata̅e̅hsen

pōhkw-	e	**-kāta̅e̅-**	-hNena̅e̅	-w
break-	EPEN	-leg-	-lie/lay/fall.AI	-3

'He/she/it falls and breaks his/her/its leg.'

c. kaeqtahkwahpesow

kaeqt-	**-āhkw-**	-ahpesi-	-w
near/close.to-	-wood/solid-	-tie.AI-	-3

'He/she/it is tied to a wooden or solid thing.'

Modifier-Medial Incorporation

Modifier-medial incorporation structures are very productive in Menominee. The same medial can combine with multiple modifier initials, as seen in (11) for the medial *-kāt-* 'leg' and in (12) for the medial *-qsahkwan-* 'nose'. The initial in these examples serves as an attribute of the medial; that is, the initial restricts the meaning of the medial.

(11) *-kāt-* 'leg'

a. kēskekata̅e̅w

kēsk-	e	**-kāt-**	-a̅e̅	-w
cut.off-	EPEN	-leg-	-AI	-3

'He/she/it lacks, is missing a leg; has a leg cut off.'

b. mamāhkekata̅e̅w

ma-	mahk-	e	**-kāt-**	-a̅e̅	-w
RED-	big-	EPEN	-leg-	-AI	-3

'He/she/it has big legs.'

c. māhkekataew

mahk-	e	**-kāt-**	-āē	-w
crippled-	EPEN	-leg-	-AI	-3

'He/she/it has a crippled leg.'

d. osāwekata̅e̅w

osaw-	**-kāt-**	-a̅e̅	-w
yellow-	-leg-	-AI	-3

'He/she/it has yellow, brown legs.'

e. tatāskikata̅e̅w

ta- taskw- e **-kāt-** -a̅e̅ -w

RED- short- EPEN -leg- -AI -3

'He/she/it has short legs.'

(12) *-qsahkwan-* 'nose'

a. kenīqsahkwan

kaenw- e **-qsahkwan-** -a̅e̅ -w

long- EPEN -nose- -AI -3

'He/she/it is long-nosed.'

b. macīqsahkwan

mat- e **-qsahkwan-** -a̅e̅ -w

ugly- EPEN -nose- -AI -3

'He/she/it has an ugly nose.'

c. mahkīqsaehkwan

mahk- e **-qsahkwan-** -a̅e̅ -w

big- EPEN -nose- -AI -3

'He/she/it is big-nosed.'

d. sāqsakīqsahkwan

sāqsakw- e **-qsahkwan-** -a̅e̅ -w

mash- EPEN -nose- -AI -3

'He/she/it has a snub nose.'

e. wākeqsāhkwan

wak- e **-qsahkwan-** -a̅e̅ -w

crooked- EPEN -nose- -AI -3

'He/she/it has a curved nose.'

The same modifier initial can also combine with multiple medials. The examples in (13) show that the initial *wēn-* 'dirty' combines with various medials. In (14), we see multiple examples of modifier-medial incorporation with *omaek-* 'scar, scab'.

(13) *wēn-* 'dirty'

a. wēnānakēqkow

wēn-	**-ānakeqkw-**	-e/ae	-w
dirty-	-eye-	-AI	-3

'He/she/it has dirty eyes.'

b. wēnekata͞ew

wēn-	e	**-kāt-**	-a͞e	-w
dirty-	EPEN	-leg-	-AI	-3

'He/she/it has (a) dirty leg(s).'

c. wēnena͞ekiw

wēn-	e	**-naehky-**	-a͞e	-w
dirty-	EPEN	-arm-	-AI	-3

'He/she has (a) dirty arm(s).'

d. wēneseta͞ew

wēn-	e	**-set-**	-a͞e	-w
dirty-	EPEN	-foot-	-AI	-3

'He/she/it has a dirty foot.'

e. wēneta͞ehpw

wēn-	e	**-taehp-**	-a͞e	-w
dirty-	EPEN	-head-	-AI	-3

'He/she/it has a dirty head.'

(14) *omaek-* 'scar, scab'

a. oma͞ekeqkow

omaek-	e	**-qkw-**	-e/ae	-w
scar/scab-	EPEN	-eye/face-	-AI	-3

'He/she has a scarred, scabby face.'

b. oma͞eketon

omaek-	e	**-ton-**	-a͞e	-w
scar/scab-	EPEN	-mouth-	-AI	-3

'He/she/it has scars, scabs on his/her/its mouth or lip.'

c. omāekeciw

omaek-	**-aecy-**	-āe	-w
scar/scab-	-round.body/belly-	-AI	-3

'He/she/it has scars/scabs on his/her/its belly.'

d. omāekepāekwan

omaek-	e	**-paehkwan-**	-āe	-w
scar/scab-	EPEN	-back-	-AI	-3

'He/she/it has scars, scabs on his/her/its back.'

e. omāekenāehciw

omaek-	e	**-naehcy-**	-āe	-w
scar/scab-	EPEN	-finger/hand-	-AI	-3

'He/she/it has scars, scabs on his/her/its hands.'

In (10)–(14) above, the verb stems are formed with abstract finals. Several concrete finals can also participate in the modifier-medial construction. Consider the examples in (15)–(18) below. (15) demonstrates that the AI concrete final *-hsenāe* 'lie, lay, fall' combines with the medials *-awhkw-* 'face/head/hair' in (a), *-qkw-* 'eye/face' in (b), *-kātāe-* 'leg' in (c), and *-āwekanāe-* in (d). A similar pattern applies to the finals *-qtā* 'body movement, activity' in (16), *-ape* 'sit' in (17), and *-kāpowe* 'stand' in (18).

(15) *-hsenāe* 'lie, lay fall'

a. āenecenaehkihsen

āenecen-	**-aehkw-**	e	-hsenāe	-w
supine-	-face/head/hair-	EPEN	-lie/lay/fall.AI	-3

'He/she/it lies on his/her/its back, face up.'

b. wāqseqkīhsen

wāqs-	e	**-qkw-**	e	-hsenāe	-w
light-	EPEN	-eye/face-	EPEN	-lie/lay/fall.AI	-3

'He/she/it lies with face showing bright.'

c. esēkāta͞ehsen

aeN-	e	**-kāta͞e-**	-hsena͞e	-w
thither/thus-	EPEN	-leg-	-lie/lay/fall.AI	-3

'He/she/it lies with legs that way.'

d. moqtawekana͞ehsen

moqt-	**-āwekana͞e-**	-hsena͞e	-w
bare-	-back-	-lie/lay/fall.AI	-3

'He/she/it lies with his/her/its back exposed.'

(16) *-qtā* 'body movement, activity'

a. kecēckekanaeqtaw

kaecēck-	e	**-kana͞e-**	-qtā	-w
creak-	EPEN	-bone-	-body.movement/activity.AI	-3

'He/she/it moves with creaking bones.'

b. nīsina͞ehcīqtaw

nīsw-	e	**-naehcī-**	-qtā	-w
two-	EPEN	-finger/hand	-body.movement/activity.AI	-3

'He/she uses both hands.'

c. wahka͞epīqtaw

wahk-	**-aepī-**	-qtā	-w
on.top-	-water/liquid-	-body.movement/activity.AI	-3

'He/she/it moves on top of the water.'

d. sēpekata͞eqtaw

sēp-	e	**-kāta͞e-**	-qtā	-w
long/slow-	EPEN	-leg-	-body.movement/activity.AI	-3

'He/she/it moves with stiff legs.'

(17) *-ape* 'sit'

a. pemētaehkipew

paemet-	**-aehki-**	-ape	-w
crosswise-	-face/head/hair-	-sit.AI	-3

'He/she/it sits crosswise.'

b. āsuakanaepew

āsaw-	**-akanāe-**	-ape	-w
across/on.the.other.side-	-bone-	-sit.AI	-3

'He/she sits with legs crossed.'

c. naehkūhkipew

naehkw-	**-aehkī-**	-ape	-w
offend-	-face/head/hair-	-sit.AI	-3

'He/she pouts, sulks, sits angry.'

(18) *-kāpowe* 'stand'

a. sākaehkikāpowew

sāk-	**-aehkī-**	-kāpowe-	-w
out.of.place-	-face/head/hair-	-stand.AI-	-3

'He/she/it stands with his/her/its head sticking up over something.'

b. ocīhcekwanekapowew

otī-	**-hcekwan-**	e	-kāpowe	-w
rear-	-knee-	EPEN	-stand.AI	-3

'He/she/it kneels.'

Shape of Medials with Concrete Finals

As can be seen in the examples in the previous two subsections, the shape of a medial sometimes varies depending on the type of final that follows it. This is also illustrated by the pair of examples in (19). In the example in (19a) with an abstract final, the medial meaning 'leg' takes the form *-kāt-*. In contrast, (19b) contains a concrete final, and the medial takes the form *-kātāe-*.

(19) a. kēskekatāew

kēsk-	e	**-kāt-**	-āe	-w
cut.off-	EPEN	-leg-	-AI	-3

'He/she/it lacks, is missing a leg; has a leg cut off.'

b. esēkātāēhsen

aeN-	e	**-katāe-**	-hsenāe	-w
thither/thus-	EPEN	-leg-	-lie/lay/fall.AI	-3

'He/she/it lies with legs that way.'

There are competing analyses for the appearance of an additional vowel after a medial with a concrete final.[5] Denny (1981) analyzes that vowel as an abstract final. Thus, examples like (19b) are instances of secondary derivation: the concrete final attaches to a complete verb stem. O'Meara (1990) and Goddard (1990) instead analyze that vowel as part of the medial, dubbing it a "postmedial." O'Meara (1990) and Goddard (1990) note that the vowel that follows medials with concrete finals is not always identical to the form of the abstract AI final that would be expected with that medial. We make a similar argument here, although the Menominee data differ from what O'Meara and Goddard provide for the languages they look at. That is, we argue that the two examples in (19) have the same structure, despite the difference in the shape of the final. This constitutes further support for our claim that medial constructions with abstract and concrete finals both have the same structure.

There are two abstract AI finals that appear with medials in Menominee. The final *-e*/*-ae* occurs after medials that end in a postconsonantal *w*, and *-āe* is used after all other medials (Bloomfield 1962:280). The examples in (20) illustrate the distribution of these two abstract finals.[6]

(20) a. kēskahāhkow

kēskah-	-āhkw-	-e/ae	-w
cut.off-	-wood/solid-	-AI	-3

'He/she cuts trees down, does logging, logs.'

b. mamāhkesetaew

ma-	mahk-	e	-set-	-āe	-w
RED-	large-	EPEN	-foot-	-AI	-3

'He/she/it has large feet.'

In (20a), the postconsonantal [w] at the end of the medial and the final *-e*/*-ae* merge to surface as [o].[7] If the final in (20a) were underlyingly *-āe*, we would expect the combination of the postconsonantal [w] with the final to yield the vowel [ī]

(Bloomfield 1962:84), contra to fact. In (20b), we see the final *-āē* appearing after the medial *-set-* 'foot'.

Given this, we might expect that these same vowels would consistently appear after medials with concrete finals if the vowels in those environments were in fact abstract finals. That is, we should always see the vowel [e/ae] between medials ending in postconsonantal [w] and concrete finals, and the vowel [āē] between other medials and concrete finals. However, this prediction is not borne out. The medial *-aehkw-* 'face, head, hair' ends with a postconsonantal [w], and thus takes the abstract final *-e/-ae* in incorporation structures. This is shown in (21a, b).

(21) a. kakīpaehkow

kakīp-	-aehkw-	-e/ae	-w
closed-	-face/head/hair-	-AI	-3

'He/she/it is blind.'

b. kesēqnaehkow

kaeseqN-	-aehkw-	-e/ae	-w
hot/warm-	-face/head/hair-	-AI	-3

'He/she/it washes his/her/its face.'

However, when *-aehkw-* 'face, head, hair' is followed by a concrete final, the vowel [āē] appears between the two components. This is exemplified in (22), where the postconsonantal [w] and [āē] combine as [ī] (Bloomfield 1962:84).

(22) enāēhkihsen

aeN-	-aehkī-	-hsenāē	-w
thither/thus-	-face/head/hair-	-lie/lay/fall.AI	-3

'He/she/it lies with his/her/its head that way.'

There is also variation in the shape of the medial with concrete finals that begin with vowels. The medial *-āhkw-* 'wood, solid' takes the abstract final *-e/-ae,* as seen in (23a). However, no vowel is added after the medial *-āhkw-* 'wood, solid' in (23b).

(23) a. wēnosāhkow

wēnos-	-āhkw-	-e/ae	-w
burn.in.blaze-	-wood/solid-	-AI	-3

'He/she burns brush, trees, wood.'

b. kaeqtāhkwahpesow

kaeqt-	-āhkw-	-ahpesi	-w
near/close.to-	-wood/solid-	-tie.AI.REFL	-3

'He/she/it is tied tight to a wooden or solid thing.'

If [e] were added, we would expect the [a] at the beginning of the final to drop, since the second of two short vowels that come together drops (Bloomfield 1962:83). Then, the combination of [w] and [e] after a consonant should yield [i] (Bloomfield 1962:84). This would happen regardless of which order vowel merger and vowel drop occur. Alternatively, if [a̅e̅] were added, we would still expect the [a] at the beginning of the final to drop, since a short vowel on either side of a long vowel drops (Bloomfield 1962:82–83).

One could potentially explain the data in (23) by positing a morphophonological restriction against adding an abstract AI final before a concrete final beginning with a vowel. However, there are medials that take this extra vowel even before a concrete final that begins with a vowel. The medial *-ton-* 'mouth' takes the final *-a̅e̅*, as would be expected in (24a). The vowel [a̅e̅] still appears after the medial *-ton-* when followed by the concrete final *-aeskā-*'by foot, body movement' in (24b).

(24) a. pāhsetona̅e̅w

pāhs-	e	-ton-	-ae	-w
swell.up-	EPEN	-mouth-	-AI	-3

'He/she has swollen lips.'

b. pōnetona̅e̅skaw

pōn-	e	-tona̅e̅-	-aeskā	-w
cease/quit-	EPEN	-mouth-	-by.foot/body.movement.AI	-3

'He/she quits talking.'

The [āē] that follows the medial *-ton-* in (24b) cannot be analyzed as the first vowel of the concrete final, since it is not in a position that would be lengthened. Instead, it must be the vowel [āē] that follows the medial.

A similar point can be made with examples with the medial *-aepy-* 'water, liquid'. The example in (25a) shows that *-aepy-* takes the abstract final *-āē* (where the postconsonantal [y] merges with the final *-āē* to yield [ī]). (25b) shows that the vowel [āē] is added between the medial *-aepy-* and the concrete final *-aehcenāē* 'immersion'.

(25) a. mōskenaepīw

mōsken-	-aepy-	-āē	-w
full-	-water/liquid-	-AI	-3

'It is full of liquid.'

b. sahsāēqsopīhcen

sah-	saeqsw-	-aepī-	-aehcenāē	-w
RED-	scatter-	-water/liquid-	-immersion.AI	-3

'He/she/it lies splashing around in the water.'

If the concrete final *-aehcenāē* were added directly to the medial *-aepy-*, we would expect the form to be *sahsāēqsopēhcen*, with the vowel [ē] between the medial and concrete final. The combination of the postconsonantal [y] of *-aepy-* plus the [ae] at the beginning of the final would yield [e] (Bloomfield 1962:85), which would then lengthen since it is in a closed syllable and the head of the foot (Bloomfield 1962:91; Milligan 2005:17). Instead, the presence of the vowel [ī] can be attributed to the result of the merger of postconsonantal [y] with the vowel [āē] (Bloomfield 1962:85).

We conclude that the extra vowel that sometimes appears between a medial and concrete final cannot be analyzed as an abstract AI final in Menominee. The vowel does not always appear in the same form as the AI final, and sometimes does not appear at all. Instead, we propose that this extra vowel is either a postmedial (as proposed by Goddard 1990 and O'Meara 1990) or forms part of an allomorph of the medial that is conditioned by the final.

In sum, we have shown that both the object incorporation and modifier-medial constructions in Menominee are productive. Furthermore, we have argued that medial constructions with concrete finals are not instances of secondary derivation.

Structure of Menominee Verb Stems with Medials

In this section, we present an analysis of Menominee verb stems with medials based on Slavin's (2012) structure of Ojicree "*e*-stems." Since her proposal is the most developed formal analysis of medial constructions, we focus on her account as a means of comparison. We argue that both abstract and concrete finals realize *v*, and that the final in modifier-medial constructions takes a small clause complement composed of the initial and medial.

Slavin (2012) proposes a syntactic structure for the Ojicree modifier-medial construction. For the verb stem in (26), she proposes that the AI final -*e* realizes *v* and takes a small clause complement. The small clause consists of the incorporated medial (*n*P) and the initial *a*P.

(26) a. oshkitaapaane

oshki- taapaan- e

new- car- AI

'He/she has a new car.' (Slavin 2012:266, (344))

b.

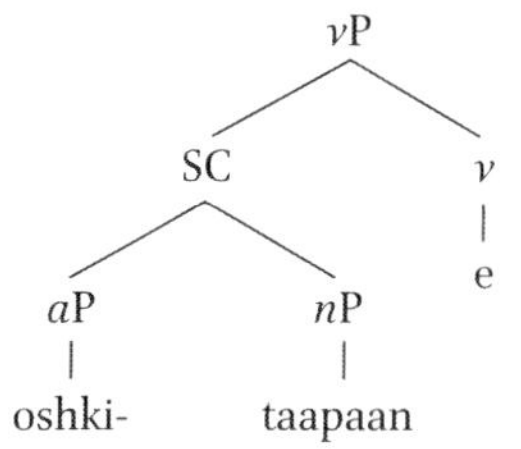

For Menominee, we propose the slightly modified structure in (27). We follow Slavin's structure for *e*-stems in Ojicree, and we argue that the initial and medial are in the complement of *v*. However, we claim that the medial in Menominee is a Root instead of an *n*P.

(27)

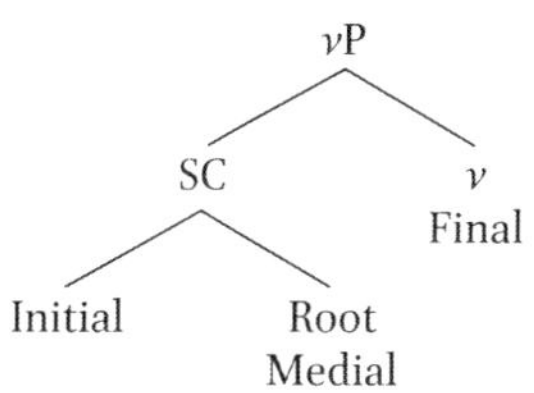

In the next two subsections, we defend the claim that the final is *v* and argue that the medial is best treated as a Root. We discuss each of these arguments in turn.

Status of the Final

In this section, we argue that both abstract and concrete finals instantiate *v* based on examples of verb stems with medials. As we saw above, modifier-medial constructions are also possible with concrete finals in Menominee. Consider (28), repeated from (16a):

(28) kecēckekanaeqtaw

kaecēck-	e	**-kanāē-**	-qtā	-w
creak-	EPEN	-bone-	-body.movement/activity.AI	-3

'He/she/it moves with creaking bones.'

If all finals are *v* as we have previously argued (Johnson and Rosen 2017), then the modifier-medial constituent will consistently be the complement to *v* for both abstract and concrete finals.

In contrast, recall that Slavin (2012) argues for a syntactic distinction between abstract finals and concrete finals. Abstract finals instantiate *v*, while concrete finals are *v*′ constituents composed of a Root (prefinal) and *v* (abstract final). Thus, under Slavin's analysis, the Menominee example in (28) would have the structure in (29).

(29)

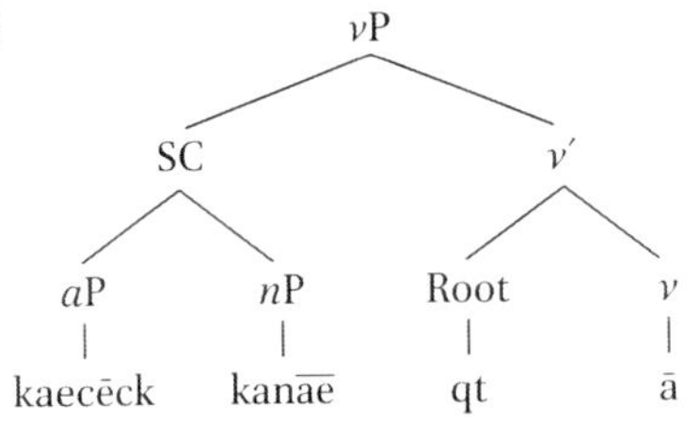

Under this analysis, the small clause composed of the initial and medial occupies a distinct position depending on the status of the final: it is in complement position with an abstract final in (26b), but in a specifier with a concrete final in (29). This is an undesirable result for Slavin. She treats the Ojicree examples of modifier-medial incorporation as analogous to possessive constructions with *have*

in English: they both involve a light verb taking a small clause complement (see, e.g., Sæbø 2009 for English).[8]

Status of the Medial: Root versus n*P*

Slavin uses two arguments to advance the analysis that medials in Ojicree *e*-stems are *n*Ps: medials are referential, and they can take stranded modifiers. This is not the case in Menominee modifier-medial constructions: the medials are not referential, and they cannot take stranded modifiers.

Medials in Menominee are not referential with either abstract or concrete finals. The medial *-set-* 'foot' in (30a) and *-kātāē-* 'leg' in (30b) cannot be interpreted as the subject of the verb in the second sentence.

(30) a. *Nepōhkoseāēm. Pāhsesew.

ne-	pōhkw-	e	**-set-**	-āē	-m	pāhs-	-aese	-w
1-	break-	EPEN	-foot-	-AI	-1	swell.up-	-AI	-3

Intended: 'I have a broken foot. It's swollen.' (MF 9/22/14)

b. *Mesāēn māēk-sākekataehsen. Maeqsiw.

Mesāēn	māēk-	sāk-	e	**-kātāē-**	-hsenae	-w
Mesāēn	SIMUL-	out.of.a.place-	EPEN	-leg-	-lie/lay/fall.AI	-3

maeqN-	-yi	-w
large-	-II	-3

Intended: 'Mesāēn is lying with a leg sticking out. It (his leg) is large.' (MF 9/22/14)

Stranded modifiers are also not possible with modifier-medial incorporation. The example in (31a) with an abstract final shows that the numeral *nīs* 'two' cannot modify the medial *-aehtawak-* 'ear'. Likewise, in (31b) with a concrete final, the demonstrative *eneh* 'that' cannot be construed with the medial *-kātāē-* 'leg'.

(31) a. *Nekākāskaehtawakaem nīs.

ne-	kā-	kāsk-	-aehtawak-	-āē	-m	nīs
1-	RED-	scrape-	-ear-	-AI	-1	two

Intended: 'My two ears/both my ears itch.' (MF 9/22/14)

b. *Nekes-pūhkikatāehsenaem eneh.

ne-	kes-	pōhkw-	e	-kātāe-	-hsenāe	-m	eneh
1-	PST-	break-	EPEN	-leg-	-lie/lay/fall.AI	-1	that.INAN

Intended: 'I fell and broke that leg.' (MF 9/22/14)

The lack of referentiality with medials is entirely expected if they are bare Roots: it is standardly assumed that *n* (or some other higher functional head) is responsible for introducing a referential argument (see, e.g., Wiltschko 2009). Roots are also by definition devoid of any functional structure, which explains the ungrammaticality of stranded modifiers with medials in Menominee. Thus, we conclude that the medial must lack functional structure.

Conclusion

In conclusion, we have examined the properties of medial incorporation in Menominee. With object incorporation and modifier-medial incorporation, both abstract and concrete finals can follow the medial. In previous work (Johnson and Rosen 2017), we argued that object incorporation constructions with concrete finals constituted an argument in favor of a homogenous account of Menominee finals. Here, we expanded this argument and argued that the ability for either abstract or concrete finals to participate in modifier-medial constructions also supports a uniform syntactic analysis of finals in Menominee: they both instantiate *v*. The arguments presented in this paper have focused on Menominee, and we leave it to future research whether they can be extended to other Algonquian languages.

NOTES

1. We are grateful to Marie Floring (MF) for providing data presented in this paper. We would like to thank Hunter Thompson Lockwood and Monica Macaulay for helpful comments and suggestions on this paper, and the Menominee Language and Culture Commission for its guidance.
2. The following abbreviations are used: 1 = first person, 3 = third person, AI = animate intransitive, EPEN = epenthetic, II = inanimate intransitive, INAN = inanimate, RED = reduplication, REFL = reflexive, SIMUL = simultaneous. /E/ represents a morphophoneme

that usually surfaces as [e], whereas /N/ is a morphophoneme that surfaces either as [n] or [s]/[ʃ] (Bloomfield 1962). All Menominee data cited in this paper without a date and speaker's initials come from Bloomfield (1975) via a database created by Monica Macaulay at the University of Wisconsin–Madison.

3. Following Valentine (2001) and Slavin (2012), we use the term "concrete final" for either monomorphemic or bimorphemic finals.
4. Slavin (2012) observes three asymmetries in Ojicree verb stems: one set of verb stems is compositional, is more productive, and consistently has *t*-palatalization. She attributes these differences to the abstract/concrete final distinction. In Johnson and Rosen (2014), we show that these asymmetries are not found in Menominee.
5. In examples like (15a), the vowel [e] appears between the medial and concrete final. Bloomfield (1962) does not ascribe any status to this vowel, and so we have glossed it as epenthetic. [e] is the epenthetic vowel in Menominee, and the presence of epenthesis in examples like (15a) would be entirely expected, as the cluster [hkwh] is not permissible. It would also be possible to analyze that vowel as a postmedial, but we know of no way to distinguish the two analyses.
6. In (19a), the initial meaning 'cut off' takes the form *kēsk-*, while in (20a) it appears as *kēskah-*. Bloomfield (1962:433–434) treats the form *kēskah-* as an "extended root" composed of *kēsk-* and the TI final *-ah* rather than as a full verb stem. Following Bloomfield, we also consider *kēskah-* to be a root.
7. The merger of [w] and [e] only surfaces as [o] when followed by another [w]; otherwise, the vowel surfaces as [i] (Bloomfield 1962:84).
8. Slavin (2012) only discusses examples of modifier-medial incorporation with the abstract AI final *-e* in Ojicree.

REFERENCES

Bloomfield, Leonard. 1962. *The Menomini language*. Ed. Charles F. Hockett. New Haven, CT: Yale University Press.

———. 1975. *Menominee lexicon*. Ed. Charles F. Hockett. Milwaukee Public Museum Publications in Anthropology and History 3.

Denny, J. Peter. 1981. Algonquian word structure from the viewpoint of logical semantics. In *Linguistique Amérindienne II: Études Algonquiennes*, ed. Lynn Drapeau, 21–29. Montreal Working Papers in Linguistics, Vol. 16. Montreal: Université du Québec à Montréal.

Goddard, Ives. 1990. Primary and secondary stem derivation in Algonquian. *International Journal of American Linguistics* 56.4:449–483.

Johnson, Meredith, and Bryan Rosen. 2014. Menominee verb stems and little *v*. Unpublished manuscript, University of Wisconsin–Madison.

———. 2017. On Menominee verb stems and the noncomplexity of verb finals. In *Papers of the forty-fifth Algonquian Conference*, ed. Monica Macaulay, Margaret Noodin, and J. Randolph Valentine. East Lansing: Michigan State University Press.

Milligan, Marianne I. 2005. Menominee prosodic structure. PhD thesis, University of Wisconsin–Madison.

O'Meara, John. 1990. Delaware stem morphology. PhD thesis, McGill University.

Sæbø, Kjell Johan. 2009. Possession and pertinence: The meaning of have. *Natural Language Semantics* 17:369–397.

Slavin, Tanya. 2012. The syntax and semantics of stem composition in Ojicree. PhD thesis, University of Toronto.

Valentine, J. Randolph. 2001. *Nishnaabemwin reference grammar*. Toronto: University of Toronto Press.

Wiltschko, Martina. 2009. Root incorporation: Evidence from lexical suffixes in Halkomelem Salish. *Lingua* 119:199–223.

Wolfart, H. C. 1973. Plains Cree: A grammatical study. *Transactions of the American Philosophical Society*, vol. 63, part 5: 1–90.

Animacy and Transitivity Alternations in Blackfoot

Kyumin Kim

Sentience plays a role in various parts of Blackfoot grammar.[1] For instance, only a sentient being (a human or an animal) can appear as the subject of a transitive verb in Blackfoot (Frantz 2009). This appears to be different from other Algonquian languages, e.g., Ojibwe, where an inanimate being can be the subject of a Transitive Animate (TA) verb (Valentine 2001). Recent studies on Blackfoot further indicate that sentience plays a significant role in the transitivity alternation (Ritter and Wiltschko 2006), in direct/inverse marking (Bliss 2013), and in the interaction between motion verbs and goal phrases (Kim 2015a).

In this paper, I argue that the obligatory presence of a sentient argument indicates the presence of a GRAMMATICAL initiator of an event described by a verb phrase. In essence, a sentient argument can be viewed as a grammatical initiator when it occupies the specifier of a functional event phrase such as FPinit(iator), where an event role of an initiator is assigned. The empirical basis of this claim mainly comes from the contrast between motion and posture verbs. The transitivity alternation—the alternation between Animate Intransitive (AI)/Inanimate Intransitive (II) and Transitive Animate (TA)/Transitive Inanimate (TI) verbs—is only possible in Blackfoot when a grammatical initiator of an event is present. I show that only inherently directed motion verbs that obligatorily license goal phrases have grammatical initiators in their structures, in contrast to manner of motion verbs, which do not require goal phrases. Consequently, unlike manner of motion verbs, inherently directed motion AI verbs with grammatical initiators show the transitivity alternation, i.e., they have TA/TI counterparts. I also show that posture AI verbs do not have a grammatical initiator in their event structure and as a result do not have TA/TI counterparts. Finally, I discuss how the proposed analysis can be extended to psych verbs and some II verbs.

The present study shares some insight with Ritter and Wiltschko (2015) in that in Blackfoot, specifiers of functional categories may pose sentience restrictions on the argument in their specifiers (they term this "H(igh)-indexation"). However, the consequences of this paper are that not every functional category may impose a sentience restriction on its argument, contrary to Ritter and Wiltschko, who argue that all functional categories impose sentience restrictions on their specifiers. This paper shows that the sentience restriction appears to be possible only when an argument has an event role of initiator by being in the specifier of FPinit. An interesting consequence is thus that the animacy of an argument is able to enter into (and is thus visible to) the narrow syntax only when the argument carries an event role. I show that in Blackfoot, a sentient argument is visible to syntax only when it carries the event role of an initiator (i.e., it is a grammatical initiator). In the rest of this paper, I refer to grammatical initiators as initiators, except where a distinction is necessary.

The Proposal: Initiators and the Transitivity Alternation

I assume that an event has two components—initiation and termination (see, e.g., van Voorst 1988; Ritter and Rosen 2000; Borer 2005)—and that these two components are represented syntactically via functional heads (e.g., Borer 2005), Finit and Fterm, as schematically illustrated in (1).[2]

(1) $[_{\text{FPinit}}$ initiator Finit $[_{\text{FPterm}}$ terminator Fterm ... $[_{\text{VP}}$...]]]

Generally, an argument in the specifier of FPinit is assigned an event initiator role and may be interpreted as having various roles that are compatible with an initiator. An argument in the specifier of FPterm is assigned an event measurer role, which is responsible for event termination or boundedness, such as a goal PP that indicates the endpoint of a motion event. A language can differ in whether it activates FPinit or FPterm. For example, some languages such as Japanese and Irish are argued to activate FPinit but not FPterm (Ritter and Rosen 2000). It is further argued by Ritter and Rosen that in such languages, FPterm can have content only if FPinit is present.

In Blackfoot, with inherently directed motion AI verbs like *oo* 'go', event measurers such as endpoint-denoting goal phrases can appear only if a sentient subject appears, as in (2) (Kim 2015a).[3]

(2) Anna saahkomaapi/*anna ainaka'si itap-oo-wa oomi isspahkoyi.
DEM boy/ DEM wagon GOAL-go.AI-3S DEM hill
'The boy went to that hill.'/*'That wagon moved to that hill.' (Kim 2015a)

By contrast, with posture AI verbs such as *ipoyi* 'stand', a locative phrase is shown not to affect event structure: the subject of those verbs can be either sentient or nonsentient, as in (3) (Kim 2015a).

(3) Anna saahkomaapi/anna ainaka'si it-ipoyi-wa anni itaisooyo'p.
DEM boy/ DEM wagon LOC-stand.AI-3S DEM table
'That boy is standing on the table.'/'That wagon is standing on the table.' (Kim 2015a)

Building on this finding, I argue that Blackfoot belongs to the class of languages where FPinit is activated. More specifically, in Blackfoot, an event can have a terminal bound (e.g., it can have an endpoint phrase) only if an initiator is present. Consider the simplified VP structure for motion and posture verbs given in (4).

(4) $[_{\text{FPinit}}$ initiator Finit $[_{\text{VP}}$ V *p*P]]

The goal phrase of a motion verb or the locative phrase of a posture verb is realized as *p*P. With an inherently directed motion verb, for instance, *p*P is licensed when an initiator is present in the specifier of FPinit. With posture verbs (as well as with manner of motion verbs), I propose that there is no initiator and thus that the FPinit in (4) is absent with those verbs. This structure will be discussed in more detail below.

I argue that the transitivity alternation is available only when an event initiator is present. Importantly, an initiator is a grammaticalized notion: an argument in the specifier of a functional phrase, i.e., FPinit in (4) is a grammatical initiator. This means that an argument NOT in the specifier of FPinit cannot be considered a grammatical initiator even if world knowledge allows the argument to be interpreted as an agent at some level, giving rise to a nongrammatical initiator interpretation. For instance, I show that in Blackfoot sentient subjects of the AI verb *oo* 'go' are grammatical initiators but sentient subjects of the AI verb *okska'si* 'run' are not.

As will be shown shortly, the functional head *p* that introduces a Figure (in the sense of Talmy 1985) does not pose a restriction on its specifier with respect to sentience. This is contrary to Ritter and Wiltschko (2015), who argue that the specifier of every functional category is specified to allow a sentient DP. I show that the specifier of *p*P can be occupied by either a sentient or nonsentient being, both of which can be grammatically animate. I also show the rather surprising fact that grammatically INANIMATE nouns can appear with some AI verbs (see (12) and (18)), and grammatically ANIMATE nouns can appear with some II verbs (see (24)). I argue that some sentient Figures can be grammatical initiators by occupying the specifier of FPinit. However, neither NONSENTIENT grammatically animate nor inanimate Figures are able to appear in the specifier of FPinit.

Motion and Posture Verbs and *p*P

This section proposes argument structure for the prepositional phrase (*p*P) and shows how motion and posture verbs can license those phrases.

There has been some work on linkers in Blackfoot. This includes Bliss et al. (2013) on locative linkers, Kim (2014a, 2015b) on instrument and associative linkers, and Kim (2014a, 2015a) on direction and locative linkers.[4] This paper is mainly built on work in Kim (2014a, 2015a), which addresses spatial linkers in the context of motion and posture verbs. I first propose argument structure for the linkers represented by *p*P, which is crucial to the understanding of the argument structure of motion and posture verbs. I then proceed to the discussion of how an initiator can license a particular type of *p*P with those types of verbs.

Argument Structure of Linker p

Blackfoot has a set of prefixes known as "linkers," which introduce oblique roles (Frantz 2009; Kim 2014a, 2015a, b). In other Algonquian languages similar types of morphemes are called "relative roots." I refer to the Blackfoot counterparts as "linkers," following the intuition of Frantz (2009) that they 'link' an argument to an event described by a verb phrase. Blackfoot also has prefixes called "nonlinkers" (Frantz 2009; Kim 2014a, c, 2015b), which, as the name suggests, do not introduce an argument to be linked to an event. Examples of the direction linker *itap-* 'to' and the nonlinker *waamis-* 'up' are illustrated in (5); examples of the locative linker *it-* and the nonlinker *ohkit* 'on' are illustrated in (6).

(5) a. Anna John itap-oo-wa anni niitahtaayi.
DEM John GOAL-go.AI-3s DEM river
'John is going to the river.'

b. Anna John waamis-oo-wa (*anni niitahtaayi).
DEM John up-go.AI-3s DEM river
'John is moving upwards.' (Kim 2015a)

(6) a. Anna John it-ohpai'piiyi-wa anni niitahtaayi.
DEM John LOC-jump.AI-3s DEM river
'John is jumping in the river.'

b. Anna John iihkit-ipoyi-wa (*anni iitaisooyo'p).
DEM John on.top-stand.AI-3s DEM table
'John will stand on top (*of the table).' (Kim 2014c)

Kim (2014a, 2015a) argues that linkers are functional *p*s while nonlinkers are lexical Ps without complements, providing evidence from various differences between linkers and nonlinkers, such as differences in idiomatic expressions, abstract nominalization, and the availability of locative derivation.

Moving this claim one step further, I propose that a linker *p* introduces a Figure in its specifier and a Ground in its complement PP.[5] To illustrate this, consider (7a) and the corresponding structure in (7b) proposed for spatial PPs (e.g., along the lines of Svenonius 2003 among many others). It is a fairly standard assumption that spatial PPs have extended projections, namely *p*, as in (7b). According to work on *p*, Figures merge in the specifier of *p*P, and Grounds appear in the complement of P.

(7) a. John went into the room.

b. [$_{VP}$ . . . [$_{pP}$ Figure *p* [$_{PP}$ P Ground]]
John to in room

A Figure is an entity in motion or an entity that is located with respect to the Ground (Talmy 1978). The Ground is a location with respect to the location of the Figure.

For instance, in (7a), 'John' is a Figure in motion occupying the specifier of *p*. The DP 'the room' is the Ground where the Figure 'John' is located, and it occupies the complement of P. As for Blackfoot spatial linkers, I propose the type of *p*P structure illustrated in (8) for the example in (5a).[6]

(8) [$_{VP}$ . . . [$_{pP}$ Figure *p* [$_{PP}$ P Ground]]
'John' *itap-* ∅ *anni niitahtaayi* 'the river'

In what follows, I discuss the argument structure of motion and posture verbs: how a grammatical initiator licenses a goal *p*P, and how FPinit can affect the transitivity alternation.

Initiator and Argument Structure of Motion and Posture Verbs

Some motion verbs require a linker *p*, but other motion verbs do not require one (Kim 2015a).[7] Inherently directed motion verbs such as *oo* 'go' or *ipikssi* 'flee' require the direction linker *p* (*itap-*), but manner of motion verbs such as *okska'si* 'run', or *ohpai'piiyi* 'jump' do not require a direction linker. Likewise, a posture verb such as *ipoyi* 'stand' requires a locative linker *p* (*it-*), while other posture verbs (*opii* 'sit' or *istsii* 'lie') do not require it (Kim 2014a). As in other studies on spatial PPs (e.g., Svenonius 2003), I argue that the obligatory linkers—path and locative *p*P—are complements of V as illustrated in (9), while optional ones are adjuncts (not shown).

(9) [$_{VP}$ [$_{pP}$ $p_{\text{PATH/LOC}}$ Figure [$_{PP}$ P Ground]]]

Blackfoot is argued to be a language where event structure is organized in terms of sentience (Bliss 2007; Kim 2014b, c, 2015a; Ritter and Wiltschko 2015). It should be noted that it is not my intention to say that grammatical animacy does not play a role in Blackfoot. What I mean to express is that grammatical animacy does not affect whether or not an event has an endpoint. Support comes from the fact that the distribution of path and locative *p*s is mediated by the presence of sentient arguments. The relevant data are in (2) and (3) above: Path *p* in (2) and locative *p* in (3). In (2), the goal of the motion verb introduced by *p* 'the hill' can appear if the subject of the verb is sentient, either a human or an animal. In contrast, *p* is not allowed if the subject is nonsentient such as 'the wagon'. In particular, both types of subjects belong to the grammatically animate noun class in the language, but they differ in their capacity to license a goal phrase of the event. The sentience of the subject appears to be crucial to the grammaticality of the sentence in (2). The sentence is ungrammatical if a nonsentient subject 'the wagon' appears; it is not the case that the sentence is infelicitous. As shown in (10), a nonsentient subject, as in (2), is possible when a goal PP does not appear.

(10) Anna saahkomaapi/anna ainaka'si wamis-oo-wa.
DEM boy/ DEM wagon up-go.AI-3S
'The boy went up.'/?'The wagon moved up.'

Moreover, the sentence in (2) with a goal PP is acceptable if the wagon is personified—for example, imagining a cartoon context such as *Thomas the Tank Engine,* as suggested by a reviewer. Thus, what is important to license a goal PP is a sentient subject—grammatical animacy is not sufficient. Unlike path *p*, a locative *p* does not show this type of sentience restriction, as indicated in (3): either a human or an object is grammatical with a locative *p*P.

Building on the claim about the sentience restriction with respect to *p*P, I argue that only those Figures that are sentient can be grammatical initiators by occupying the specifier position of FPinit, as illustrated in (11a). (Subscript s indicates sentience, and N-S indicates nonsentience).

(11) a. $[_{\text{FPinit}}$ DP_{S} Finit... $[_{\text{VP}}$ $[_{p\text{P}}$ $\langle\text{DP}_{\text{S}}\rangle$ p_{PATH} $[_{\text{PP}}$ P Ground]]]]

b. *$[_{\text{FPinit}}$ $\text{DP}_{\text{N-S}}$ Finit... $[_{\text{VP}}$ $[_{p\text{P}}$ $\langle\text{DP}_{\text{N-S}}\rangle$ p_{PATH} $[_{\text{PP}}$ P Ground]]]]

c. $[_{\text{VP}}$ V $[_{p\text{P}}$ Figure p_{LOC} $[_{\text{PP}}$ P Ground]]]

Nonsentient Figures cannot occupy the specifier position of FPinit because Finit does not allow nonsentient arguments, as in (11b). For instance, in (2), the sentient Figure 'the boy' occupies the specifier of FPinit where the head Finit imposes the sentience restriction on its specifier. On the other hand, the nonsentient Figure 'the wagon' cannot occupy the specifier position of FPinit due to the sentience restriction. Locative *p* is inert to event structure, i.e., there is no sentience restriction, as discussed previously. I argue that this inertness indicates that a Figure of locative *p*P cannot be a grammatical initiator, and propose that there is no FPinit projected in the event structure of posture verbs as in (11c). The sentence in (10) without a goal PP where a nonsentient subject is allowed will have a similar structure to (11c), i.e., no FPinit is projected.

The current analysis is in line with Ritter and Wiltschko (2015), who also recognize that the sentience restriction ("H-animacy" in their terms) plays a role in various parts of Blackfoot phrase structure. However, this paper departs from their proposal by arguing that not every argument-hosting functional category is restricted based on sentience. The data in this section (and the results of the current paper) seem to suggest that not every functional category can pose a sentience restriction, but rather only those categories (e.g., FPinit) that host a grammaticalized event role such as an initiator.

Additional evidence for this claim comes from posture verbs. As proposed in (11c), these verbs do not have Fpinit, and they allow either a sentient or nonsentient entity in the specifier of *p*P that does not impose a sentience restriction. If this is so, then the specifier of *p*P may be able to host a grammatically INANIMATE subject, which is always nonsentient in the language. This is borne out by the data in (12):

(12) Anni saakokotoissko it-a-ipoy-wa anni iitaisooyo'p.
DEM bottle.INA LOC-DUR-stand.AI-3S DEM table.INA
'The bottle is standing on the table.' (Kim 2014c)
(in a context where the bottle is in vertical position on the table)

Although it is surprising in that an AI verb allows a grammatically inanimate subject, the example in (12) shows that the specifier of a functional category such as *p*P is inert to the sentience restriction. Importantly, these data, in conjunction with other data from motion verbs in this paper, suggest that the sentience restriction of an argument is active in the narrow syntax when the argument bears an event role such as a grammatical initiator. A similar type of evidence from II verbs is provided in the next section.

The Transitivity Alternation and Initiators

This section discusses how the argument structure of the verbs discussed in the previous section can interact with the transitivity alternation by providing data from various types of verbs. This section also discusses some II verbs with respect to the proposed account.

It is well known that in Blackfoot, only sentient beings may be subjects of TA/TI verbs (Frantz 2009). Consistent with this fact, examination of a dictionary of Blackfoot (Frantz and Russell 1995) reveals that AI-TA/TI pairs or AI-TI-TA triples almost always have sentient subjects (Ritter and Wiltschko 2006).[8]

In this section, I argue that the previous observation can be accounted for by the analysis proposed earlier. Recasting those observations within the current analysis, verbs that show the transitivity alternation have grammatical initiators (i.e., they have sentient DPs in the specifier of FPinit), while verbs that do not show the transitivity alternation have no initiators in their structure. Moreover, I provide novel evidence from different types of motion AI verbs that supports the correlation between an initiator and the transitivity alternation argued for in this paper.[9] With posture verbs that appear with a locative *p*P, as shown above, there is no initiator; thus, no TA/TI verbs are expected. This is true in the language, and I do not further discuss this type of verb.

In the sections that follow, I discuss inherently directed motion verbs, manner of motion verbs, psych verbs, and some II verbs.

Initiators and Transitivity Alternation

As shown in (2) and (11a), inherently directed motion verbs such as 'go' have initiators. The proposed account for the transitivity alternation predicts that the AI verb 'go' will have TA/TI counterparts. This is borne out by the data in (13). To avoid confusion, it should be noted that TA/TI forms of the verbs in Blackfoot determine the GRAMMATICAL ANIMACY of the OBJECT, not the sentience of the subject.

(13) a. Nit-(*itap-)iistap-aaat-a-yi **anniksi** **pookaiksi**/*annistsi naapioyisistsi.
1-GOAL-away-go.TA-TH-3PL DEM children/ DEM houses
'I went away from those children/*those houses.'

b. Nit-(*itap-)iistap-aatoo-'p-wa **anni** **naapioyis**/*anna pookaa.
1-GOAL-away-go.TI-TH-3S DEM house/ DEM child
'I went away from that house/*that child.'

In (13a), the TA verb *aaat* 'go' is presented, and in (13b) the TI verb *aatoo* 'go' is presented. These are full-fledged transitive verbs like other transitive verbs in the language. Unlike their AI counterparts, which require direction linkers introducing goal phrases, these transitive verbs have path DP objects: 'those children' in (13a) for the TA verb and 'that house' in (13b) for the TI verb without a direction linker *itap-*. In fact, the sentences are ungrammatical if the linker appears, as indicated in (13). Moreover, each transitive verb shows agreement in animacy with its respective path DP object. With the TA verb in (13a), a grammatically animate path object DP 'those children' appears, but a grammatically inanimate path DP 'those houses' is not allowed. In (13b) with the TI verb, a grammatically inanimate path DP 'that house' appears, but a grammatically animate path DP 'that child' is not allowed. The verbs are also marked with theme suffixes and person and number agreement, which appear only with TA/TI verbs in Blackfoot (Frantz 2009). For instance, the TA verb in (13a) shows plural agreement (*-yi*) with its object 'those children', while the TI verb in (13b) shows singular agreement (*-wa*) with its object 'that house'. TA/TI verbs in Blackfoot have DP objects consisting of a demonstrative and an NP, but are ungrammatical with an NP object (Ritter and Rosen 2010), which is the case with the TA/TI of the verb 'go' in (13): the TA/TI with a corresponding NP object is ungrammatical as shown in (14). Thus, the data presented in (13) constitute strong evidence that the AI verb *oo* 'go' shows the transitivity alternation of TA/TI verbs.

(14) a. *nit-iistap-aaat-a-yi **pookaiksi** TA
Intended interpretation: 'I went away from those children.'

b. *nit-iistap-aatoo-'p-wa **naapioyis** TI
Intended interpretation: 'I went away from that house.'

Before we move to the discussion of the manner of motion verbs, a word on the non-linker *iistap* 'away' is in order. As far as Blackfoot is concerned, the prefix *iistap* is a nonlinker (Frantz 2009), and it is not the same type as a linker such as *itap*- 'to' (Frantz 2009; Kim 2015a). It has been shown that nonlinkers including *iistap*- cannot introduce a goal DP, as illustrated in (15), which is adapted from Kim (2015a).

(15) Nit-yaak-**iistap**-ohpai'piiyi (*anni niitahtaayi).
I-will-away-jump.AI (DEM river)
'I will jump away (*from the river).'

Moreover, in (13), it is not the case that the presence of the linker (*itap*-) is blocked because of the presence of the nonlinker (*iistap*-). As shown in (16), the presence of the linker alone without the nonlinker cannot make the sentence grammatical.

(16) *nit-itap-aaat-a-yi anniksi pookaiksi
Intended meaning: 'I went (away) from those children.'

Manner of motion AI verbs, unlike the inherently directed motion verbs in (15), do not require goal *p*Ps (Kim 2014c, 2015a), as illustrated in (17).[10] They are only optional. The example in (17b) is adapted from Kim (2014c, 2015a).

(17) a. Anna saahkomaapi (itap)-inn-inaka'si-m-wa (oomi isspahkoyi).
DEM boy.AN GOAL-down-roll.AI-??-3S DEM hill
'That boy rolled down (to the hill).'

b. Anna saahkomaapi (itap)-okska'si-wa (oomi isspahkoyi).
DEM boy.AN GOAL-run.AI-3S DEM hill
'That boy ran (to the hill).'

According to Kim (2015a), building on Levin (1993), the contrast between inherently directed motion and manner of motion verbs with respect to *p*P is due to the lexical semantic difference between the two types of verbs. The former has a direction meaning built into it requiring a direction phrase, while the latter does not have such a meaning in its lexical semantics, thus not requiring a direction phrase. In the current analysis, this difference with respect to the direction phrase can be accounted for by the absence of a grammatical initiator with manner of motion verbs, in contrast to inherently directed motion verbs. In the absence of such an initiator, manner of motion verbs do not license a direction *p*P; the direction *p*P is optional with this type of verb. The absence of a grammatical initiator further suggests that manner of motion verbs do not require a sentient subject, which is borne out by (18). Here, the subject ('that wagon') is nonsentient, although it is grammatically animate. It should be mentioned that this AI verb also allows a grammatically INANIMATE subject ('that bottle'), like the posture verbs discussed earlier (see (12)), which is predicted by the proposed analysis.

(18)	Anna	ainaka'si/anni	saakokotoissko	(itap)-inn-inaka'si-m-wa
	DEM	wagon.AN/DEM	bottle.INA	GOAL-down-roll.AI-??-3S

	(oomi	isspahkoyi).
	DEM	hill

'That wagon/bottle rolled down (to that hill).'

As predicted by the current analysis, the verb in (18) does not have TA/TI counterparts, lacking the transitivity alternation (which is true for the manner of motion verbs in (17)). An interesting contrast to the verb *inaka'si* 'roll' in (18) is *inakataki* 'roll', another AI verb:

(19)	a.	**Anna**	**saahkomaapi**	inakataki-wa	(pokon)
		DEM	boy	roll.AI-3S	(ball)

'That boy rolled (a ball).'

b.	*__Anna__	**ainaka'si**	inakataki-wa	(pokon)
	DEM	wagon	roll.AI-3S	(ball)

'That wagon rolled (a ball).' (Intended meaning: 'That wagon made a ball roll.')

In (19), the verb is a manner of motion AI verb 'roll' just like the AI verb *inaka'si* 'roll' in (18). However, unlike the verb *inaka'si* 'roll' in (18), this verb allows a sentient subject only (19a); the nonsentient subject 'that wagon' is not allowed, as the ungrammaticality of sentence (19b) shows. In fact, this verb is a pseudotransitive verb (in the sense of Ritter and Rosen 2010), allowing an optional NP object such as 'ball'. I argue that the sentience restriction on this verb together with its being pseudotransitive indicates that the subject is a grammatical initiator. The prediction is that this verb (*inakataki* in (19a)) will have a TA/TI counterpart, unlike the verb *inaka'si* 'roll' in (18), which is confirmed by the data in (20):

(20) a. Nit-inakat-a-wa anna saahkomaapi. TA
1-roll.TA-TH-3S DEM boy
'I rolled that boy.'

b. Nit-inakatoo-'p-wa anni saakokotoisskoyi. TI
1-roll.TI-TH-3S DEM bottle
'I rolled that bottle.'

Finally, I propose that psych predicates belong to the same type as the pseudotransitive AI *inakataki* 'roll' in that they require grammatical initiators. Consider the data for AI psych verbs where a human is an experiencer. Unlike pseudotransitive AI verbs, AI psych verbs do not allow optional NPs, but their subjects must always be sentient, like pseudotransitives (Kim 2014b).

(21) Nit-a'ka-i'taki.
1-hate-AI
'I have hatred.' (i.e., I am in the state of disliking/hating) (Kim 2014b)

As expected, in addition to a human experiencer as in (21), an animal can also appear as an experiencer subject:

(22) Anna poos a'ka-i'taki-wa.
DEM cat hate-AI-3S
'That cat has hatred.'
(Context: A cat is brought into a room containing a dog, and is angry about it.)

The defining property of the sentient subjects of AI psych verbs in the language is that they behave syntactically just like agents, i.e., sentient subjects of TA/TI verbs (see Kim 2014b for some diagnostics). I propose that these facts can be accounted for if agentlike experiencers are grammatical initiators.[11] This view also captures the fact that they have TA/TI counterparts, as illustrated in (23):

(23) a. Nit-a'ka-imm-a-wa [amo mamii]/*mamii. TA
1-hate-TA-TH-3S DEM fish.AN/ fish.AN
'I hate this fish/*fish.'

b. Nit-a'ka-i'tsi-'p-wa [anni akoopis]/*akoopis. TI
1-hate-TI-TH-3S DEM soup.INA/ soup.INA
'I hate that soup/*soup.' (Kim 2014b)

Inanimate Intransitive (II) Verbs and Initiators

The analysis proposed in this paper predicts that II verbs in Blackfoot may not have initiators in their event structure. This is because II verbs by their morphological classification (Bloomfield 1946) have a grammatically inanimate subject, which is an inanimate object in the real world. That is, grammatically inanimate nouns are not sentient. Thus, grammatically inanimate subjects of II verbs cannot be initiators of events, and II verbs may not have corresponding transitive counterparts. The previously mentioned study of the dictionary of Blackfoot (Ritter and Wiltschko 2006) appears to support this prediction. II verbs are found to have AI counterparts, lacking transitive counterparts. Moreover, some AI pairs of the same meaning, e.g., *ihkssoyi* vs. *ihkssaki* 'dry (AI)', have different stems that are counterparts of IIs and TA/TIs, respectively.

My fieldwork findings on II verbs are thus far in line with previous findings and the predictions made by this paper: II verbs have grammatically inanimate subjects, and there are no corresponding TA/TI verbs. A surprising and novel finding, however, is that some II verbs can have grammatically ANIMATE subjects (either sentient or nonsentient), which is inconsistent with their morphological classification. For instance, consider the II verb 'float' illustrated in (24):

(24) Anni saakokotoissko/anna saahkomaapi itap-yiistsi-wa anninaapioyis.
DEM bottle.INA / DEM boy GOAL-float.II-3S DEM house
'The bottle/the boy floated down toward the house (by the shore).'

In (24), the II verb 'float' allows a grammatically inanimate subject 'bottle', consistent with its morphological classification. Unexpectedly, however, it also allows a grammatically animate human subject (i.e., sentient), which shows a morphological mismatch like AI posture verbs that allow grammatically inanimate subjects (see (12) and 18)).[12] Although surprising, this type of data is predicted by the account proposed in the previous section: it is proposed that intransitives may have TA/TI forms if their subjects are grammatical initiators. The II verb in (24) does not have corresponding TA/TI forms, which suggests that its subject is not a grammatical initiator. One possible subject of this II verb is sentient, i.e., a human 'that boy', and thus in our world knowledge, the subject might exert energy to initiate an event. Importantly, however, it fails to do so when it appears with this type of II verb. Although it is sentient, it cannot appear in a grammatical initiator position such as the specifier of FPinit.[13] Another supporting fact for this account is that II verbs like that in (24) do not require a direction *p*P like AI manner of motion verbs that have no initiator arguments. The data shown in this section provide further support for the view that sentient arguments can be visible to the syntax only when they have the event role of an initiator.

Concluding Remarks

I have proposed that the transitivity alternation is possible when a grammatical initiator is present, providing evidence from motion, posture, and psych verbs, as well as from some II verbs. The results of the current study suggest that not all semantically animate arguments are visible to the syntax. As shown with various types of verbs, only sentient beings that are grammatical initiators can interact with the syntax. It remains to be seen how a grammatical initiator can affect the syntax of event structure or other related parts of the syntax in parallel to or differently from grammatical delimiters (that mark telicity) in languages like English.

NOTES

1. I would like to thank Sandra Many Feathers (formerly Crazybull) and Brent Prairie Chicken for sharing their language with me, and Betsy Ritter for her comments at various stages of this research. Of course, all errors are my own. Unless otherwise noted, all data presented in this paper are from my own fieldwork. The data presented come from the

Kainaa (Blood) dialect.

2. Various functional heads have been proposed for these two components in the literature. I employ FPinit and FPterm, but the proposal made in this paper does not depend on this choice.
3. The following abbreviations are used: 1/3 = first/third person, AI = animate intransitive, AN = animate, DEM = demonstrative, DUR = durative, II = inanimate intransitive, INA = inanimate, LOC = locative, PL = plural, S = singular, TA = transitive animate, TH = theme, TI = transitive inanimate.
4. Bliss et al. (2013) propose that the locative linker is a functional adposition adjoined to IP, and thus their focus is different from that of the present paper.
5. A non-linker PP is a PP without a complement (i.e., a Ground) (Kim 2015a).
6. For now, I assume that P is null. Alternatively, it may be the case that a linker moves from P to *p*. This issue does not significantly affect the proposal in this paper.
7. In fact, inherently directed motion or posture verbs require either a linker *p* or a non-linker P (Kim 2015a). However, as I have shown, a non-linker P does not require a sentient subject, unlike a linker *p*. I do not further discuss non-linker Ps here.
8. According to Ritter and Rosen (2010), the Blackfoot dictionary lists six verbs that are exceptions to this generalization. However, this classification is not based on formal criteria. See Ritter and Rosen (2010) for discussion of this issue.
9. At this stage, it is not clear how this correlation can be formalized. More research on other types of verbs is required.
10. My fieldwork shows that the suffix *-m* on the verb 'roll' in (17a) appears when a subject is third person singular animate, and it cannot appear when a subject is first or second person. This suffix may not indicate that this AI verb is used as a TI verb. For example, this verb is unable to have an object, as shown in (i): the intended object 'that bottle' cannot appear. This fact may suggest that the morpheme *-m* may not be a TI theme suffix. As in (17b), this suffix does not appear with all manner of motion AI verbs. I leave the exact status of this suffix for further research, and for now, gloss it as '??'.

(i)	Anna	saahkomaapi	inaka'si-m-wa	(*anni	saakokotoissko).
	DEM	boy.AN	roll.AI-??-3S	DEM	bottle.INA

'That boy rolled (* that bottle).'

11. Their interpretation is not exactly like the initiator of a canonical agentive verb, which would result from the encyclopedic information of the verb.
12. Johansson (2008) shows that a grammatically INANIMATE noun can be the subject of an

AI verb only if it is personified, i.e., treated as a sentient being. However, in (24), what is surprising is that a HUMAN noun can be the subject of an II verb.

13. In the encyclopedic knowledge, a subject of the verbs 'float', 'be hated', or other statives are all stative subjects, i.e., non-initiators, as implied by the lexical semantics of the verbs. However, as argued in this paper, only the subject of psych predicates like 'be hated' can be grammatical initiators by being in the specifier of FPinit.

REFERENCES

Bliss, Heather. 2007. Object agreement in Blackfoot: Sentient and non-sentient controllers. In *Papers of the thirty-eighth Algonquian Conference*, ed. H. C. Wolfart, 11–28. Winnipeg: University of Manitoba Press.

———. 2013. The Blackfoot configurationality conspiracy: Parallels and differences in clausal and nominal structures. PhD thesis, University of British Columbia.

Bliss, Heather, Rose-Marie Déchaine, and Tomio Hirose. 2013. Locative PPs in Blackfoot and Plains Cree. Paper presented at the 2013 *Annual Meeting of the Canadian Linguistic Association*.

Bloomfield, Leonard. 1946. Algonquian. In *Linguistic structures of Native America*, ed. Harry Hoijer et al., 85–129. New York: Viking Fund Publications in Anthropology 6.

Borer, Hagit. 2005. *The normal course of events*. New York: Oxford University Press.

Frantz, Donald. 2009. *Blackfoot grammar*. 2nd ed. Toronto: University of Toronto Press.

Frantz, Donald, and Norma J. Russell. 1995. *Blackfoot dictionary of stems roots and affixes*. Toronto: University of Toronto Press.

Johansson, Sara. 2008. The status of nominal gender in Algonquian: Evidence from psych verbs. In *Proceedings of the 2008 CLA*, ed. Susie Jones. Vancouver: University of British Columbia.

Levin, Beth. 1993. *English verb classes and alternations: A preliminary investigation*. Chicago: University of Chicago Press.

Kim, Kyumin. 2014a. Refining the syntax of non-core arguments: P, applicative, and functional *p*. In *Proceedings of 44th NELS*, ed. Jyoti Iyer and Leland Kusmer, 205–219. Amherst, MA: GLSA Publication.

———. 2014b. PERSON all the way in Blackfoot: Evidence from psych-predicates. In *Proceedings of the 2013 CLA*, ed. San Luo. Victoria, BC: University of Victoria.

———. 2014c. Spatial PPs in Blackfoot with motion and posture verbs. Unpublished manuscript. University of Ottawa, Ottawa, ON.

———. 2015a. Spatial PPs and structure of motion verbs in Blackfoot. In *Proceedings of the*

19th WSCLA, ed. Natali Weber and Sihwei Chen, 125–139. Vancouver: UBC Working Papers in Linguistics.

———. 2015b. The instrument linker *iiht-/oht-* in Blackfoot as a functional *p*. In *Proceedings of the 18th WSCLA*, ed. Natali Weber and Sihwei Chen, 35–49. Vancouver: UBC Working Papers in Linguistics.

Ritter, Elizabeth, and Sara Rosen. 2000. Event structure and ergativity. In *Events as grammatical object*, ed. Carol Tenny and James Pustejovsky, 187–238. Stanford, CA: CSLI Publication.

———. 2010. Animacy in Blackfoot: Implication for event structure and clause structure. In *Syntax, lexical semantics and event structure*, ed. M. Rappaport-Hovav, E. Doron, and I. Sichel, 124–152. Oxford: Oxford University Press.

Ritter, Elizabeth, and Martina Wiltschko. 2006. Relating verb stems in Blackfoot: The contribution of argument structure to stem agreement. Poster presented at the 2006 Algonquian Conference, Vancouver, BC.

———. 2015. Animating the narrow syntax. *Linguistic Review* 32.4: 869–908.

Svenonius, Peter. 2003. Limits on P: Filling in holes vs. falling in holes. *Nordlyd* 31:431–445.

Talmy, Leonard. 1978. Figure and ground in complex sentences. In *Universals of Human Language*, Vol. 4, ed. J. H. Greenberg, 625–649. Stanford, CA: Stanford University Press.

———. 1985. Lexicalization patterns: Semantic structure in lexical forms. In *Language Typology and Syntactic Description*. Vol. 3, *Grammatical Categories and the Lexicon*, ed. T. Shopen, 57–149. Cambridge: Cambridge University Press.

Valentine, J. Randolph. 2001. *Nishnaabemwin Reference Grammar*. Toronto: University of Toronto Press.

van Voorst, Jan. 1988. *Event Structure*. Amsterdam: John Benjamins.

Negation and Indefinite Pronouns in Mi'gmaq

Carol-Rose Little

This paper describes negation and indefinite pronouns in Mi'gmaq, an Eastern Algonquian language spoken in eastern Canada.[1] The focus of this paper is on standard negation, or the negation "apply[ing] to the most minimal and basic sentences . . . characteristically main clauses and consist[ing] of a single predicate with as few noun phrases and adverbial modifiers as possible" (Payne 1985:198), with a particular emphasis on the past, present, and future intransitive forms. The second part of the paper gives an overview of indefinite pronouns, or pronouns that do not refer to a specific person or thing, and their interaction with negation.

The paper is structured as follows. The next section presents an overview of negation markers and where they occur. I discuss negation in the present, direct and indirect past, and future tenses. I also discuss other preverbal negation particles. In the third section, I introduce indefinite pronouns in the scope of negation as well as their interrogative and existential readings. The last section concludes the paper.

Overview of Negation Particles

In negative sentences, there are obligatorily two markers of negation, a preverbal negation particle and a negative suffix. The *World Atlas of Language Structures* (WALS) calls this type of negation system "double negation" (Dryer 2013a) (not to be confused with "double negation" in propositional logic). Dryer (2013a) cites the Algonquian languages Menominee and Ojibwe as having this type of negation. Mi'gmaq is not included in WALS, though it also has a double negation system composed of Neg [V-Neg], or a preverbal negation particle and a negative suffix (Dryer 2013b). The preverbal negative marker is *mu* 'not' and the negative suffix is *-w* or *-u* after a consonant. I return to other preverbal negation particles co-occurring with the negative suffix below. The following examples show the affirmative (1) and negative (2) with negation markers bolded.

(1) *Affirmative*

a. Mijji-n.
   eat.VAI-2
   'You eat.'[2]

b. Mijji-'t-'p.
   eat.VAI-2-PAST.DIR
   'You ate.'

(2) *Negative*

a. **Mu** mijji-**w**-'n
   NEG eat.VAI-**NEG**-2
   'You don't eat.'

b. **Mu** mijji-**w**-t-'p.
   NEG eat.VAI-**NEG**-2-PAST.DIR
   'You didn't eat.'

The negative suffix comes from the Proto-Eastern Algonquian negative suffix *-(o)w(i) (Goddard 2006:167). All Algonquian languages except Miami-Illinois have an obligatory negative particle or preverb (Goddard 2006:163).

If the verb is transitive then the negation marker comes after the verb root and any theme sign. The theme sign is sensitive to the animacy and transitivity of the verb as well as inverse and direct alignment. For example, the theme sign *-a-* shows direct alignment. Due to a phonological change, the theme sign in the affirmative is not pronounced.

(3) *Affirmative*

a. Gesal-t.
love.VTA-2
'You love him/her.'

b. Gesal-i-n.
love.VTA-1-2
'You love me.'

(4) *Negative*

a. **Mu** gesal-a-**w**-t.
NEG love.VTA-TH-**NEG**-2
'You don't love him/her.'

b. **Mu** gesal-i-**w**-n.
NEG love.VTA-1-**NEG**-2
'You don't love me.'

For the remainder of this section, I focus on intransitive verb paradigms.

Order of the Negative Particle

Polysynthetic languages are known for having highly flexible word orders (Baker 1996); Mi'gmaq is not excluded. Elements like the direct object and subject can intervene between the preverbal negation particle *mu* and the verb as shown in example (5a). Other word orders are also grammatical as in (5b) and (5c).

(5) a. **Mu** Mali almalga-**gu**-p.
NEG Mary dance.VAI-3.NEG-PAST.DIR
'Mary didn't dance.'

b. **Mu** amalga-**gu**-p Mali.

c. Mali **mu** almalga-**gu**-p

The negation particle cannot follow the verb, as in the ungrammatical examples in (6).

(6) a. *Amalga-**gu**-p **mu** Mali

b. *Amalga-**gu**-p Mali **mu**

c. *Mali amalga-**gu**-p **mu**

Present Tense

The following tables show the present tense of the VAI verb *mijji-* 'to eat' and the negative present tense. Person marker morphemes are separated by hyphens. Negation makers are bolded. There is no morpheme that overtly marks present. The *-ulti* morpheme marks the plural form (more than two) and *-ig* marks nonsingular third person (Table 1).

Note in Table 2 that the pluralizer is closest to the stem, as per its apparent historical derivational origins (see Goddard 1980 for discussion). The negative suffix follows *-ulti*.

The first person inclusive seems to have no *-w* as a suffix: *mijji'gw* 'we (inclusive) eat' and *mu mijjigw* 'we (inclusive) don't eat'. The verb forms are, however, distinguished by a shortening of the vowel in the negative form. The phonetic details of this are not yet fully understood, and the first person exclusive negative form could be *mu mijjiggw* [k] where the negative suffix has assimilated to a velar stop in the [k^w]. I have found a form where the velar stop is a geminate in the plural inclusive with an indirect evidential, as shown in (8), which is subject to speaker variation. Compare this with the affirmative form in (7) where there is no geminate velar stop.

TABLE 1. Mi'gmaq present tense intransitive verb paradigm

	SG	DU	PL
1	Mijji	Mijji-eg	Mijj-ulti-eg
12	—	Mijji-'gw	Mijj-ulti-'gw
2	Mijji-n	Mijji-oq	Mijj-ulti-oq
3	Mijji-t	Mijji-j-ig	Mijj-ulti-j-ig

TABLE 2. Mi'gmaq present tense negative intransitive verb paradigm

	SG	DU	PL
1	**Mu** mijji-**w**	**Mu** mjji-**w**-eg	**Mu** mijj-ulti-**w**-eg
12	—	**Mu** mijji-**gw**	**Mu** mijj-ulti-'gw
2	**Mu** mijji-**w**-'n	**Mu** mijji-**w**-oq	**Mu** mijj-ulti-**w**-oq
3	**Mu** mijji-**gw**	**Mu** mijji-'**gw**	**Mu** mijj-ulti-'**gw**

(7) Mijj-ulti-'gu-s
eat.VAI-PL-1.INCL-PAST.INDIR
'We (incl.) apparently ate.'

(8) **Mu** mijj-ulti-g-g-u-s
NEG eat.VAI-PL-**NEG**-1.INCL-PAST.INDIR
'We (incl.) (apparently) didn't eat.'

The gemination could also be due to the shortening of the vowel *i*, where the remaining timing slot is filled by the velar stop [k] (orthographically <g>). For the purposes of this paper, I leave this question open.

In the third person, the negative marker follows the third person suffix, instead of preceding it as in other person markings. This is realized as a labialized velar [k^w]. This is a historical metathesis of the third person marker and the negation suffix as discussed by Goddard 1969.

(9) **Mu** mijji-**gw**
NEG eat.VAI-**3.NEG**
'He doesn't eat.'

In some forms, the third person negative suffix is realized phonetically as [k], as in (10). The *-u-* found here is a connecting vowel from the Proto-Eastern Algonquian connecting vowel <*-ō-> (Goddard 2006:167), which became *-u-* in Mi'gmaq.

(10) **Mu** eim-u-**g**.
NEG be.VAI-LV-**3.NEG**
'He is not here.'

In (11), when the past tense marker *-p(n)* is suffixed to the verb in (10), the form is similar to past tense, as in (12).

(11) **Mu** eim-u-**gu**-p.
NEG be.VAI-LV-**3.NEG**-PAST.DIR
'He/she was not here.'

(12) **Mu** mijji-**gu**-p.
NEG eat.VAI-**3.NEG**-PAST.DIR
'He/she didn't eat.'

For the purposes of this paper, I gloss *-gw* and its variant *-gu* as the third person (*-g*) and negation marker (*-w*); '3.NEG'.

Past: Direct and Indirect Evidentials

Other morphemes, like the direct past tense evidential marker *-p(n)*, come after person marking. The direct past tense marker is used when the speaker has witnessed information firsthand, via any of the senses, or when the speaker is certain about such information. The use of both the direct and indirect evidential always occurs in past tense environments. I first illustrate the direct past tense:

(13) *Affirmative Direct Past*

a. Mijji-a-p.
eat.VAI-1-PAST.DIR
'I ate.'

b. Mijji-oq-op.
eat.VAI-2.PL-PAST.DIR
'You (dual) ate.'

c. Mijji-p.
eat.VAI-PAST.DIR
'He ate.'

(14) *Negative Direct Past*

a. **Mu** mijji-**w**-ap.
NEG eat.VAI-**NEG**-1-PAST.DIR
'I didn't eat.'

b. **Mu** mijji-**w**-oq-op.
NEG eat.VAI-**NEG**-2.PL-PAST.DIR
'You (dual) didn't eat.'

c. **Mu** mijji-**gu**-p.
NEG eat.VAI-3.**NEG**-PAST.DIR
'He didn't eat.'

TABLE 3. Mi'gmaq direct past tense intransitive verb paradigm

	SG	DU	PL
1	Mijji-a-**p**	Mijji-eg-'**p**	Mijj-ulti-eg-'**p**
12	—	Mijji-'gu-**p**	Mijji-ulti-'gu-**p**
2	Mijji-'t-'**p**	Mijji-oq-**op**	Mijj-ulti-oq-**op**
3	Mijji-**p**	Mijji-**pn**-ig	Mijj-ulti-**pn**-ig

TABLE 4. Mi'gmaq negative direct past tense intransitive verb paradigm

	SG	DU	PL
1	**Mu** mijji-**w**-a-p	**Mu** mijji-**w**-eg-'p	**Mu** mijj-ulti-**w**-eg-'p
12	-	**Mu** mijji-**w**-gu-p	**Mu** mijj-ulti-**w**-gu-p
2	**Mu** mijji-**w**-t-'p	**Mu** mijji-**w**-oq-op	**Mu** mijj-ulti-**w**-oq-op
3	**Mu** mjji-**gu**-p	**Mu** mijji-**gu**-pn-ig	**Mu** mijj-ulti-**gu**-pn-ig

The indirect evidential—also referred to as suppositive by Inglis (2003)—marks information acquired through means other than firsthand. It is also used in interrogative contexts in the past. The indirect evidential is marked by *-s('p(n))*.

TABLE 5. Mi'gmaq indirect past tense intransitive verb paradigm

	SG	DU	PL
1	Mijji-a-s	Mijji-eg-'s	Mijj-ulti-eg-'s/Mijj-ulti-eg-s'**p**
12	—	Mijji-'gu-s	Mijj-ulti-'gu-s
2	Mijji-'s'**p**	Mijji-oq-s'**p**	Mijj-ulti-oq-s'**p**
3	Mijji-s	Mijji-**sn**-ig	Mijj-ulti-**sn**-ig

TABLE 6. Mi'gmaq negative indirect past tense intransitive verb paradigm

	SG	DU PL	
1	**Mu** mijji-**w**-a-s	**Mu** mijji-**w**-eg-'s	**Mu** mijj-ulti-**w**-eg-'s
12	—	**Mu** mijji-**w**-gu-s	**Mu** mijj-ulti-**w**-gu-s/ **Mu** mijj-ulti-g-gu-s
2	**Mu** mijji-**w**-s'p	**Mu** mijji-**w**-oq-s'p	**Mu** mijj-ulti-**w**-oq-s'p
3	**Mu** mijji-**gu**-s	**Mu** mijji-**gu**-sn-ig	**Mu** mijj-ulti-**gu**-sn-ig

Tables 4 and 6 show that the negative suffix *-w* is internal to the verb morphology.

Future and Negation

Above, I have shown that the negation particle follows the verb stem, the theme sign, and any pluralizer like *-ulti*. Evidential markers, like the direct and indirect, and person markers then follow the negative suffix. However, the future morpheme *-te* does not co-occur with the negative suffix *-w*.

(15) *Affirmative Future*
Mijji-tes(g).[3]
eat.VAI-FUT.2
'You will eat.'[4]

(16) *Negative Future*
Ma' mijji-w-'n.
NEG.FUT eat.VAI-NEG-2
'You won't eat.'

The future suffix *-tes(g)* in (15) does not appear in the negative version in (16). In (17) (negative present tense) and (16) (negative future tense), the verbs are the same but the negative particles are different. The preverbal negative particle *mu* seen in present (17) and past (14) is *ma'* in the future:

(17) Mu mijji-w-'n.
NEG eat.VAI-NEG-2
'You don't eat.'

Furthermore, the process of initial change (where *ə* becomes *e* in certain contexts) happens in the past and present but not in the future. The phonological process of initial change on the verb marks realis clauses (like past and present verbs) and no initial change marks irrealis clauses (like future tense verbs). For example, the verb *'pgisin-* 'to arrive' becomes *pegisin-* in the present and past (examples (18a) and (18b)) (see Costa 1996 for more on initial change).[5] In the negative future with *ma'* the verb stem remains *'pgisin-* (19c), the unchanged form. In negative present and past (examples (19a) and (19b)) the verb stem is the changed form *pegisin-*.

(18) a. *Direct Past*

Pegisin-u'-t-'p.
arrive.VAI-LV-2-PAST.DIR
'You arrived.'

b. *Present*

Pegisin-n.
arrive.VAI-2
'You arrive.'

c. *Future*

'Pgisin-tes(g).
arrive.VAI-FUT.2
'You will arrive.'

(19) a. *Negative Direct Past*

Mu pegisin-**u**-t-'p.
NEG arrive.VAI-**NEG**-2-PAST.DIR
'You didn't arrive.'

b. *Negative Present*

Mu pegisin-**u**-'n.
NEG arrive.VAI-**NEG**-2
'You haven't arrived.'

c. *Negative Future*

Ma' 'pgisin-**u**-'n.
NEG.FUT arrive.VAI-**NEG**-2
'You won't arrive.'

In subordinate clauses, marked by the suffix -n (referred to in (20) and (21) as conjunct), person suffixes are like in the present indicative. In these examples there is no initial change of the verb stem. Recall that initial change marks realis, while no initial change marks irrealis clauses. The negative suffix *-w* comes after the verb and its theme sign.

(20) *Affirmative Conjunct*
Newt tluisi-a-n . . .
once named.VAI-1-CONJ
'Once my name is . . .'

(21) *Negative Conjunct*
Newt **mu** tluisi-**w**-a-n
once **NEG** named.VAI-**NEG**-1-CONJ
'Once my name is not . . .'

Table 7 shows the future paradigm for the VAI verb *mijji-* 'to eat'. The future markers are bolded.

TABLE 7. Mi'gmaq future intransitive verb paradigm

	SG	DU	PL
1	Mijji-tes/mijji-a's[1]	Mijji-tes-nen	Mijjulti-tes-nen
12	—	Mijji-tes-nu	Mijji-ulti-tes-nu
2	Mijji-tes(g)	Mijji-toqs'p	Mijj-ulti-toqs'p
3	Mijji-tew	Mijji-taq	Mijj-ulti-taq

1. *Mijjia's* is preferred over *mijjites* for the first person singular future in Listuguj.

TABLE 8. Mi'gmaq negative future intransitive verb paradigm.

	SG	DU	PL
1	**Ma'** mijji-**w**	**Ma'** mijji-**w**-eg	**Ma'** mijji-ulti-**w**-eg
12	—	**Ma'** mijji-**gw**	**Ma'** mijj-ulti-**gw**
2	**Ma'** mijji-**w**-n	**Ma'** mijji-**w**-oq	**Ma'** mijj-ulti-**w**-oq
3	**Ma'** mijji-**gw**	**Ma'** mijji-'**gw**	**Ma'** mijj-ulti-'**gw**

Further differentiating the future from the past and present tenses are the person suffixes. The person suffixes in the future for first person plural exclusive are more like possessive suffixes, unlike in the paradigms given for past and present. The example in (22) shows a possessive suffix for the first person plural exclusive, while (23) shows the future first person dual exclusive. Compare with the first person exclusive suffix of the present in (24).

(22) *Possession*
'n-tus-**inen**
1-daughter-**EXCL**
'our daughter'

(23) *Future*
Mijji-tes-**nen.**
eat.VAI-FUT-**EXCL**
'We will eat.'

(24) *Present*
Mijji-**eg.**
eat.VAI-**EXCL.1**
'We eat.'

Other Negative Particles

Table 9 presents a summary of the negative particles occurring in the Mi'gmaq online dictionary and those found in fieldwork. These particles all obligatorily co-occur with the negative suffix *-w*.

TABLE 9. Mi'gmaq preverbal negative particles

NEGATIVE PARTICLE	TRANSLATION
gesgmnaq	'Before'
ma'	Future negation particle
(me')mnaq	'Never, not yet'
mu	Negation marker
mutt (mukk in some dialects)	Imperative negation marker

Below are examples of other negative markers. Note that the negative suffix also appears in these contexts.

(25) **Mnaq** ne'w ajie-**gw.**
not.yet four advance.VTA-**3.NEG**
'It's not yet four o'clock.' (Mi'gmaq Online Dictionary (2014) entry 2489)

(26) Tetaqa'si, **gesg-mnaq** apaja'si-**gw.**
rush.IMP.SG, **over-not.yet** return.VAI-**3.NEG**
'Hurry up, before he/she gets back'. (Mi'gmaq Online Dictionary (2014) entry 1246)

(27) a. *Affirmative Dual Imperative*
Mijji-gw!
eat.VAI-IMP.2
'Eat (dual)!'

b. *Negative Dual Imperative*
Mutt mijji-**new!**
NEG eat.VAI-IMP.2.NEG.PL
'Don't eat (dual)!'[6]

In conclusion, negation requires two elements: both a preverbal negation particle and the negative suffix *-w*.

Indefinite Pronouns and Negation

This section concerns the indefinite pronouns *goqwei* 'what' and *wen* 'who', which, when preceded by a negative marker, mean 'nothing' and 'no one', respectively. This is similar to other Algonquian languages such as Cheyenne (Murray 2012) and Cree (Wolfart 1996). For negative indefinite pronouns 'no one' or 'nothing', the negation particle must precede both the indefinite pronoun and the verb, and the verb must have the agreeing negative suffix on the verb.

'Nothing'

The negative pronoun 'nothing' is expressed with the inanimate interrogative pronoun *goqwei* and the negative particle *mu* or future negative particle *ma'*. The indefinite pronoun *goqwei* must come after the negative particle for it to mean 'nothing'. The examples in (28) show the indefinite pronoun within the scope of negation in the direct past, the present and the future tenses. (29) gives the forms for the existential pronoun and (30), the interrogative.

(28) *Negative Indefinite*

a. Mu goqwei eten-u-gu-p.
NEG what be.VII-LV-3.NEG-PAST.DIR
'Nothing was here.'

b. Mu goqwei eten-u-g.
NEG what be.VII-LV-3.NEG
'Nothing is here.'

c. Ma' goqwei ten-u-g.
NEG.FUT what be.VII-LV-3.NEG
'Nothing will be here.'

(29) *Existential*

a. Nat goqwei ete-g-'p.
EXT what be.VII-3-PAST.DIR
'Something was there.'

b. Nat goqwei ete-g.
EXT what be.VII-3
'Something is there.'

c. Nat goqwei te-tew.
EXT what be.VII-3.FUT
'Something will be there.'

(30) *Interrogative*

a. Goqwei ete-g's/ete-g-s'p?
what be.VII-3-PAST.INDIR/BE.VII-3-PAST.INDIR
'What was there?'

b. Goqwei ete-g?
what be.VII-3
'What is there?'

c. Goqwei te-tew?
what be.VII-3.FUT
'What will be there?'

In the examples above, the negative particle must precede the indefinite pronoun for a negative indefinite reading.

'Nobody'

'Nobody' is expressed with the indefinite pronoun *wen* 'who' after the negative particle *mu* or the future negation particle *ma'*. (31) gives the paradigm for 'nobody' in the direct past, present, and future. The existential forms are in (32), and the interrogative forms are in (33).

(31) *Negative Indefinite*

a. Mu wen eim-u-gu-p.
NEG who be.VAI-LV-3.NEG-PAST.DIR
'Nobody was here.'

b. Mu wen eim-u-g.
NEG who be.VAI-LV-3.NEG
'Nobody is here.'

c. Ma' wen i'-m-u-g
NEG.FUT who be.VAI-LV-3.NEG
'Nobody will be here.'

(32) *Existential Pronoun*

a. Na'tuen eig-'p.
EXT.who be.VAI-PAST.DIR
'Someone was there.'

b. Na'tuen ei-g.
EXT.who be.VAI-3
'Someone is there.'

c. Na'tuen i'-tew.
EXT.who be.VAI-3.FUT
'Someone will be there.'

(33) *Interrogative*

a. Wen ei-g-'s?
who be.VII-3-PAST.INDIR
'What was there?'

b. Wen ei-g?
who be.VAI-3
'Who is there?'

c. Wen i'-tew?
who be.VAI-3.FUT
'Who will be there?'

In questions, the interrogative *wen* is the first element (34a). When an NP precedes the interrogative *wen*, speakers find the sentence awkward, as exemplified in (34b).

(34) a. Wen Mali-al mu nemi-a-gu-sn-n?
who Mary-OBV NEG see.VTA-TH-3.NEG-PAST.INDIR-OBV
'Who didn't see Mary?'

b. ?? Mali-al wen mu nemi-a-gu-sn-n?
Mary-OBV who NEG see.VTA-TH-3.NEG-PAST.INDR-OBV
Intended: Who didn't see Mary?

However, if the indefinite pronoun is not preverbal, it is not an interrogative but an indefinite. In the example below, this is translated as the generalized term "people"; however, the indefinite pronoun *wen* is used.

(35) Ei-g **wen** na'jiga-j suliewei.
be.VAI-3 **who** yearn-3.RFM money
'There are people very desirous of money [who yearn after money].'
(Mi'gmaq Online Dictionary 2014: entry 2569)

Furthermore, when *wen* is within the scope of another negative particle like *mnaq* 'not yet', it also means 'nobody'. (36) gives an example with the indefinite pronoun *wen* in the scope of *mnaq* 'not yet'. I discuss scope further in the next section.

(36) **Mnaq** wen wette'ge-**gw**
yet who win.VAI-**3.NEG**
'Nobody has won yet.'

Order of Negative Particles and Negative Pronouns

This section discusses the ordering of the negative particle in relation to the indefinite pronouns. The negative particle must come before the pronoun for the pronoun to be interpreted as an indefinite pronoun within the scope of negation. If the indefinite pronoun comes before the negative particle, the sentence is interrogative.

(37) gives the sentence 'He/she didn't give anything to anyone' and some of the possible word orders.

(37) a. **Mu** ignm-u-a-**gu**-pn-n wen-n goqwei.[7]
NEG give.VTA-APPL-TH-**3.NEG**-PAST.DIR-OBV who-OBV what
'He/she didn't give anything to anyone.'

b. Mu ignmuagupnn goqwei wenn.

c. Mu goqwei ignmuagupnn wenn.

d. Mu wenn ignmuagupnn goqwei.

In (38a) the preverbal particle precedes the indefinite pronoun, thus the meaning is 'nobody'. When the order is changed such that the negative particle follows the indefinite pronoun, the utterance is interpreted as a question, as in (38b).

(38) a. **Mu** wen eim-u-g.
NEG who be.VAI-LV-3.NEG
'Nobody is here.'

b. Wen **mu** eim-u-g?
who NEG be.VAI-LV-3.NEG
'Who is not here?'

Furthermore, the preverbal negative marker cannot occur more than once. Thus the sentence in (39) is ungrammatical.

(39) *__Mu__ ignm-u-a-**gu**-pn-n **mu** goqwei wen-n.
NEG give.VTA-APPL-TH-3.NEG-PAST.DIR-OBV NEG what who-OBV
Intended: 'She didn't give anything to anyone.'

Another question particle, the pronoun *tegen* 'which/which one', cannot be preceded by negation, as shown in (40). Compare (40a) to (40c) where 'someone' has wide scope relative to negation.

(40) a. Tegen mu eim-u-g?
which NEG be.VAI-LV-3.NEG?
'Which one isn't here?'

b. *Mu tegen eim-u-g?
NEG which be.VAI-LV-3.NEG

c. Na'tuen mu eim-u-g
EXT.who NEG be.VAI-LV-3.NEG.
'Someone is not here.'

The data demonstrate that the indefinite pronouns *goqwei* 'what' and *wen* 'who' must follow the negative particle *mu* (or other negative particle like *ma'* 'future negator', *mnaq* 'not yet', etc.) to mean 'nothing' or 'nobody'. *Tegen* 'which/which one' cannot follow the negative particle.

Conclusion

This paper has provided an overview of the standard negation system in Mi'gmaq as well as indefinite pronouns in the scope of negation. Mi'gmaq marks negation with two obligatory markers, a preverbal negation particle and a verb-internal suffix. There are also other preverbal particles like 'not yet' and 'never' that appear with the negation suffix. Finally, I have discussed the indefinite pronouns *goqwei* 'what' and *wen* 'who' and the environments in which they are understood as negative, interrogative, or existential.

Of course, this is just the first step in the study of negation in Mi'gmaq. McCulloch (2012) notes that the preverb *me'si* 'fail to, have difficulty with, be unable to' can have negative scope over the indefinite pronoun as shown in example (41).

(41) **Me'si**-nemi'g-'p wen.
fail-see.VTA-PAST.DIR who
'I couldn't see anyone.' (Adapted from McCulloch (2012:7))

This is different from the negative particles discussed above because *me'si* does not occur with the negative suffix *-w*. The preverb *me'si* has scope over *wen*, and thus *wen* is understood as 'nobody'. *Me'si* patterns with preverbs as it attaches to the verb stem and is not a particle, further differentiating it from the other negative particles discussed above. It is thus necessary to investigate queries such as: Are there any other inherently negative particles that do not occur with the negative suffix? And how do they pattern with indefinite pronouns? These and other questions are reserved for future research.

NOTES

1. First and foremost, I would like to gratefully acknowledge Mi'gmaq speakers and experts Mary Ann Metallic, Roger Metallic, Janice Vicaire, and Joe Wilmot. Without them, this paper would not have been possible. I would also like the thank Miloje Despić, Sarah Murray, Conor Quinn, the members of the Cornell Syntax Circle, and the audiences of the Forty-Sixth Algonquian Conference for comments during various stages of this paper. Unless otherwise cited, the data from this paper comes from the author's fieldwork in the Mi'gmaq First Nations community of Listuguj, Quebec. All Mi'gmaq text has been adapted to the Listuguj orthography by the author. Glosses are also the author's. Any errors are the

author's. An apostrophe (') is used to mark vowel length and represent a schwa (ə); <g> is used to represent the velar stop, in place of the <k> seen in other orthographies (e.g., Smith-Francis); <gw> word finally is realized as a labialized velar stop [k^{w}].

2. Abbreviations: 1 = first person, 2 = second person, 12 = first person inclusive, 3 = third person, APPL = applicative, CONJ = conjunct, DIR = direct, DU = dual, EXT = existential, FUT = future, IMP = imperative, INAN = inanimate, INDIR = indirect evidential, LOC = locative, LV = linking vowel, NEG = negative, PAST = past tense, PL = plural, PSN = person, RFM = relativization feature marker (marks features of relativized element), SAP = speech act participant, SG = singular, TH = theme sign, VAI = verb animate intransitive, VII = verb intransitive inanimate, VTA = verb transitive animate.
3. Speakers in Listuguj prefer the form *mijjites* for second person singular in the future 'you will eat'.
4. The future affirmative second person series also are understood as commands, as in *Mijjites!* 'Eat!'. However, the future negative second person forms cannot be used as commands. To say 'Don't eat!' a speaker would say *Mutt mijjiw!*
5. Early Algonquianists working on Mi'gmaq analyzed this vowel insertion as vowel deletion. Fidelholtz (1968) states that there is contraction in the stem in irrealis contexts. I follow Costa (1996), among others, who says that initial change is vowel insertion.
6. Fidelholtz (1968:248) analyzes *-ne* as the plural morpheme and *-w* as negation. However, the *-w* found in the dual and plural imperative could also be analyzed as a non–first person pluralizer (Conor Quinn, personal communication) as in *g-ipit-**u**-a* 'your (PL) tooth', where the bolded *u* is the non–first person pluralizer. Compare *n-ipit-**l*** 'my teeth', where the bolded *l* marks the plural of 'tooth'.
7. For this sentence, some speakers prefer:

(i)	Mu	ignm-u-a-gu-p	wen-n	goqwei.
	NEG	give-APPL-TH-3.NEG-PAST.DIR	who-OBV	what

'She/he didn't give anything to anyone.'

Note that both the *n* of the direct past (*-p(n)*) as well as the obviative marker *n* on the verb drops.

REFERENCES

Baker, Mark. 1996. *The polysynthesis parameter*. New York: Oxford University Press.

Costa, David J. 1996. Reconstructing initial change in Algonquian. *Anthropological Linguistics*

38.1:39–72.

Dryer, Matthew S. 2013a. Negative morphemes. In *The world atlas of language structures online*, ed. M. S. Dryer and M. Haspelmath. Leipzig: Max Planck Institute for Evolutionary Anthropology.

———. 2013b. Order of negative morpheme and verb. In *The world atlas of language structures online*, ed. Matthew S. Dryer and Martin Haspelmath. Leipzig: Max Planck Institute for Evolutionary Anthropology. .

Fidelholtz, John. 1968. Micmac morphophonemics. PhD thesis, Massachusetts Institute of Technology.

Goddard, Ives. 1969. Delaware verbal morphology: A descriptive and comparative study. PhD thesis, Harvard University.

———. 1980. Eastern Algonquian as a genetic subgroup. In *Papers of the eleventh Algonquian Conference*, ed. W. Cowan, 143–158. Ottawa, ON: Carlton.

———. 2006. The Proto-Algonquian negative and its descendants. In *Papers of the thirty-seventh Algonquian Conference*, ed. H. C. Wolfart, 161–158. Winnipeg: University of Manitoba.

Inglis, Stephanie. 2003. The deferential evidential in Mi'kmaq. In *Papers of the thirty-fourth Algonquian Conference*, ed. H. C. Wolfart, 193–200. Winnipeg: University of Manitoba.

McCulloch, Gretchen. 2012. Practical uses of typological semantics: Mi'gmaq indefinite pronouns. Presentation at the Oklahoma Workshop on Native American Languages (OWNAL).

Mi'gmaq Online Dictionary. 2014. http://mikmaqonline.org/.

Murray, Sarah. 2012. Quantificational and illocutionary variability in Cheyenne. In *Proceedings of SULA 6: Semantics of under-represented languages in the Americas*, ed. Bogal-Allbritten, 149–170. Amherst, MA: GLSA Publications.

Payne, J. R. 1985. Negation. In *Language typology and syntactic description, 1*, ed. Timothy Shopen, 197–242. Cambridge: Cambridge University Press.

Wolfart, H. C. 1996. Sketch of Cree, an Algonquian language. In *Handbook of North American indians*, Vol. 17, ed. Ives Goddard, 90–439. Washington, DC: Smithsonian Institution.

Revisiting Potawatomi Derivational Morphology

Hunter Thompson Lockwood

The purpose of this paper is to reexamine Potawatomi derivational morphology, given new research with remaining speakers in northern Wisconsin and changes to the Bloomfieldian framework put forward by Goddard (1990 and elsewhere). This is sorely needed; currently the Potawatomi community relies on descriptive grammars of neighboring Ojibwe to fill their documentary gaps.

This paper provides some phonological background on Potawatomi, walks through previous morphological analyses of Potawatomi, and then provides updates and corrections to every initial, medial, and final positively identified in Hockett's 1939 dissertation, to which I add components and examples not present in Hockett's works.

Potawatomi Phonology in Brief

This section begins with a summary of the segment inventory of Potawatomi before moving into a brief overview of syncope. The consonant inventory is presented in Table 1.[1]

TABLE 1. Consonant inventory (from Forest County Potawatomi 2014; fortis on the left, WNALP in parentheses)

	BILABIAL	DENTAL	ALVEOLAR	POST-ALVEOLAR	PALATAL	VELAR	GLOTTAL
Stop	p, b	t, d				k, g	ʔ (ʻ)
Nasal	m		n				
Fricative			s, z	ʃ, ʒ (sh, zh)			h
Affricate				tʃ, dʒ (ch, j)			
Glide	w				j (y)		

Potawatomi has a series of consonant contrasts typically labeled fortis-lenis. The fortis-lenis contrast is eliminated word-finally, as examples (1) and (2) below illustrate.

(1) mak 'loon'

(2) magok 'loons'

In (1) 'loon' is underlyingly /mag/, but appears to end in the fortis (voiceless) velar stop consonant [k]. After adding the plural suffix in (2), it surfaces as lenis /g/.

The vowel inventory of Potawatomi is given in Table 2.

TABLE 2. Vowel inventory (adapted from Forest County Potawatomi 2014; WNALP in parentheses)

iː (i)		
		o, oː (o)
	ə (e)	
ɛː (é)		
		a (ɑː)

There are six phonemes; these are /iː, ə, ɛː, o, oː, ɑː/, where /iː, ɛː, oː, ɑː/ are long (or strong, to use Hockett's terminology) and /ə, o/ are short.[2] This differs from Hockett's (1939) analysis only slightly; they observed the length contrast in rounded vowels but did not label it as phonemic. Syllables are parsed iambically, from left to right, and the heads of iambs receive secondary stress, short vowels in strong position are lengthened, and main stress is generally antepenultimate.

Unstressed vowels are subject to syncope and do not surface. Syncope was a major focus of Hockett's dissertation (1939) and produces complex consonant clusters on the surface, as in (3) and (4) below.

(3) gkedon! 'Hide it! (in.)'

(4) ngekdon 'I hide it (in.).'

The underlying form of this verb meaning 'hide' is /gə.kə.do:n/, but only one /ə/ surfaces due to syncope. I do not cover syncope in detail here (see Lockwood 2012).

Potawatomi and Algonquian Morphology

Potawatomi nouns come in two genders: animate and inanimate. These genders can be common sense (animals are animate, e.g.), but generally must be memorized. Verbs in Potawatomi are classified along the traditional lines, according to the animacy of the ergative argument and transitivity (VII, VAI, VTI, VTA).

The most thorough analysis of Potawatomi morphology comes from Hockett's dissertation (1939) and the series of articles (1948a–d) derived from it. In these he presents a description based on early drafts of Bloomfield's 1946 sketch of Algonquian grammar. In his dissertation, he treats a derived primary stem as consisting of an initial, a medial, and a final. An example of a word with all three is given in (5), and its structure is given in (6).

(5) gnwabyéya
genw-abyé-ya-∅
long-string-VII-3
'IT (IN.) IS LONG (OF STRING)'

(6) [INITIAL]–[MEDIAL]–[FINAL]

The word in (5) shows all three components: an initial /genw-/ or /geno-/ 'long,' a medial /-abyé-/, which indicates that the long object referenced by the verb is 'stringlike' (e.g., rope, thread, vines, etc.), and a final /-ya/, which indicates that the verb takes only one, inanimate argument.

Only an initial or a medial is required in Hockett's approach, with multiple initials and multiple medials allowed (1948a:7). Some stems are monomorphemic, but whether these are distinct from a regularly derived stem or are simply initials or medials is unclear (Hockett 1948a:6–7, 1948b:63–64). Like Bloomfield, Hockett counts dependent noun stems as medials. So for Hockett, a word like (7) consists of only a medial and inflection.

(7) nzed
n-zed
1-foot
'my foot'

This classification is made on the basis of comparison with other forms, such as the form in (8).

(8) mishzedé
mish-zed-é
hair-foot-vai
'He has hairy feet.'

Hockett and Bloomfield argued that an example like (7) contains only a medial and no initial because of words like (8), where /zed/ 'foot' is an unambiguous medial, sitting between a well-attested initial and final.

Goddard (1990) offers a series of subtle but important changes to the analysis of Algonquian languages. Goddard formulates his rules for derivation as a series of "if-then" statements (1990:450), yielding the allowable stem types given in (9) through (11).

(9) [initial]

(10) [initial]-[final]

(11) [initial]-[medial]-[final]

Goddard (1990) greatly limited the number of allowable primary stem configurations, which presents a number of changes in the way we analyze stems provided by Hockett. Dependent noun stems, as in (7) 'foot,' are now seen as containing an initial, rather than a medial.

Data and Discussion

The lexicon in Hockett's dissertation (1939) lists around 100 components. Starting from Hockett's lexicon, I reexamine, verify, and emend his analysis, supplementing it with examples gathered from fieldwork toward the dictionary (Forest County Potawatomi 2014), which contains about 5,000 words (and more in the database).

Several issues inspire this reexamination. The first issue is Goddard's set of changes discussed above. The second issue is the morphophonemic transcription Hockett uses for his dissertation that relies on an idiosyncratic set of vowel signs. Hockett's signs may have been due to typographical limitations. For example, Hockett (1948, a–d) uses /u/ for /ə/, whereas in his dissertation (1939) /ə/ appears freely and alpha (α) appears for schwa in morphophonemic representations. This makes cross-comparing Hockett's various publications with each other and with documentation from other, related languages a cumbersome task. The third issue is the way voicing is inconsistently transcribed. The sections that follow present underlying forms in the Wisconsin Native American Languages Project orthography, which mirrors the International Phonetic Alphabet (IPA) transcriptions much more closely.

Initials

Initials are generally seen in Algonquian morphology as the most open class. Hockett's lexicon offers evidence from several important subcategories of initials; I begin by listing the relative roots.

(12) eko-, ekew- 'to such extent, as long as'
Iw ékozet.
'That's how tall he is.' (VAI)

(13) epit- 'inasmuch as, while, degree, yet'
pitnegwet
'It is so heavy.' (VII)

(14) eN- 'thus'
nazo
'It (an.) is a certain color.' (VAI)

(15) deN- 'where, while, how'
dzhikazo
'He/she/it (an.) is in the middle of doing something.' (VAI)

(16) wed-, wej- 'why, from'
wjegé
'It (an.) is leaking out.' (VAI)

Hockett only offers preverb forms for each of the forms above except (13). Lexical evidence from new fieldwork shows that they can all be initials as well, as expected.

The next group of initials Hockett recognized, but I have emended.

(17) jig- 'next to, nearby'
jigakwa
'at the edge of the woods' (PART)

(18) bem- 'along'
nbemwedon
'I take it along.' (VTI)

(19) byéd- 'come, toward, arriving'
byédasen
'It blows this way.' (VII)

(20) bid- 'come, toward, arriving'
nbidapkowébna
'I put it (an.) in the oven.' (VTA)

(21) nam- 'under'
namsek
'under the floor, in the basement' (PART)

(22) enem- 'away'
nemashe
'it (an.) leaves soaring' (VAI)

(23) begem- 'in this direction, toward here'
bgembi
'S/he arrives drunk.' (VAI)

(24) dekem- 'across'
dkemashe
'He sails across (the water).' (VAI)

Hockett classified the morphemes in (17) through (24) as roots, but did not include numerical roots, presented below.

(25) negod- 'one'
ngodek
'once' (PART)

(26) nizh- 'two'
nizhdiyé
'It (an.) has two butts.' (VAI)

(27) neso- 'three'
nesodbé
'It (an.) has three heads.' (VAI)

(28) nyéw- 'four'
nyéwek
'four times' (PART)

(29) nyan- 'five'
nyanek
'five times' (PART)

(30) negodwadeso- 'six'
ngodwadsomdenne
'sixty' (NUMBER)

(31) no'ek- 'seven'
no'ek-dsomdenne
'seventy' (NUMBER)

(32) shwadso- 'eight'
shwadsomdenne
'eighty' (NUMBER)

(33) zhag- 'nine'
zhak-dswak
'nine hundred' (NUMBER)

(34) medadeso- 'ten'
mdadsosegos
'ten thousand' (NUMBER)

Hockett did not list any forms at all for the numbers 4, 5, 7, or 8.
The biggest group of initials recognized by Hockett all have verbal readings.

(35) geg- 'hide'
ngegdon
'I hide it (in.).' (VTI)

(36) gek- 'think, decide, know'
ngekéndan
'I know, recognize, remember it (in.).' (VTI)

(37) mek- 'find'
nmekwa
'I find, discover it (in.).' (VTI)

(38) nedo- 'try, look for'
ndobyéngé
'He searches through water for things.' (VAI)

(39) gemod- 'steal, sneak'
gmode
'He steals it (in.).' (VAIO)

(40) nad-, naN- 'go, fetch'
nadapkwé
'He goes after liquor.' (VAI)

(41) bashk- 'burst'
bashkjédé
'It explodes (by heat).' (VAI)

(42) bok- 'break'
nbokwnejéshen
'I fall and break a hand / have a broken hand due to falling.' (VAI)

(43) wéb- 'begin, inceptive'
wébakso
'It (an.) catches fire.' (VAI)

(44) nege- 'melt, thaw'
ngedé
'It (in.) melts, thaws.' (VII)

Hockett gave (39) as an AI verb rather than a component.

The next group of initials all have adjectival or adverbial readings but generally surface as components of verbs.

(45) (be)beshk- 'bald'
peshkwdebé
'He is bald-headed.' (VII)

(46) ziw- 'sour'
ziwabo
'juice, cider, lemonade, sour liquid, soda' (NI)

(47) déb- 'sufficient'
dépsémget
'That's enough.' (VII)

(48) wab- 'white'
wabshkya
'It (in.) is white.' (VII)

(49) gezh- 'warm, hot'
gzhabkezgen
'stove' (NI)

(50) nok- 'soft'
noka
'It (in.) is soft.' (VII)

(51) wzam- 'too much'
ndozamgwam
'I oversleep.' (VAI)

In this section we have seen that initials can serve many disparate roles. In the next section we examine medials, and find a much more limited set of concepts.

Medials

The first class I discuss are classificatory medials, which Hockett partially recorded.

(52) -ekw-, -akw- 'wood, sticklike'
zhoshkakwed
'It (in.) is slippery, smooth.' (VII)

(53) -abek-, -apek- 'inorganic solid'
tkwabkeze
'It (an.) is short.' (VAI)

(54) -abyé-, -abig-, -abyég- 'stringlike'
gnwabyéya
'It is long.' (VAI)

(55) -(y)ég- 'sheetlike'
nokyéget
'It (in.) is soft.' (VII)

(56) -agem- 'liquid'
gzhagmedé
'It (in.) is warm.' (VII)

In the 'stringlike' medials (54) we see evidence of Ojibwe's influence. Generally speaking, **Cye·* inherited from Proto-Algonquian is preserved in Potawatomi but shifts to *Cii* in Ojibwe, an observation first made by Hockett (1943).[3] That means in Potawatomi we generally expect /-abyék-/ or /-abyé-/ but not /-abig-/, which we should only see in borrowings from Ojibwe; compare Ojibwe *ginwaabiigad* 'it is long and stringlike' with Potawatomi forms *gnwabyéya* 'it is long string' and *gnwabigze* 'he is long of body.'

A few derivational components that Hockett called medials I either have limited evidence for or would be analyzed differently by Goddard's standards.

(57) -jé- 'round object (globular)'
bashkjédé
'It explodes (by heat).' (VAI)

(58) -ad- 'exist'
bmadze
'It (an.) lives, is alive.' (VAI)

There is little evidence for systematic use of a 'berrylike' or 'round object' classifier in Potawatomi. Other than the forms in (41) and (57), our data has few other examples.

On the other hand, /-ad-/ 'exist' is frequent in Potawatomi, but different from the shape- and material-based classificatory medials given above. I assume that /-ad-/ is a prefinal, rather than a medial, aligning with Valentine's analysis for the cognate morpheme in Ojibwe (Valentine 2001:397–398).

The other major category of medials is the body part medials. Hockett's treatment of body part morphemes in Potawatomi is inconsistent. He gives body part components sometimes as roots and other times as medials, but more often offering no categorization. Following Goddard (1990:465 and elsewhere), I offer the following morphemes as medials, given that they are attested in medial position. I do not give a list of body part initials for reasons of space.

(59) -jan- 'nose'
winjané
'He has a dirty nose.' (VAI)

(60) -gad- 'leg'
mbowgadé
'His leg is numb, paralyzed.' (VAI)

(61) -nej- 'hand'
winnejé
'His hand is dirty.' (VAI)

(62) -zed- 'foot'
mishzedé
'He has hairy feet.' (VAI)

(63) -déb- 'head'
mkedéwdebé
'His head is black.' (VAI)

(64) -don- 'mouth'
mskwedonégabo
'He stands with a red mouth.' (VAI)

(65) -teweg- 'ear'
gizhotewgé'wen
'earmuffs' (NI)

There is widespread allomorphy with the body part medials due to interactions with the final /-é/, which historically followed incorporated nominal goals (cf. Valentine 2001:386–389, 2002:86, 113–115; Goddard 1990:466–467). This leads to complex, contrasting cases; in some words, like (64) mskwe**doné**gabo 'stand with a red mouth, stand with lipstick on,' the form /don-é/ together behaves like a medial. In other cases, like (63) *mishzed*é 'have hairy feet,' /-zed-/ is a medial and /-é/ is a final.[4]

Finals

This section of the paper departs most significantly from the list offered in the appendix of Hockett's (1939) dissertation. The amount of data that has been collected for the Potawatomi dictionary enabled me to find more robust patterns, especially when it comes to concrete finals. Hockett only provided five concrete finals; the rest are abstract. The result is that Hockett's list of finals is a long list of abstract finals, generally appearing as single phonemes, without accompanying examples.

I begin with a discussion of abstract VAI finals before moving into concrete verb and noun finals. I do not discuss VAI verbs that take objects or other complex cases.

(66) -i 'VAI final'
tkemi
'He goes across (water or ice).' (VAI)

(67) -a 'VAI final'
ndezhya
'I go.' (VAI)

(68) -eze 'VAI final'
ngekades
'I am wealthy.' (VAI)

(69) -é 'have a body part that is . . .'
wizhgdé'é
'He is brave.' (literally 'strong-hearted') (VAI)

(70) -gé 'indefinite object'
gojegé
'He hangs things.' (VAI)

(71) -n 'VAI final'
gojen
'It hangs.' (VAI)

(72) -di 'reciprocal'
wéwépshedi
'They wrestle each other.' (VAI)

(73) -wé 'indefinite object'
batawé
'He tells (on someone).' (VAI)

(74) -we 'verb of being'
wgemawe
'He is the leader.' (VAI)

VAI finals, in the canonical cases, indicate that the verb takes a single, animate argument, which can be an underlying agent (unergative) as in (70) 'he hangs things' or patient (unaccusative) as in (71) 'it hangs.' Hockett and other sources following him traditionally refer to the final in (67) as *a/é* because in certain contexts (third person singular and plural) it appears as /é/ and in others as /a/ (first and second person singular).

The following examples illustrate concrete VAI finals.

(75) -gwam 'sleep'
bbam*s*égwam
'He sleepwalks.' (VAI)

(76) -be 'sit'
jibdebe
'He sits down.' (VAI)

(77) -beto 'run'
dkembeto
'He runs across.' (VAI)

(78) -osé 'walk'
bgemsé
'He arrives walking.' (VAI)

(79) -ashe 'blown, moved by wind'
dkemashe
'He sails across.' (VAI)

(80) -abe 'sees, capable of sight'
débabe
'He can see (into the distance).' (VAI)

(81) -shka, -shké[5]
bmashka
'He soars, flies, ascends.' (VAI)

(82) -shen 'fall down, lower, undergo, lie down'
atwashen
'He lies supine.' (VAI)

(83) -énd+em 'think, recall, mental activity'
néndem
'He thinks such.' (VAI)

(84) -gedaze 'mad, angry'
ndewzamgedas
'I am too mad.' (VAI)

(85) -nekazo 'be named'
zhenkazo
'He is named such.' (VAI)

(86) -wéwé 'make noise"
bonwéwé
'It (an.) stops making noise.' (VAI)

The following VII finals appear in verbs that describe the weather, the environment, and properties and actions of inanimate nouns. Few of Hockett's originally identified finals appear here.

(87) -byésa 'rain'
pichbyésa
'It rains such an amount.' (VII)

(88) -asen 'blown'
majiyasen
'It (in.) is blown in the wind.' (VII)

(89) -sen 'fall down, lower undergo, lie down'
atwasen
'It (in.) lies right-side up.' (VII)

(90) -nekadé 'be named'
zhenkadé
'It (in.) is so named.' (VII)

(91) -ya 'VII final'
gsenya
'It is cold.' (VII)

(92) -shka 'VII final'
bmashka
'It soars (not on its own power).' (VII)

(93) -shen 'fall down, lower, undergo, lay down'
atwasen
'It lies supine.' (VII)

(94) -wéwé 'make noise'
bonwéwé
'It (an.) stops making noise.' (VII)

Here we have evidence of paired VAI and VII finals in Potawatomi; compare examples (79) and (88), (82) and (89), and (85) and (90).

What follows are a handful of examples of Potawatomi VTI finals, both abstract and concrete.

(95) d+on 'VTI final'
njisbedon
'I pinch it (in.).' (VTI)

(96) -abed+an 'see it (in.)'
nwabdan
'I see it (in.).' (VTI)

(97) -énd+an 'think, recall, mental activity'
mikwéndan
'He remembers it (in.).' (VTI)

(98) -myad+an 'smell'
nbyéjmyadan
'I smell it (in.).' (VTI)

The examples below present several VTA finals, including some parallels of VTI finals above, again both abstract and concrete.

(99) -abem 'see it (an.)'
nwabma
'I see it (an.).' (VTA)

(100) -énem 'think, recall, mental activity'
nmikwénma
'I remember it (an.).' (VTA)

(101) -myam 'smell'
nbyéjmyama
'I smell him (an.).' (VTA)

(102) -ew 'applicative'
tkemnashkewa
'He chases it (an.) across.' (VTA)

I do not discuss transitive verbs for reasons of space.

Though frequently monomorphemic, nouns can appear with an overt final. The following examples show some of the diversity of noun finals, attaching to nouns, verbal roots, and adjectival roots.

(103) -weyan 'skin, hide'
wabozowyan
'rabbitskin, blanket' (NI)

(104) -abo 'liquid'
gonabo
'meltwater from snow' (NI)

(105) -egen 'N final'
dbe'gen
'hour, yard, mile, measuring instrument' (NI)

(106) -wegemekw 'house, building'
tadiwgemek
'casino' (NI)

(107) -egawesh 'plant, bush'
mskwemnegawesh
'raspberry bush' (NA)

(108) -wen 'N final'
dopwen
'table' (NI)

Conclusion

In this paper I have presented, updated, emended, and commented on every component morpheme for primary derivation (initial, medial, and final) positively identified by Hockett in his dissertation (1939). Beyond the components Hockett identified, I have added many that were either implicit in Hockett's corpus or altogether absent. This work is part of a continuing effort to update and render more accessible existing Potawatomi documentation in light of the changes to the traditional Algonquianist model offered by Goddard (1990) and others since Hockett first conducted his fieldwork. By expanding on Hockett's work, I have provided the stepping stone necessary to proceed on to a fuller description of Potawatomi morphosyntax, and toward a better picture of the historical changes that separated Potawatomi and Ojibwe. This will ultimately benefit not just Algonquianists, but the community of Potawatomi speakers who still lack an accessible descriptive grammar and must rely on descriptive materials written for neighboring Ojibwe.

NOTES

1. All examples are given in the Wisconsin Native American Languages Program (WNALP) Orthography, which is one of several writing systems in use by the Forest County Potawatomi. It is used here because it is close to phonemic, and it is used in the 2014 dictionary. Abbreviations used in this paper: an. = animate, in. = inanimate, PART =

particle, VAI = animate intransitive verb, VAIO = animate intransitive verb, plus object, VII = inanimate intransitive verb, VTA = transitive animate verb, VTI = transitive inanimate verb, 1 = first person, 2 = second person, 3 = third person, 3' = third person, obviative, sg. = singular, pl. = plural.

2. There is significant variation in the pronunciation of the schwa phoneme in Potawatomi, the extent of which is not yet completely understood.
3. I thank an anonymous reviewer for helping me understand this.
4. Alternatively, /-zed-é/ could be a complex final.
5. Cf. *gwénbeshké* 'he turns over, changes'.

REFERENCES

Bloomfield, Leonard. 1946. Algonquian. In *Linguistic Structures of Native America*, ed. Harry Hoijer et al., 85–129. New York: Viking Fund Publications in Anthropology 6.

Forest County Potawatomi. 2014. *Ézhebmadzimgek gdebodwéwadmizheshmomenan* 'How Our Potawatomi Language Lives' Potawatomi Dictionary. Crandon, WI: Forest County Potawatomi.

Goddard, Ives. 1990. Primary and secondary stem derivation in Algonquian. *International Journal of American Linguistics* 56(4):449–483.

Hockett, Charles F. 1939. The Potawatomi language. PhD thesis, Yale University.

———. 1943. The Position of Potawatomi in Central Algonkian. In *Papers of the Michigan Academy of Science, Arts, and Letters*, 38:537–542.

———. 1948a. Potawatomi I: Phonemics, morphophonemics, and morphological survey. *International Journal of American Linguistics* 14(1):1–10.

———. 1948b. Potawatomi II: Derivation, personal prefixes, and nouns. *International Journal of American Linguistics* 14(2):63–73.

———. 1948c. Potawatomi III: The verb complex. *International Journal of American Linguistics* 14(3):139–149.

———. 1948d. Potawatomi IV: Particles and sample texts. *International Journal of American Linguistics* 14(4):213–225.

Lockwood, Hunter. 2012. Revisiting Potawatomi syncope. Paper given at the Forty-Fourth Algonquian Conference, Chicago.

Valentine, J. Randolph. 2001. *Nishnaabemwin reference grammar*. Toronto: University of Toronto Press.

———. 2002. Variation in body-part verbs in Ojibwe dialects. *International Journal of American Linguistics* 68(1):81–119.

Discontinuous Constituents in Ojibwe: Accounting for Two Preverbal Words

Cherry Meyer

A well-known construction in Algonquian languages, referred to as a discontinuous constituent, involves separation of associated nominal elements whereby the initial element occurs preverbally and the remaining nominal material is postverbal (Tomlin and Rhodes 1992; Tourigny 2008; Meyer 2015 for Ojibwe; Dahlstrom 2003 for Meswaki; Russell and Reinholtz 1996 for Swampy Cree; Johnson and Rosen 2011 for Algonquian).[1] In the example below, *gakina igiw adikwag* 'all those caribou' forms a nominal constituent. The universal quantifier *gakina* appears preverbally and separated from the associated demonstrative and noun, shown in bold.[2]

(1)

Mii	igo	**gakina**	imaa	gii-akoshinowaad	**igiw**	**adikwag.**
it.is	EMPH	all	there	PST-pile.up.VAI.CONJ.3P	those.AN.P	caribou.AN.P

'So all those caribou were piled up.' (Nichols 1988:171 [54])

There are cases where this simple description at first glance does not seem entirely accurate, cases in which it appears that two elements are preverbal instead of one. This was first pointed out by Kathol and Rhodes (1999), and their example is given in (2). The nominal, shown in bold, seems to consist of a preverbal quantifier and noun and a postverbal relative clause, shown in brackets.

(2) **Kina** gegoo wii-waabndahdim [**wezhtood** aw
all thing.0 FUT-display.it.IND.VAI.X which.he.makes.CCNJ.3-0 that.AN

Nishnaabe].
Indian.AN
'**Everything that the Indians produce** will be on display.' (Kathol and Rhodes 1999:82 [30b])

It is suggested by Kathol and Rhodes that discontinuous examples of this sort pose a problem for movement-based approaches. Lochbihler's (2009) configurational account of discontinuity standardly assumes only a single element may occur preverbally, and such examples are indeed unmentioned. To further complicate matters, it appears that these examples may also be split by the verb, with only the quantifier preverbal, as shown in (3).

(3) **Kina** dash gaa-giizhtood **gegoo** . . .
all EMPH PST-finish.making.VTI.CCNJ.3-0 thing.IN
'After she had finished making **everything** . . .' (Kathol and Rhodes 1992:82 [30a])

Further analysis of texts from the Southwestern, Eastern, and Ottawa dialects reveals that while such examples are not uncommon, they are limited to specific lexical items. The first item consists of the quantifiers *gaa* 'not', *akina* 'all', or *anooj* 'various, all kinds', and the second consists of either the animate indefinite pronoun *waya* 'someone' or the inanimate indefinite pronoun *gegoo* 'thing'. Those formed with the negative quantifier, *gaa waya* and *gaa gegoo,* translate as 'no one/anyone' and 'nothing/anything'; those formed with the universal quantifier, *kina waya* and *kina gegoo*, translate as 'everyone' and 'everything' (Valentine 2001:126). Valentine (2001:594) labels these as indefinite negative and universal pronouns, respectively. The quantifier *anooj* also occurs in combination with *gegoo* to mean 'various things' (Valentine 2001:597), though examples of this are rarer than those formed with the negative or universal quantifiers.

I propose that the aforementioned constructions constitute multiword phrases with the syntactic category of a quantifier. This allows the existing characterization of discontinuity in configurational accounts to be maintained, as well as several other constraints, including a limit on the number of elements in a nominal and the placement of second-position clitics. This account also distinguishes between discontinuous constituents with one or two words in preverbal position.

Language Background

The following sections discuss certain properties of nominals, quantification, and relative clauses in Ojibwe that aid in the identification of constituents in their continuous and discontinuous realizations. These include constraints on the number of nominal elements and their relative ordering, the position of quantifiers in the clause, and morphological markers of relative clauses.

Properties of Nominals

The basic word order of Ojibwe is taken to be VOS (Tomlin and Rhodes 1992), but nominals may occur in preverbal position for considerations of information structure (Tomlin and Rhodes 1992; Tourigny 2008; Meyer 2015). The relative order of elements in a nominal is shown in (4). Every element is optional, including the head noun. An overt nominal may consist of one of these elements or a combination of multiple elements, but there may be only one element of each kind in a nominal (Kathol and Rhodes 1999).

(4) Order of nominal elements in Ojibwe
Demonstrative : Quantifier > Noun > Relative clause
(Kathol and Rhodes 1999:78 [21])

The order of demonstratives and quantifiers is permutable, symbolized by the colon, but the ordering may change the available readings. An inclusive reading specifies a group, while a partitive reading picks out a subset of the group (Kathol and Rhodes 1999; Valentine 2001). Both inclusive and partitive readings are available with the demonstrative > quantifier order, but the reverse order forces a partitive reading (Kathol and Rhodes 1999). The order of the demonstrative preceding the universal quantifier is unattested (Valentine 2001:575).[3]

The relative ordering of nominal elements, as well as a description of possible permutations, is provided in order to assist in identification of discontinuous constituents. Crucially, discontinuity may be distinguished from after-thought or recapitulative constructions in that the strict limit to one type of each nominal element must be maintained in the former, and the order must remain constant between the continuous and discontinuous realizations (Kathol and Rhodes 1999:83). In (5), for example, the head noun cannot occur preverbally to the exclusion of the numeral.

(5) **Nswi** wgii-nsaan **giigoonyan.**
three PST-kill.VTA.IND.3-3' fish.AN.OBV
'He killed **three fish.**'
***Giigoonyan** wgii-nsaan **nswi.** (Kathol and Rhodes 1999:82 [29])

Properties of Quantification

The negative quantifier is represented by the preverbal particle *gaa*. The verb is also marked with the suffix *-sii*(*n*) or allomorphs thereof. Both forms of negation are obligatory in the independent order (6). In the conjunct order, the suffix *-si*(*w*) may suffice (Valentine 2001; Tourigny 2008). *Gaa* sometimes combines with the contrastive particle *wii* to form *gaawii*(*n*), as shown below.

(6) **Gaawii** dash o-gii-waabanda-**zii**-n.
not but 3-PST-see.VTI.IND-NEG-0
'But he did **not** see it.' (Nichols 1988:158 [32])

Similarly, other quantifiers usually occur preverbally, even if this creates a discontinuous constituent, though they may also occur postverbally.[4] The negative quantifier has a fixed preverbal position, whether serving as a nominal or verbal modifier, so it is not usually discussed as an element of nominal structure proper, though Lochbihler (2009) includes it in her account of discontinuous constructions. The fixed preverbal position may simply reflect Jesperson's "Neg First" principle (Jespersen 1917:5, as cited in Horn 1989:449), which captures the tendency for negation to appear early in a clause, for clarity and, presumably, considerations of scope. In the next section, a brief description of relative clauses serves to guide the reader in differentiating this type of nominal element from matrix verbs and adverbial clauses.

Properties of Relative Clauses

Relative clauses are identified by bearing inflection of the conjunct order and initial change. Valentine (2001:579) says all of the inflectional possibilities of verbs, such as tense and mode, are also available in relative clauses. He describes them as hybrids between verbs and nouns, since they may have both verbal and nominal inflection, especially when referencing a third person. In the following example, the changed conjunct form of the verb has a suffix complex *-jig*, which consists of the verbal third person suffix /-d/, palatalized to [-j], which is visible in the simple conjunct form, as well as the nominal plural suffix *-ig*.

(7)	Animate Intransitive Verb:	maadzi	'live, be alive'
	Simple Conjunct 3P:	bmaadzi-**waa-d** verb-animate.P-3	'(when) they live'
	Changed Conjunct 3P:	bemaadzi-**j-ig** IC.verb-3-animate.P	'those who live'

Discontinuous Constituents

Much progress has been made toward understanding the motivation and mechanism underlying discontinuous constituents in Algonquian languages. In both configurational and nonconfigurational accounts of word order in Algonquian, motivation for discontinuous constituents is discussed in terms of information structure. Discontinuity results when the first element, usually a quantifier or demonstrative, of a nominal in postverbal continuing topic position occurs in preverbal focus position, separated from the remaining postverbal elements (Tomlin and Rhodes 1992; Meyer 2015 for Ojibwe; Dahlstrom 2003 for Meswaki). Discontinuity does not alter the order of elements, as the same availability of inclusive and partitive readings remains, nor does it appear to affect scope (Lochbihler 2009).

A gap in the literature on discontinuity concerns examples in which it appears that two elements are preverbal, in contrast to the single element usually permitted. In the next section, I show further data confirming that such constructions are not a rarity. I outline the relevant constraints that place these constructions in accord with configurational accounts, as well as propose a distinction between discontinuous constituents of the relevant lexical items with one (as in (3)) or two (as in (2)) words in preverbal position.

Discontinuous Constituents with Two Preverbal Words

The following examples illustrate discontinuous constituents that are identical in structure to that offered by Kathol and Rhodes (1999), with a preverbal quantifier and indefinite pronoun and a postverbal relative clause.

(8) . . . mii aazhəgo gii-dagshinwaad giw Nishnaabeg aapji go
it's already PST-come.in.VAI.CONJ.3P those.AN.P Indians.AN.P very much

kina gegoo shkahii *gaa-zhitoowaad*
all thing.AN new PST-made.VTI2.CCNJ.3P-0

[waa-biiskamwaad] . . .
FUT.which-they.wear.VTI.CCNJ.3P-0
'. . . the Indians were starting to come in, having made **everything they were to wear** brand new . . .' (Nichols 1988:76 [2])

(9) **Kina** go **gegoonh** *ngii-biidmawaa* **[eteg**
all EMPH thing.AN PST-bring.VTA.IND.1-3 which.is.VII.CCNJ.0

taaswining].
in.the.cupboard
'One by one I brought to her everything that was in the cupboard.'
(Nichols 1988:52 [7])

(10) **Gakina gegoo** *ogii-wiindamaagoon* niigaan
all thing.AN PST-told.VTA.IND.3'-3 in.the.future

[ge-ani-izhiwebizid maaba inini].
FUT-henceforth-how.fare.VAI.CCNJ.3 this.AN man.AN
'He was told everything by them which happened ahead.'
Alt. translation: 'They told this man everything which would happen to him in the future.' (Nichols 1988:131 [40])

(11)

Nooj	**gegoo**	sa	*gii-zhichge*	maaba	shkinwe	sa
various	thing.IN	EMPH	PST-do.so.VAI.IND.3	this.AN	young.man.AN	EMPH

[**ge-zhimdaagwenmigod**	**nonda**	sa	**shkiniigkwen**
FUT-so.that.thus.like.VTA.CCNJ.3'-3	this.OBV	EMPH	young.woman.AN.OBV

waa-kwebnigjin].
PST-who.put.under.love.spell.VTA.CCNJ.3'-3
'This young man did all kinds of things in order to gain the affections of this young woman who had put him under the love spell.' (Valentine 2001:597 [236])

Despite the minor differences in distribution discussed above, there is enough similarity between the negative quantifier and other quantifiers in the constructions under consideration to warrant a comparison, as the same pattern is observable with negation, shown below.

(12) a.

Adoopowinensing	onabi'id,	**gaawiin**	**gegoo**	*niwaabandanziin*
at.a.little.table	seat.VTA.CONJ.3-1	not	thing.AN	not.see.VTI.IND.1-0

[**de-miijiyaambaan**].
could-eat.VTI3.CCNJ.1-0
'She seats me at a little table, but I don't see **anything I could eat.**

b.

Aanish	**gaawiin**	sa	**gegoo**	odayaanziin
well	not	EMPH	thing.AN	not.haveVTI4.IND.3-0

[**ded-ashamipan**].
could-feed.VTA.CCNJ.3-1
'Well, she doesn't have **anything at all that she could feed me.**'
(Nichols 1988:276 [7-8])

As the order of nominal elements in (4) showed, relative clauses follow the nouns they modify. It is insufficient to appeal to a special property of relative clauses in the environment of quantification that would cause them to be postverbal to the exclusion of other associated nominal elements in a discontinuous constituent. They may also occur preverbally in continuous realizations:

(13)	**Gaa**	**waya**	[**ekwaabid**]	nwaabmaasii.
	not	someone.AN	who.keep.watch.VAI.CCNJ.3	not.see.VTA.IND.1-3

'I do not see anyone keeping watch.' (Valentine 2001:580 [174])

(14)	**Anooji**	**gegoo**	**maanda**	[**nayaangang**]
	various	thing.IN	this.IN	which.is.light.VII.CCNJ.0

ogii-maajiidoonaawaa.
PST-take.along.VTI2.IND.3P-0
'They took various light things.' (Nichols 1988:153 [7])

As discussed in the next section, relative clauses are also not the only postverbal elements found in discontinuous constituents with two preverbal words.

Differing Syntactic Distributions

This distribution of *waya* 'someone' and *gegoo* 'thing', taken together with the distribution of the aforementioned quantifiers in combination with these indefinites, and the restriction to one type of element per nominal explain the apparent exception in discontinuous constituents with two preverbal words and illuminates a subtle distinction between discontinuous constituents with one or two words preverbally.

First, note that the indefinite pronouns may function in a clause as nouns; specifically simple indefinites (Valentine 2001:595). Examples are given for *waya* (15) and *gegoo* (16) below.

(15)	. . . **waya**	gii-mdwe-noondaagzid,	"Gzakzomi!"
	someone.AN	PST-in.the.distance-shout.VAI.CONJ.3	on.fire.VAI.IND.21

'. . . **somebody** shouted in the distance, "We're on fire!"' (Valentine 2001:596 [229])

(16)	**Gegoo**	dash	wii	go	wgii-gkendaanaawaa...
	something.IN	but	indeed	EMPH	PST-learn.VTI.IND.3P-0

'They really learned **something** . . .' (Valentine 2001:596 [230])

This is not the only syntactic function of these words, however. Valentine (2001:596) says *waya* and *gegoo* are not strictly pronominal, but may modify nouns as well. He notes that speakers do not inflect the indefinites for number or obviation in such contexts. They serve as quantificational elements, rather than nouns, in such constructions.

(17) **Waya** na **giigoonh** ggii-debnaa?
anyone.AN yes/no.question fish.AN PST-catch.VTA.IND.2-3
'Did you catch **any fish**?' (Valentine 2001:596 [231])

(18) **Gegoo** na gdayan **"bmaaknigewaans"** . . .
something.IN yes/no.question have.VTI.IND.2-0 rule.IN
'Do you have **some rule** . . . ? (Valentine 2001:596 [233])

The phrases *gaa waya/gegoo* 'no one, anyone/nothing, anything', *kina waya/ gegoo* 'everyone/everything' and *anooj gegoo* 'various things' may also be followed by an associated noun (cf. Valentine 2001:598 for *gaa waya/gegoo,* 2001:608 for *kina gegoo*). Observe the occurrence of an associated noun following the negative quantifier and the indefinite in a continuous realization in (19):

(19) . . . **gaa** **wii** **gegoo** **mzinhigan** gii-yaasnoon.
not EMPH thing.IN book.IN PST-not.exist.VII.IND.0
'. . . there was no book.' (Valentine 2001:599 [240])

In (20), the nominal is discontinuous and the quantifier and indefinite are preverbal, associated with a postverbal demonstrative and noun. This example also shows that postverbal elements in such constructions are not limited to relative clauses.

(20) **Kina** **gegoo** wii-yaamgadoon **niw** **games** . . .
all thing.IN FUT-be.there.VII.IND.0P those.IN.P games.IN.P
'There will be everything in the way of games . . .' (Valentine 2001:608 [277])

Given the above distributions and the restriction to one manifestation of each type of element per nominal, which disallows two associated head nouns, it follows that the quantifier and indefinite may form a quantificational phrase as a single nominal element. This analysis is compatible with the ordering of nominal elements given in (4), whereby quantifiers may precede demonstratives and always precede nouns, as well as the occurrence of second-position clitics following the first word of the quantificational phrase, seen in (9) and (12b).

The distinction between possible realizations of discontinuous constituents, whether it appears that one or two words occur preverbally, is also explained by these differing syntactic categories. If the indefinite functions as part of a quantificational phrase, both the quantifier and indefinite will be preverbal. If the indefinite instead functions as a noun, the quantifier will be preverbal and the indefinite will be postverbal. The following examples, along with (3), show that in discontinuous constructions with a preverbal quantifier and postverbal indefinite, there is no additional associated noun.

(21)	**Gaa**	dash	wikaa	ogii-wanendaziin	**gegoo**	a'aw	Anishinaabe.
	not	and	ever	PST-not.forget.VTA.IND.3-0	thing.IN	that.AN	Indian.AN

'That man never forgot **anything**.' (Nichols 1988:131 [42])

(22)	**Gaawiin**	niin	ndaagkinoohmaagsii	**waya**
	not	me	not.teach.VTA.IND.3-1	anyone.AN

ge-zhignawenmag	aw	nnooshenh.
FUT-how.take.care.of.VTA.CCNJ.1-3	that.AN	my.grandchild.AN

'**No one** can tell me how to raise my grandchild.' (Valentine 2001:598 [238])

Previous Accounts of Discontinuity

The possibility of two preverbal words in discontinuous nominals might at first appear to pose a problem for Lochbihler's (2009) configurational account. She proposes that A'-movement to a preverbal position is motivated by a contrast feature. Demonstratives and quantifiers are adjoined to DP arguments. The fact that only the first element may be preverbal is captured by the fact that this feature can only appear at the highest DP level. Under her analysis, when the two words form a QP, the contrast feature can motivate the dislocation of both the quantifier and the indefinite. When the indefinite is part of the NP, rather than the QP, it may remain in situ.

Kathol and Rhodes (1999) use Head-Driven Phrase Structure Grammar to account for discontinuous constituents, which allows for LIBERATED phrase structure. The combinatorics are stated independently of linearization, which is determined by the feature INFORMATION STRUCTURE. Discontinuity is achieved when part of the phrase structure is marked as liberated. A FOCUS value for the information structure feature on the liberated element(s) and a GROUND value on the rest of the constituent explain the linearization. The advantage of allowing for both one or two preverbal words in these constructions is mitigated by the fact that it is not immediately clear what principle, if any, distinguishes between the two possible realizations.

Conclusion

I have proposed that discontinuous constituents that have two words in preverbal position, as opposed to the single element standardly accounted for with configurational approaches, may be explained by the formation of a multiword quantificational expression. These phrases are limited to the quantifiers *gaa, kina,* and *anooj* as the first word, followed by the indefinite pronoun *waya* or *gegoo* as the second word. These quantificational phrases act as a single nominal element, allowing current configurational approaches to capture their behavior, as well as a principled way to distinguish discontinuous constituents with only the quantifier as preverbal to the exclusion of the indefinite. When the indefinite occurs postverbally and discontinuous from the quantifier, it serves as the head noun within the nominal structure.

NOTES

1. I would like to thank Amy Dahlstrom as well as attendees of the Forty-Sixth Algonquian Conference and reviewers for their very helpful comments and suggestions. All remaining errors are my own.
2. Abbreviations: 1 = first person, 2 = second person, 21 = second person inclusive, 3 = third person proximate, 3' = third person obviative, X = unspecified actor, 0 = inanimate actor, AN = animate gender, CCNJ = changed conjunct, CONJ = conjunct order, EMPH = emphatic, FUT = future, IC = initial change, IN = inanimate gender, IND = independent order, NEG = negative, OBV = obviative, P = plural, PST = past, VAI = animate intransitive verb, VII = inanimate intransitive verb, VTA = transitive animate verb, VTI = transitive inanimate verb.
3. Valentine describes *kina* 'all' as "universally inclusive" (2001:575). Given that the

universal quantifier only precedes demonstratives, it may be more accurately described as "universally partitive." It requires that the subset drawn be the entire set and so obligatorily occurs preceding the demonstrative.

4. Additionally, the universal quantifier may function as an adverbial modifier if following a noun (Valentine 2001:607 (271)):

   (i) Gegzhebaawgak *goon* **kina** gii-nkaabaawe.
   when.morning.0 snow.3 all PST-melt.away.3
   'By morning, the snow had **all melted** away.'

REFERENCES

Dahlstrom, Amy. 2003. Focus constructions in Meskwaki (Fox). In *Proceedings of the LFG03 Conference*, ed. Miriam Butt and Tracy Holloway King, 144–163. Stanford, CA: CSLI Publications.

Horn, Larry. 1989. *A Natural history of negation*. Chicago: University of Chicago Press.

Jespersen, Otto. 1917. Negation in English and other languages. In *Selected writings of Otto Jespersen*, 3–151 London: Allen and Unwin.

Johnson, Meredith, and Bryan Rosen. 2015. The syntax of discontinuous noun phrases in Algonquian languages: Left branch extractions and focus movements. In *Papers of the forty-third Algonquian Conference*. New York: SUNY Press.

Kathol, Andreas, and Richard Rhodes. 1999. Constituency and linearization of Ojibwe nominals. In *Proceedings of workshop on structure and constituency in languages of the Americas* 4:75–91. Vancouver, BC.

Lochbihler, Bethany. 2009. Discontinuous DP constructions. In *Proceedings of Canadian Linguistics Association*. Ottawa, ON.

Meyer, Cherry. 2015. Word order and information structure in Ojibwe. Presentation at the Society for the Study of the Indigenous Languages of the Americas, Portland, OR

Nichols, John D. 1988. *An Ojibwe text anthology*. London, ON: Centre for Research and Teaching of Canadian Native Languages, University of Western Ontario.

Russell, Kevin, and Charlotte Reinholtz. 1996. Hierarchical structure in a non-configurational language: Asymmetries in Swampy Cree. In *Proceedings of the fourteenth West Coast Conference on Formal Linguistics*, 431–445. Stanford, CA: Center for the Study of Language and Information.

Tomlin, Russell S., and Richard Rhodes. 1992. Information distribution in Ojibwa. In *Pragmatics of word order flexibility*, ed. Doris L. Payne, 117–135. Typological Studies of

Language 22. Amsterdam: John Benjamins.

Tourigny, Hélèn. 2008. Configurationality in Ojibwe: Focus on word order. MA thesis, University of Ottawa.

Valentine, J. Randolph. 2001. *Nishnaabemwin reference grammar*. Toronto: University of Toronto Press.

Obviation, Inversion, and the Notion of Topic in Algonquian

Richard A. Rhodes

This paper addresses questions that arise in understanding the morphosyntax of Algonquian texts, as it applies to reference tracking. While the paper itself focuses on Plains Cree and Ottawa (Ojibwe), much, if not all, of what is proposed here generalizes widely across the Algonquian family. At issue are two morphosyntactic patterns that are at the heart of Algonquian typology: obviation and inversion.

Theoretical Background

Much of what is in this paper has been said before in various places, especially Tomlin and Rhodes (1979) and Rhodes (1991). What is new is that I draw several lines of analysis together to focus on the concept of TOPIC. I use a definition of topic as ABOUT-NESS. But rather than looking just at sentences, or conversational excerpts (see Lambrecht's work, e.g., 1987), I take whole texts as the scope of about-ness. This view follows work on text analysis most fully articulated in Grimes (1975) and Jones (1977). Their approach treats monologic texts as planned (i.e., not spontaneous) wholes.

Following Jones (1977), I distinguish two kinds of about-ness: THEMATICITY, the about-ness that can only be expressed as a clause or as a whole sentence, and TOPICALITY, the about-ness properties that simple referents can possess. The usefulness of this distinction has been recognized in, for example, Özsoy (1983) and de Lecerda (1983). I will note in passing that Lambrecht (1987, among others) is more nuanced in his understanding of thematicity, which encompasses two clearly distinct things, sentence focus and predicate focus—concepts crucial in dialogue, but more limited in monologic text. I also note that a significant line of study of issues related to theme and topic, especially in the Algonquian literature, has focused on the higher level questions of how attention is directed when proximate is reassigned (e.g., Russell 1996; Bliss 2005), and discussed under the rubric of POINT OF VIEW. But my first concern here is with a more basic text-level syntactic question: within a proximate span, how do inversion and obviation interact? Although point of view presents an extremely interesting line of inquiry that I touch on later, I maintain that our primary concern represents a more fundamental question that needs to be answered before questions about the meanings of proximate shift can be readily answered. And I claim that we can answer the basic question using only the nominal (simple reference) kind of about-ness, i.e., topicality as a scalar entity, as developed in the earlier literature.

Preliminaries

Two of the most distinctive features of Algonquian grammar are obviation and inversion. They were recognized early because they realize inflectional categories in Algonquian grammar that have no ready correspondents in languages that the early students of Algonquian knew. Both have long been recognized to be sensitive to both syntactic configuration and discourse level distinctions in information flow in various languages (Goddard 1984, 1990; Dahlstrom 1987, 1991, 1995, 1996; Rhodes 1976, 1991; Russell 1991; inter alia). Because of significant parallels among Fox, several varieties of Cree, and several varieties of Ojibwe, I propose a framework that will, I hope, be able to serve as the basis of accounts across the family. To that end I cite data from several languages, but mostly Plains Cree and Ottawa. I expect that a family-wide framework is possible precisely because some parameters vary almost as much between speakers and texts within languages as they do across languages, and the differences in the variants are parallel across speakers, across texts, and across languages. I am encouraged to think this way because they share similarities—like the uses of preverbal position for nominals and the use of "unnecessary" nominals (henceforth PLEONASTIC nominals) to manage information flow—and at the same time they share differences in the scope of obviation.

The conventional wisdom has been that obviation is in some way directly reflective of topic, as illustrated by the Plains Cree text excerpt in (1). In the passage in (1) there are three textually significant referents: the boy, his father (the chief), and a group of men from the boy's tribe. At the point this passage opens the boy is proximate for the first half of the excerpt. But then the fronted (and pleonastic) NP in line 7 resets the obviation, and from that point on the men are proximate and the boy is obviative. This reset is called a PROXIMATE SHIFT. The stretch of text over which the assignment of a single referent as proximate is constant has traditionally been called a PROXIMATE SPAN.[1]

(1)	tāpwē pimitisahwēw.	'Accordingly he PROX followed them OBV.'
	itē ēh-otākosiniyik,	'At the place [they reached] toward evening OBV,
	ē-wīh-minahoyit,	as they OBV were about to kill game,
	wīsta ēkotē takohtēw.	he too PROX arrived there.'
	namoya kiskēyimik ōhtāwiya,	'His father OBV did not know [of him PROX]
	ē-sipwēhtēt.	that he PROX had gone off.'
	ēkwa ōki nāpēwak	'And those men PROX,
	kāh-minahocik,	when they PROX had killed game
	kā-takohtēyit ōhi nāpēsisah,	and the boy OBV arrived,
	nisitawēyimēwak ōhtāwiyiwa	they PROX recognized him OBV
	ēh-okimāwiyit.	as the chief OBV's son OBV.'
	namoya nānitaw wīh-itēwak.	'They PROX did not care to say anything to him.'
	ēkos' ēh-kīsitēpocik,	'So, when they PROX cooked their meal
	ē-wīh-mīcisocik,	and [they PROX] were about to eat,
	miyw-asamēwak ōhi nāpēsisah	they PROX gave the boy OBV plenty of food.'

(BC T18. A Brave Boy, §7)[2]

At first glance it appears that within a proximate span, direct and inverse verbs are used in such a way as to maintain the proximate status of the single referent, as in the fifth line of (1), repeated here as (2):[3]

(2) namoya kiskēyimik ōhtāwiya, ē-sipwēhtēt.

namoya	kiskēyim-ikw-w	w-ōhtāwiy-ah	ē-sipwēhtē-t
NEG	know-INVER-3.SBJ	3.POSS-father-OBV	COMP-leave-3.SBJ

'His father OBV did not know [of him PROX] that he PROX had gone off.'

Such a view of inversion is consistent with the conventional analysis of direct and inverse in sentences like those in (3).[4]

(3) a. Direct verb

'Waabm**aa**n 'gwisan.

o-waabam-**aa**-an	o-gwis-an
3.ERG$_i$-see-**DIR**-OBV$_j$	3.POSS$_i$-son$_j$-OBV

'He$_i$ PROX sees his$_i$ son$_j$ OBV.'

b. Inverse verb

'Waabm**igoo**n 'gwisan.

o-waabam-**igo**-an	o-gwis-an
3.ERG$_i$-see-**INV**-OBV$_j$	3.POSS$_i$-son$_j$-OBV

'His$_i$ son$_j$ OBV sees him$_i$ PROX.'

The meaning in (3a) cannot be expressed with an inverse verb, and the meaning in (3b) cannot be expressed with a direct verb. The usual conclusion is that the assignment of proximate drives the choice of direct or inverse. The sentence in (2) is an instance of the structure (3b), with the boy's father as the notional subject of the verb and the boy as the notional object, and the verb is inverse.

But the view that proximate status drives the choice of direct or inverse has problems. Consider the following sentence cluster from another Plains Cree text, *The Story of Skirt* (BC, T15).

(4) kītahtawē wāpamēw iskwēwa ē-wayawīyit,	'Then he saw a woman come out [of a tent].'
ē-kī-nipahimiht onāpēmiyiwa,	'Her husband had been killed.'
ē-kī-nipahikowit kāhkākiwacēna.	'He had been killed by the Crow.'

In English there is no easy way to match the structure in the translation. In Cree the use of *ēh-* marks these clauses as belonging together. Bloomfield gets halfway there by treating the second two as a complex relative clause. But that is not what is of interest to us. This sentence cluster has four referents: the man (the title character), the woman (whom he will end up with), her late husband, and the Crow. This cluster is part of a larger proximate span with the man as the topic/proximate. But the problem is in the third clause, given a full analysis in (5).

(5) ē-kī-nipahikowit kāhkākiwacēna.
 ēh=kīh=nipah-iko-iyi-t káhkákiwacen-ah
 COMP=PST=kill-INV-OBV 3.SBJ-Crow-OBV
 'He [=her OBV husband OBV] had been killed by the Crow OBV.'

Here, unlike in (3b), we have only obviatives, and the one that is notionally the possessed referent (*onāpēmiyiwa* 'her husband', here realized only by verb agreement) is the one in what I call the PREFERRED POSITION. Notice that to get the desired emphasis in English one has to translate it as passive. Clearly it cannot simply be the assignment as obviative that is driving the choice of direct or inverse.

Sentences and sentence clusters with embedded or dependent clauses with two obviative arguments are not all that rare. The single long sentence from an Ottawa text in (6) shows the same thing.

(6)	Wgii-gnahmawaan niw wgwisan	'He PROX warned his son OBV,
	gaa wii nkwetwaasig niw	not to respond to him OBV
	bi-ggwejmigod mandaagninwan	if the fancy-man OBV comes to ask him OBV
	iw ji-zhwenmigod.	if he OBV could bless him OBV [the son].'
		(BO T31:6 p. 213)

The English gloss in the second clause in (6) is a little misleading. There are no subjectless transitive clauses in Algonquian languages.[5] After the first clause in (6), all the clauses have both arguments in the obviative. In the second clause this is less obvious because modern Ottawa has lost the morphology marking the subject as obviative, so the verb form in the second clause is not *nkwetwaaswinid* with the obviative subject marker *ini* in it (although some older speakers recognize the conservative form).

The traditional analysis for handling proximate spans with more than two arguments is to invoke a notion FURTHER OBVIATIVE (Hockett 1966). That will work for proximate spans with three arguments, such as (6), with the problem that in languages like twentieth-century Ottawa, further obviatives are entirely unmarked. However, the span in (4) has four arguments, and that would require the positing of a further, further obviative. I argue that this apparent conundrum can be resolved by appealing to a notion of topichood proposed by Grimes (1975). He argues that in texts about-ness is not just binary. Referents are not topic or nontopic. Rather topichood in whole texts is multidimensional, having both local and global dimensions. Along both dimensions topichood is scalar. Some referents are more highly ranked than others. The ultimate assignment of topic rank is according to factors like empathy or point of view, but at the moment this is not the issue. The prior question is what mechanism we need to give a full account for the assignment of inversion. So in the passage in (4) the topic ranking (i.e., ranking of about-ness) is as in (7a), and in the passage in (6) the topic ranking is as in (7b).

(7) a. Skirt > the woman > the woman's husband > Crow

b. the father > his son > the fancy-man (an undesirable spirit guide)

The rule for assigning obviation is that the highest ranked topic in a section is proximate and everything else is obviated. This is not significantly different from the proposals that have been around for years (Dahlstrom 1996; Goddard 1990; Russell 1991, etc.). What is new is the rule for assigning direct and inverse.

The traditional hierarchy for assigning inverses has three cases, as in (8).[6]

(8) second person > first person > third person
(notional) animate > (notional) inanimate
proximate > obviative (> further obviative)

If the notional subject outranks the notional object according to (8), then the verb is direct. If the notional object outranks the notional subject according to (8), then the verb is inverse. The problem is that the traditional approach in (8) implies a limitation to three (relevant) characters in a proximate span, when in principle more are possible, as in (4). What I am proposing is to adjust the third clause to read as in (8').[7]

(8') second person > first person > third person
(notional) animate > (notional) inanimate
higher ranked topic > lower ranked topic

The formulation in (8') accounts for the distribution of direct and inverse in both (4) and (6) as outlined in (9):

(9) a. Skirt > the woman > the woman's husband > Crow (see [4])

kītahtawē **wāpamēw** iskwēwa ē-wayawīyit,	'Then [Skirt PROX] **saw** DIR a woman OBV come out [of a tent].'

Topic: Skirt > the woman
Syntax: Skirt [acted on] the woman: DIR

ē-kī-**nipahimiht** onāpēmiyiwa,	'Her OBV husband OBV **had been killed** PASS.'

Topic and Syntax: the woman's husband

ē-kī-**nipahikowit** kāhkākiwacēna.	'[Her husband OBV] **had been killed** INV OBV by the Crow OBV.'

Topic: the woman's husband > Crow
Syntax: Crow [acted on] the woman's husband: INV

b. the father > his son > the fancy-man (undesirable spirit-guide) (see [6])

Wgii-**gnahmawaan** niw wgwisan	'He PROX **warned** DIR his son OBV,

Topic: the father > his son
Syntax: the father [acted on] his son: DIR

gaa wii **nkwetwaasig** niw	not to **respond** DIR to [the fancy man OBV]

Topic: his son > the fancy-man
Syntax: his son [acted on] the fancy-man: DIR

bi-**ggwejmigod** mandaagninwan	if the fancy-man OBV **comes to ask** INV him OBV

Topic: his son > the fancy-man
Syntax: the fancy-man [acted on] his son: INV

iw ji-zhwenmigod.	if he OBV could bless INV [the son OBV]'

Topic: his son > the fancy-man
Syntax: the fancy-man [acted on] his son: INV

As is obvious from (9), all the verbs where the alignment matches the topicality scale are direct.

The formulation in (8') also gives a satisfying account for unusual (but perfectly grammatical) sentences like that in (10). You do not have to claim any participant in a clause is the topic, only that it has a higher rank than the other.

(10) Wiijkiwenyan **wgii-dkamgoon** niw gnebgoon.

w-iijakiweny-an	**o-gii-dakam-igo-an**	iniw	ginebigw-an
3.POSS-friend-OBV	**3.SBJ-PST-BITE-INV-OBV**	that.OBV	snake-OBV

'The snake OBV bit INV his friend OBV.' (BO S359 p. 158)

However, there are two significant problems that must be addressed. One has to do with how topichood is understood in the case of proximate shifts like those in (2) and the other is the matter of how to account for the restrictions between inversion and obviation, in (3). Let me address the second matter first.

As is shown in (3) (repeated here as (11)), there are no options between direct and inverse.

(11) a. Direct verb
'Waabm**aan** 'gwisan.
o-waabam-**aa**-an o-gwis-an
3.ERG$_i$-see-**DIR**-OBV$_j$ 3.POSS$_i$-son$_j$-OBV
'He$_i$ PROX sees his$_i$ son$_j$ OBV.'

b. Inverse verb
'Waabm**igoon** 'gwisan.
o-waabam-**igo**-an o-gwis-an
3.ERG$_i$-see-**INV**-OBV$_j$ 3.POSS$_i$-son$_j$-OBV
'His$_i$ son$_j$ OBV sees him$_i$ PROX.'

There are, however, plenty of examples of direct clauses with possessed notional subjects, like the second clause in (6), or the Miami example in (12):

(12) Meehci weentamawaaci paapankamwa ahseensali mahweewali **iši-kati sakinaalici** kiihkoneehsahi.
iši-kati-sakin-aa-ili$_j$-t$_j$-i
thus-FUT-catch-DIR-OBV$_j$-3.SBJ$_j$-CONJ
'After Fox$_i$ PROX tells DIR his$_i$ older brother$_j$ OBV Wolf$_j$ OBV how to **catch** DIR fish$_k$ OBV.'

There are also examples of inverse clauses with possessed notional objects, as in (10).

The crucial feature of clauses like those in (11) is that there is coreference between the possessor of the one argument and the other argument. The reason there are no options with the sentences in (11) is that there is a constraint, something analogous to a crossover constraint, given in (13) (see Rhodes 1993).

(13) Possessor Constraint
No sentence is good in which the syntax requires that a clausemate coreferent of a possessor be obviated by its possessee.

The Possessor Constraint is stated in this way because it obtains for configurations of clausemate nominals other than just subject and primary object. It also accounts for grammaticality facts like those in (14).

(14) Ngii-mkamwaa kiwenziinh niw wgwisan.

ni-gii=mak-amaw-aa	akiwenziinh	*niw*	*o-gwis-an*
1.SBJ-PST=find-BEN-DIR	old man_i	$that_j$.**OBV**	3.$POSS_i$-son_j-**OBV**

'I found the old man_i's son_j for him_i.'

*'I found the old man_i for his_i son_j.'

(14) shows that in Ottawa, where primary objects outrank secondary objects for the purposes of control of obviation, the Possessor Constraint applies in a way parallel to the way it applies between subjects and objects.

It turns out that the Possessor Constraint is not unique to Algonquian. Aissen (1997) observes a completely parallel constraint that either blocks or requires passives in Mayan clauses containing possessors with coreferent clausemates.

That leaves only the question of how to account for proximate shifts in a topic ranking system. For example, in (2) the cast of characters remains the same: a boy, his father, and men from their village, but in the first half of the passage the boy is the proximate and in the second half the men are. Proposals to deal with these shifts have attempted to raise two kinds of notions, one being empathy (e.g., Dahlstrom 1996:122, pointing back to Kuno 1987) and the other point of view (e.g., Russell 1996).

As Grimes (1975) points out, topicality is both local and global. That is, there are two dimensions of topic rank: referents have global ranking in whole texts, but the actual information structure of a text is governed by the local overlay of ranking among the main characters. In our example of the "Brave Boy," the proximate spans of the first chapter and the beginning of the second chapter (from which (2) is excerpted) are given in (15).

(15) Whole story synopsis:
Young teen son of the chief sneaks out following a raiding party and saves a man wounded in an ambush and kills Blackfeet, steals their horses, and hunts successfully while bringing the injured man back to the village.

PROXIMATE	THEME
a. men of a raiding party §1–5.1	planning a raid on Blackfeet
b. chief's son §5.2–7.1 . . . §7.2–7.4	boy desires to go . . . and goes
c. men of the raiding party §7.5–9	they discover the boy, camp for a week
d. one of the raiding party §10–11	a Cree shoots a buffalo
§12.1	Blackfeet hear the shot

e.	Blackfoot raiding party §12.2	Blackfeet investigate
f.	men of the raiding party §12.3–7	Blackfeet ambush and wound a Cree
g.	chief's son §12.8-§15	Boy stays to help wounded Cree

Globally the story is mostly about the chief's son. But where he does not drive the plot, as in §7.5–12.7, he is not the local topic and so is backgrounded, until he begins to drive the plot again starting at §12.8.

While there is not space to discuss the point in detail, there is widespread evidence that global high rank can have subtle effects in the assignment of obviation, as exemplified in the pairs of Ottawa sentences in (16) and (17). (See Rhodes 1991 for a fuller discussion.) In the (a) sentences, the expected obviative pattern obtains, and the subject of a subordinate clause is obviated by the subject of the main clause. But in the (b) sentences expected obviation does not occur—in (16b) because the subject of the main clause, which would control obviation, is very low ranked globally, and in (17b) because the potential victim of obviation is very high ranked globally.

(16) a. . . . gye go wgii-kendaanaawaa sa waa-bi-dgoshnoomgad**ni**g niigaan.

gye	go	o-gii-gikend-am-naa-waa	sa
and	EMPH	3.ERG-PST=know-INAN.OBJ-OBJ-3.PL	EMPH

CHANGE-*wii=bi=dagoshinoo-magad-**ini**-g*	*niigaan.*
REL-FUT=come=arrive-INAN-**OBV**-3SBJ.	ahead

'. . . and they knew what OBV was going to come in the future.' (B T23:10)

b. Aanii-sh mii sa go gii-kendmowaad iidig gaa-zhiwebak.

aanii-sh	mii	sa	go	gii=gikendamo-waa-d	iidig
EMPH-EMPH	CLEFT	EMPH	EMPH	PST=know-3.PL-3.SBJ	DUB

CHANGE-gii=izhiwebad-g.
COMP-PST=happen-3.SBJ
'Well, they must have known what PROX had happened.' (Rl 2.41 p. 117)

(17) a. Gii-boonii dash maa ddibew mtigoonskaanig.
gii=boonii-w dash maa dVdibew mitigoonsikaa-**ini**-g.
PST-land=3.SBJ EMPH there on.the.shore be.bushes-**OBV**-3.SBJ
'Then she landed on the shore where there were bushes.' (B T35.21)

b. . . . gye go gii-dbaajmod gaa-dgoshing widi endaawaad.
gye go gii=dibaajimo-d CHANGE-gii=dagoshin-g
and EMPH PST=tell-3.SBJ COMP-PST=arrive-3.SBJ

widi CHANGE-daa-waa-d
there REL-live-3.PL-3.SBJ
'. . . and she told the story as soon as she got to where they PROX lived.' (B T31:10)

Unfortunately, the limits of space also preclude a full exposition, but it is worth noting there is a local topic effect in the "Brave Boy" story. In (15e) the Blackfeet have their own proximate span because they are driving the plot and the Cree are not mentioned. But there is a proximate shift in (15f) when the Cree are again mentioned, in spite of the fact that the Blackfeet are still driving the plot. The Blackfeet are the antagonists, so the Cree rank higher. This is, of course, amenable to an empathy-based account, but such an account does not have the explanatory value that comes with recognizing topicality as two dimensional.

Conclusion

In conclusion, I want to draw the above observations together in a single point. Obviation and inversion are only surface markers. They are sensitive to deeper structures of information flow that are best modeled as scalar rather than binary properties. Such mechanisms alone will not account for everything. The insights that come from understanding the role of empathy in assigned global topic rank and the role of point of view in local shifts of topic rank are crucial. However, the key points here remain: first, topichood is scalar, and second, one must attend to both local and global dimensions of rank assignment.

NOTES

1. The apparatus for citing examples from published sources is as follows: The sources are: R1 = Kaye et al. (1971), R2 = Piggot and Kaye (1973), BO = Bloomfield (1958), BC = Bloomfield (1934). BO contains both texts and sentences these are distinguished by T vs. S. The next number is the number of the text or example sentence. If the citation is from a text, the number of the sentence following the punctuation of the published version is given preceded by a colon and the page number is given. In the case of R1 and R2, I have listened to the original tapes from which the texts were transcribed and restored the taped version if there is a difference.
2. Bloomfield's sectioning in *Plains Cree Texts* frequently makes no sense in terms of discourse structure. In the section marked off as (7), the first line clearly belongs with the last line of the previous section. One can only speculate, but it is likely that Bloomfield was responding to intonational breaks and pause features that are frequently mismatched with structural and notional breaks in monologues to serve as turn maintenance devices.
3. Glossing is by Leipzig rules, with the following added abbreviations: AN = animate, CHANGE = initial change, CLEFT = cleft marker, DIR = direct, DUB = dubitative, EMPH = emphatic, INAN = inanimate, INV = inverse, OBV = obviative, PROX = proximate.
4. Generally I would gloss *-aa* in (3a) as 3.AN.OBJ, consistent with the syntactic analysis of inversion that I have argued for in Ottawa consistently since Rhodes (1976). However, since the point of this paper is intended to transcend the difference between those languages with morphological inversion and those with syntactic inversion, I use the traditional gloss of DIR here, and use the language of morphological inversion throughout.
5. There is some question whether the indefinite subject forms of transitive stems should be counted as truly transitive. That is not at issue here. All the verb forms of interest have two true referents.
6. There are attempts to conflate the clauses of (8) into a single large scale. For a variety of reasons I think that idea is misguided. Even if such an approach can be made to work, for the sake of clarity, I treat the subcases of inversion assignment as quasi-independent.
7. I am explicitly rejecting the notion of further obviative. It was hypothetical when Hockett proposed it (1948:8), and it has since been repeatedly confirmed that no such morphological entity exists. His student, H. C. Wolfart, correctly observes that the morphology thought to mark further obviative, i.e., the reflex of PA **-eli-*, actually marks the obviation of the possessor (1973:29).

REFERENCES

Aissen, Judith. 1997. On the syntax of obviation. *Language* 73.4: 705–750.

Bliss, Heather. 2005. Topic, focus and point of view in Blackfoot. In *Proceedings of the twenty-fourth West Coast Conference on Formal Linguistics*, ed. John Alderete, Chung-hye Han, and Alexei Kochetov, 61–69. Somerville, MA: Cascadilla Press.

Bloomfield, Leonard. 1934. *Plains Cree texts*. New York: G. E. Stechert.

———. 1958. *Eastern Ojibwa: Grammatical sketch, texts and word list*. Ed. Charles F. Hockett. Ann Arbor: University of Michigan Press.

Dahlstrom, Amy. 1987. Discontinuous constituents in Fox. In *Native American languages and grammatical typology*, ed. Paul D. Kroeber and Robert E. Moore, 53–73. Bloomington: Indiana University Linguistics Club.

———. 1991. *Plains Cree morphosyntax*. New York: Garland.

———. 1995. *Topic, focus, and other word order problems in Algonquian*. The Belcourt Lecture 5, Winnipeg: Voices of Rupert's Land.

———. 1996. Narrative structure of a Fox text. In *Nikotwâsik iskwâhtêm, pâskihtêpayih! Studies in Honour of H. C. Wolfart*, ed. John D. Nichols and Arden C. Ogg, 113–162. Winnipeg: Algonquian and Iroquoian Linguistics.

de Lecerda, Celia Mendonca. 1983. The article in Brazilian Portuguese narrative discourse. PhD thesis, University of Michigan.

Goddard, Ives. 1984. The obviative in Fox narrative discourse. In *Papers of the fifteenth Algonquian Conference*, ed. William Cowan, 273–286. Ottawa, ON: Carleton University.

———. 1990. Aspects of the topic structure of Fox narratives: Proximate shifts and the use of overt and inflectional NPs. *International Journal of American Linguistics* 56:317–340.

Grimes, Joseph. 1975. *The Thread of Discourse*. Janua Linguarum, Series Minor 207. Berlin: Walter de Gruyter.

Hockett, Charles. 1948. Potawatomi I: Phonemics, morphophonemics, and morphological survey. *International Journal of American Linguistics* 14:1–10.

———.1966. What Algonquian is really like. *International Journal of American Linguistics* 32:59–73.

Jones, Linda Kay. 1977. *Theme in English expository discourse*. Lake Bluff, IL: Jupiter Press.

Kaye, Jonathan, Glyne L. Piggot, and Kensuke Tokaichi, eds. 1971. *Odawa Language project: First report*. University of Toronto, Anthropological Series 9. Toronto: University of Toronto.

Kuno, Susumo. 1987. *Functional syntax: Anaphora, discourse and empathy*. Chicago: University of Chicago Press.

Lambrecht, Knud. 1987. Sentence focus, information structure, and the thetic-categorical distinction. In *Proceedings of the thirteenth annual meeting of the Berkeley Linguistics Society*, 366–382. Berkeley, CA: Berkeley Linguistics Society.

Özsoy, A. Sumru. 1983. Kendi-reflexivization in Turkish: A syntactic, semantic and discourse analysis. PhD thesis, University of Michigan.

Piggot, Glyne L., and Jonathan Kaye, eds. 1973. *Odawa language project: Second report*. Centre for Linguistic Studies, Series 1. Toronto: University of Toronto.

Rhodes, Richard A. 1976. The morphosyntax of the Central Ojibwa verb. PhD thesis, University of Michigan.

———. 1991. Obviation, inversion, and topic rank in Ojibwa. In *Berkeley Linguistic Society parasession to the Sixteenth Annual Meeting*, ed. D. Costa, 101–115. Berkeley, CA: Berkeley Linguistic Society.

———. 1993. The Possessor Constraint. Paper presented at the Twenty-Sixth Algonquian Conference, Ottawa, ON, October 19.

Russell, Kevin. 1991. Obviation as discourse structure in a Swampy Cree âcimowin. In *Papers of the twenty-second Algonquian Conference*, ed. William Cowan, 320–335. Ottawa, ON: Carleton University.

———. 1996. Does obviation mark point of view? In *Nikotwâsik iskwâhtêm, pâskihtêpayih! Studies in honour of H. C. Wolfart*, ed. John D. Nichols and Arden C. Ogg, 367–382. Winnipeg: Algonquian and Iroquoian Linguistics.

Tomlin, Russell, and Richard Rhodes. 1979. An introduction to information distribution in Ojibwa. *Chicago Linguistic Society* 15:307–320.

Wolfart, H. C. 1973. *Plains Cree: A grammatical study.* Philadelphia: American Philosophical Society.

Algonquian Naming, Power, and Relationality in a Rare Native Love Poem

Melissa Tantaquidgeon Zobel

Narragansett Indian Medicine Woman Ella Wilcox Sekatau (1928–2014) was "a teacher of culture, language, and traditional arts and crafts" (Santiago 2014).[1] In *Dawnland Voices: An Anthology of Indigenous Writing from New England*, her poem "Sometimes I Wish I Could Rage Like You" (Sekatau 2014) considers the deeply loving and stormy relationship she shared with her husband, John Brown. This rare first-person Native love poem contributes to the canon of regional New England Native literature in several ways, the most significant of which is its structuring of indigenous names (written in English) in a way that sheds light on traditional Algonquian language concepts of power and relationality. Because a well-known traditional leader pens the poem in a manner that deeply reflects Algonquian philosophy, it may well be viewed as an important traditional tale by future generations.

Firefly Song of Wind is Sekatau's Narragansett name. Brown is called Mountain Thunder. Both indigenous names can be inferred from her poem. Firefly Song of Wind is suggested in the phrases: "I'll soar on your mighty wild winds. My soul must fly with you again." The tempestuous demeanor of her husband, Mountain Thunder, is evident in the line, "Oh Storm King, where did you come from with raging winds and pouring rain . . . ?" (Sekatau 2014:517–518). These formidable indigenous names are best understood from the perspective of what Paula Gunn Allen describes as the Universe of Power, a universe that is "alive with what is to rationalist sight unseen, a world pulsing with intelligence. . . . There are numerous kinds of beings who regularly inhabit the universe of power . . . [such as] animals or weather beings like Thunder" (Allen 1991:5–20).

Sekatau describes her actions and those of her husband from within this highly relational state of being. Her poem shows the importance of this relationality as it illuminates the notion of animacy within the Universe of Power. Linguist Margaret Noodin offers insight on this subject, explaining that nothing in Algonquian is inherently animate or inanimate: "Most fluent speakers would tell you . . . it depends on their relationship to that object in their particular discourse" (Mead 2014:50). Anishinaabemowin speaker Howard Kimewon elaborates, "There is no animate and inanimate. People just bring that along. I could make anything alive. . . . It's how you talk about it" (Mead 2014:50–51).

Sekatau demonstrates kinship with Noodin's and Kimewon's sense of the importance of relationships in designating animacy by representing herself and her husband as animate beings within a supremely interconnected universe. Not only does she carry the traditional name Firefly Song of Wind while her husband calls himself Mountain Thunder; this couple's embodiment of their names involves multiple connections within the poem. Their names each include a unified dual entity—firefly/wind and mountain/thunder. These unified beings ritually shift in form and function with and within the verses, which focus on their multiple aspects as animal, landform, weather, and wind, with phrases like "Scatter my hurts like your rain," "rage like you," "distant reign," "mighty wild winds," "Storm King," "raging winds and pouring rain," and "my soul must fly with you again."

To highlight the differences between this interconnected Algonquian world and the nonrelational mainstream world, it is helpful to consult the research of Jarrad Reddekop at the University of Western Ontario, who defines nonrelational mainstream philosophy as follows:

> [a] materialist, atomistic, Christianized (and then secularized) ontology, framing modern epistemological premises, gives rise to certain ways of partitioning phenomena such that only certain kinds of beings can count properly as beings. . . . Of those beings recognized, mineral ones such as mountains and stones are worth no special moral consideration in themselves, being inanimate matter. But then,

> neither particularly are plants and animals, for though these are alive they lack the moral status of personhood. (2014:118–120)

In this atomistic/mainstream world, a mountain is a dead rock pile, and thunder is nothing but particles vibrating from electricity. By contrast, from an Algonquian perspective, Mountain Thunder may not only be animate but may be connected to a broad relational field of entities. To reiterate Noodin, what is animate "depends on their relationship to that object in their particular discourse" (Mead 2014:50). Reddekop further elaborates on the fluidity of animate relationships in this description of Algonquian animacy:

> In this world full of persons, no sharp line can be drawn between the personhood of human beings, or of animals, or of other-than-human "grandfathers." . . . It is assumed that it is both possible and desirable to develop a range of social relationships—including relations of exchange, of empathy and nurture and obligation, and so on—with many of these persons. . . . To say that a particular thing is animate is less to embark upon a taxonomic venture than to describe the positioning of something "within a relational field" in which the speaker herself is always presumed to be immersed. (2014:188–122)

One can also read relational eroticism into Sekatau's fluid words when she says, "Oh Storm King, where did you come from with raging winds and pouring rain . . . ? Her passion illuminates yet another attribute of the Universe of Power: it allows Indians to be sexy as/with other-than-human beings and in/with noncolonized gender roles.

Michelle McGough's discussion of Anishnaabe artist Norval Morriseau in *Me Sexy* expands our understanding of these other-than-human sexual relations in Algonquian terms, noting that Morriseau physically juxtaposes people with other-than-human beings in erotic poses, presenting women as birds, bears, and the earth mother. McGough says, "this image of Mother Earth, humans and other-than-human beings illustrates Anishnaabe notions of the connection between the earth and women and of the interconnections marking relationships between the humans and other-than-human beings" (2008:67). Like Sekatau, "Morrisseau's depiction of the female form speaks of an active sexuality that is profoundly creative and gives us a glimpse of woman as an autonomous sexual being who is both a subject and an object of desire" (McGough 2008:67). Morrisseau's nudes lack the passivity of classic European female nudes. They are engaged and relational. Likewise, Sekatau's spousal role is engaged and relational.

She also displays passion for Algonquian names. She once told me she did not change her anglicized married surnames Brown and Thomas to the old Narragansett name Sekatau because the translation of that Algonquian word meant something special to her. In fact, she never mentioned its translation to me, only that it was an old Narragansett surname that she wished to preserve. I understand this impetus, having changed my own paternal surname Fawcett to my maternal Mohegan family's dying surname Tantaquidgeon. Like Sekatau, the translation of my adopted/reclaimed Algonquian name is imprecise. My great aunt Medicine Woman Gladys Tantaquidgeon told me her last name means "going along fast on land or in the water." How exactly it breaks down linguistically, I do not know. Algonquian languages were rarely spoken in southern New England during the mid to late twentieth century when Ella and I were young adults, which is precisely why we both assumed old Algonquian names.[2]

Sekatau's promotion of an Algonquian surname was but part of her general advocacy for indigenous nomenclature. She wrote an award-winning academic paper about her tribe's past efforts to preserve their Narragansett name called "The Right to a Name: the Narragansett People and Rhode Island Officials in the Revolutionary Era," coauthored with Ruth Wallis Herndon (1997). This article decries Rhode Island's disposal of the Narragansett tribe's name in the eighteenth century, arguing that the state "declared the Narragansett people 'extinct' and illegally took away the tribal status of people who still called themselves by that name" (Herndon and Sekatau 1997:433). Trying to strip the tribe of their name, Charlestown town leaders referred to the Narragansett, diminutively, as the "Tribe of Indians belonging to this Town" (Herndon and Sekatau 1997:443). The enforcement of this diminution is evident in the testimony of tribal member Mary Fowler to local officials. She is denied the use of her Narragansett Tribe's name when they say "her Mother was one of the Tribe of the Indians in Charlestown" (Herndon and Sekatau 1997:448).

In *The Names,* N. Scott Momaday says that "a man's life proceeds from his name, in the way that a river proceeds from its source" (1987:ii). Similarly, Sekatau considered her tribe's name to be essential, partly because it connected tribal people to their indigenous homeland. It is therefore significant that Los Angeles Times reporter Joan Nathan records Sekatau as stating that *Narragansett* means "bay Indians" (Nathan 1994).[3] But the depth of the tribe's link between geography and citizenry can only be fully appreciated by understanding southern New England

Algonquian possessive terminology, related to the land. Wampanoag linguist Jessie Little Doe Baird described the importance of Native American connections to New England places at the 2014 New England American Studies Association conference in Bristol, Rhode Island. She explains (Baird et al. 2014) that when the Wampanoag word *ahkee* 'land' becomes *nutahkeem* 'my land,' the suffix shows that the indigenous people connect to their land in a physical way.

Connections to personal names have a similar level of traditional significance and attachment for Native people throughout southern New England. Samson Occom, a traveling eighteenth-century Mohegan educator, records the importance and associated foofaraw of tribal naming ceremonies among the Montauk, a tribe closely associated with his own and the nearby Narragansett—not only then, but now:[4]

> They used to make great dances or frolicks. They made great preparations for these dances, of wampum, beads, jewels, dishes, and cloathing, and liquors, &c. Sometimes two of three families join in naming their children, so make great preparation to make a great dance. When they have got all things ready, they will call their neighbours together, very often send to other towns of Indians, and when they have all got together, they will begin their dance, and to distribute their gifts, and every person that receives the gifts or liquors, gets up and pronounces the name that a child is to be called by, with a loud voice three times. But sometimes a young man or woman will be ashamed to pronounce the name, and they get some other person to do it. Very often one family will make small preparations, and call few old people to name a child; and it was very common with them to name their children two or three times over by different names, and at different times, and old people very often gave new names to themselves. (Brooks 2005:48–49)

Algonquian naming ceremonies dwindled by the mid-twentieth century due to the pressures of colonialism. But the magnitude of such ceremonies has risen in southern New England over the last few decades, as has the number of Natives using indigenous Algonquian names. Examples of traditional Algonquian naming in the Narragansett Tribe are notably strong among Sekatau's grandchildren and great-grandchildren, many of whom use Algonquian first names as their primary legal names. Sekatau was able to suggest many of these names because she was a language teacher among her people, even though she was not a fluent speaker. She possessed a deep understanding of the relationships and concepts inherent in Algonquian words. For example, when passing Weekapaug, Rhode Island, one day, I mentioned to her that Samson Occom recorded a Mohegan cure containing a similar word, *weecup*, but confessed that I did not know the translation of that word. She explained to me that *weecup* was 'basswood,' and that a large stand of that tree once grew in Weekapaug.

Sekatau seized any opportunity to educate people on southern New England traditions and the Algonquian perspective. In a February 17, 1987, interview in the *Roger Williams University Messenger*, she offered her thoughts on a contentious local weathervane that depicted an Indian. While some Native and non-Native people found it offensive, Sekatau contrarily chose to convey to the media her positive relational appreciation of that weathervane, based on her deep connection between human, animal, mineral, plant, and wind beings. She said, "Indians were so in tune with nature—the wind, the tides, and the weather in general, that it seems very natural to me to depict one on a weather vane" (Mongillo 1987:1). This Medicine Woman spoke out about that weathervane because she had an intimate relationship with the wind that she was proud to share. She wasn't just a firefly; she was Firefly Song of Wind.

She and Mountain Thunder chose to exist in a profoundly animate space wherein the lively incarnation of another being is normal and fluid. In this way, their experiences not only reflect Algonquian relationality; they echo the writings of several celebrated writers in the broader Native American literary canon. In Leslie Marmon Silko's tale of "Yellow Woman," she depicts a modern Pueblo woman and her lover, a couple that seems remarkably close to the characters in an ancient Pueblo story about a woman engaged in a relationship with a mountain wind spirit. According to Robin Cohen, Silko's modern woman "is not just like Yellow Woman; she is Yellow Woman" (Cohen 1995:141–147). Her protagonist incarnates an ancient/timeless being who behaves according to her nature and acts within the Universe of Power. Similarly, Firefly Song of Wind behaves in a timeless elemental way when she rides the emotional storm of Mountain Thunder/her husband. Yet the difference between the two tales is noteworthy. Sekatau's poem is autobiographical, whereas Silko's prose appears to be describing someone other than herself. Nonetheless, by offering this tale of Whirlwind Man and Yellow Woman, Silko demonstrates that she, too, understands the kind of relationship between humans and other-than-human persons found in Sekatau's poem.

Silko further describes her perception of the interconnectedness of humans and the landscape in a straightforward way as follows:

> "A portion of territory the eye can comprehend in a single view" does not correctly describe the relationship between the human being and his or her surroundings. This assumes the viewer is somehow outside or separate from the territory she or he surveys. Viewers are as much a part of the landscape as the boulders they stand on. There is no high mesa edge or mountain peak where one can stand and not immediately be part of all that surrounds. . . . The land, the sky, and all that is within them—the landscape—includes human beings. (Silko 1997:5–7)

Simon Ortiz and N. Scott Momaday say much the same thing about indigenous human relationships with the land, water, and sky. According to Smith, Ortiz claims that "the young are frequently reminded by their elders; these lands and waters and all parts of Creation are a part of you, and you are a part of them; you have a reciprocal relationship with them" (Smith 2005:222). Likewise, Momaday addresses the importance of relationality and landforms for Native people when he says, "I am interested in the way that a man looks at a given landscape and takes possession of it in his blood and rain" (Momaday 1998:166–167). Firefly Song of Wind specifically echoes Momaday's connection with the rain when she says to Mountain Thunder: "Sometimes I wish I could rage like you and scatter my hurts like your rain" (Sekatau 2014:517).

Sekatau's description of her marriage to Mountain Thunder also evokes images akin to those found in Marilou Awaikta's poem "Selu and Kanati: Marriage." It portrays another deep conjugal relationship between other-than-human beings, this one between a peaked mountain and its rounded mountain mate. Rader quotes Daniel Heath Justice as saying of Awaikta's work, "the mountains . . . are the Chimney Tops . . . in the great smoky mountains. One is softly rounded, one is sharp. Their beauty is their balance. . . . For Awaikta, as with other Native poets, this description is not mere symbol or metaphor, her poetic relationships are real and tangible" (Rader 2003:74–75). Like Silko, Awaitka is recounting the story of something/someone separate from herself. Sekatau's work thus stands out because she is embodying her own name in her poem, as well as offering a true modern Native love story that may be retold to future Narragansetts as a traditional tale.

Having passed on in 2014, Sekatau leaves behind a profound legacy as a Medicine Woman and teacher in her community. Her son and mentee, current Narragansett Medicine Man John Brown III, carries the relational name of West Wind. That name evokes the spirits of his ancestors, for the west is the direction through which we pass into the Spirit Land. Like his mother, Brown's relationship to his name is powerful, as he spent years working as his tribe's Historic Preservation Officer, protecting the ancient burials of his people that face in a westerly direction.

When West Wind and I discussed his mother's poem, he noted the stormy yet heartfelt nature of his parents' union. We also discussed their relational names, especially his father's name of Mountain Thunder. I noted that some in the linguistics community say the inanimacy or animacy of thunder is unwavering, whereas Noodin says, "It depends on their relationship to that object in their particular discourse." West Wind agreed with Noodin, saying the difference between existing within the relational paradigm of the Algonquian/Narragansett universe and what Reddekop (2014) calls the atomistic world can be understood, viscerally, by the felt "difference between thunder [in the abstract] and [being/deeply feeling thunder] Thunder/ing."

Medicine Woman Sekatau's poem affords readers a sample of that felt experience by drawing them into her relational animate Universe of Power.

While mainstream love poems and lyrics about Indians are often written outside the Universe of Power and represent a kitsch literary trope, à la "Running Bear Loves Little White Dove," Sekatau's refined poem dives inside that deeper universe. In so doing, it reflects elements of other well-known writings within the canon of Native American literature, offers specific insights into naming and relationality in Native New England literature and Narragansett literature, and provides a rare example of a renowned indigenous community leader's powerful, passionate, and personal love poem.

As well as being a Medicine Woman, Sekatau carried the tribal title of "ethnohistorian," publishing a major article in the journal *Ethnohistory* (Herndon and Sekatau 1997). History mattered to Sekatau, as it did to other local traditional leaders of her generation. My great-uncle, Mohegan Chief Harold Tantaquidgeon, used to postscript every big Mohegan event by saying that we were "making history." This sense of knowing one's place in the course of one's tribal history was well understood by Sekatau. She spoke about it frequently, once insisting I not shy away from using my title of Medicine Woman because such ancient titles reflect a different perspective. She told me that our old word for Medicine Person, written variously in different Algonquian orthographies and commonly anglicized to *powwow*, means 'the one who dreams' for the people. Here again, she offered an understanding of an Algonquian word and concept from within the mighty and relational Universe of Power.

Sekatau succeeded in making history for her people in many ways. In an obituary published on April 10, 2014, the *Westerly Sun* stated that her research and traditional knowledge are "credited with helping to ensure the tribe's federal recognition in 1983." She also dedicated herself to preserving and sharing Narragansett history, stories, poetry, and prose, all of which preserved and expounded upon her people's traditional lifeways. It is therefore no surprise that she created this poem recounting her traditional love story in order to create something historical for future generations.

NOTES

1. I wish to thank Narragansett Medicine Man John Brown III for allowing and encouraging me to write this paper on his mother's poem, as well as sharing his understandings of its content. I am indebted to Lisa Brooks for her insights on Silko's "Yellow Woman" and to Siobhan Senier and Marge Bruchac for their general comments on the paper. A special thank you to Rachel Sayet at the Mohegan Library for suggesting I read Paula Gunn Allen's book on Medicine Women. Finally, I wish to thank the late Narragansett Medicine Woman Ella Sekatau for sharing her bold spirit and wisdom with the world, and I offer my respect to her family and tribe.
2. According to Mohegan Elder Stephanie Fielding, *Tantaquidgeon* (also written *Tawaqueesen* by Mohegan Medicine Woman Gladys Tantaquidgeon) could be composed of *towu* 'he flies/moves through the air' and *qihso* 'he jumps.'
3. There are other translations of the word *Narragansett,* including 'people of the small bay.'
4. Spelling in the original preserved here.

REFERENCES

Allen, Paula Gunn. 1991. *Grandmothers of the light: A medicine woman's sourcebook.* Boston: Beacon Press.

Baird, Jessie Little Doe, Amy Den Ouden, Jacquelyn Grey, Kehaulani Kauanui, Jean M. O'Brien, Trudie Lamb Richmond, Rachel Sayet, and Ruth Garby Torres. 2014. *Indigenous sovereignty, conquest mythology, and Indian policy histories and futures in New England.* Bristol, RI:Roger Williams University.

Brooks, Joanna, ed. 2005. *The collected writings of Samson Occom, Mohegan.* New York: Oxford University Press.

Cohen, Robin. 1995. Landscape, story, and time as elements of reality in Silko's Yellow Woman.

Weber Studies: An Interdisciplinary Humanities Journal 12:141–147.

Herndon, Ruth Wallis, and Ella Wilcox Sekatau. 1997. The right to a name: The Narragansett people and Rhode Island officials in the Revolutionary era. *Ethnohistory* 44:433–462.

Hallowell, A. Irving. 2002. Ojibwa ontology, behavior, and world view. *Readings in Indigenous Religions* 22:17.

McGough, Michelle. 2008. Norval Morrisseau and the erotic. In *Me sexy: An exploration of Native sex and sexuality*, ed. Drew Hayden Taylor, 109–123. Vancouver: Douglas and McIntyre.

Mead, Chelsea. 2014. Zeziikizit kchinchinaabe: A relational understanding of Anishinaabemowin history. PhD thesis, Arizona State University.

Mongillo, John, 1987. Vane atop police blotter. http://docs.rwu.edu/the_messenger/60/.

Momaday, N. Scott. 1987. *The names: A memoir*. Vol. 16. Tucson: University of Arizona Press.

———. 1998. *The man made of words: Essays, stories, passages*. New York: Macmillan.

Nathan, Joan. 1994. An early Thanksgiving. http://articles.latimes.com/1994-11-17/food/fo-63996_1_early-thanksgiving.

Rader, Dean. 2003. The epic lyric: Genre and contemporary American Indian poetry. In *Speak to me words: Essays on contemporary American Indian poetry*, ed. Dean Rader and Janice Gould, 123–142. Tucson: University of Arizona Press.

Reddekop, Jarrad, 2014. Thinking across worlds: Indigenous thought, relational ontology, and the politics of nature; or, if only Nietzsche could meet a Yachaj. PhD thesis, University of Western Ontario.

Santiago, Ellyn. 2014. Narragansett medicine woman remembered as "wisdom-keeper." http://www.thewesterlysun.com/news/charlestown/4174737-129/narragansett-medicine-woman-remembered-as-wisdom-keeper.html.

Sekatau, Ella Wilcox. 2014. Sometimes I wish I could rage like you. In *Dawnland voices: An anthology of indigenous writing from New England*, ed. Siobhan Senier, 517–518. Lincoln: University of Nebraska Press.

Silko, Leslie Marmon. 1997. Interior and exterior landscapes: The Pueblo migration stories. In *Speaking for the generations: Native writers on writing*, ed. Simon Ortiz, 2–24. Tuscon: University of Arizona Press.

Smith, Patricia Clark. 2005. Simon Ortiz: Writing home. In *The Cambridge companion to Native American literature*, ed. Joy Porter and Kenneth M. Roemer, 220–232. Cambridge: Cambridge University Press.

CONTRIBUTORS

Heather Bliss received her PhD from the University of British Columbia in 2013. Since 2003, she has been working with elders and other speakers in the Siksiká and Kaináá communities on Blackfoot language documentation and analysis. Her research focuses primarily on the syntax of Blackfoot, but she has also investigated properties of the phonetics, morphology, semantics, and pragmatics of the language, and has done comparative work looking at Blackfoot in relation to Plains Cree, Nishnaabemowin, and other Algonquian languages. She started a Banting postdoctoral fellowship in September 2016, which focuses on building an online archive of Blackfoot personal stories and conversations.

Vincent Collette is a sessional lecturer in linguistics at First Nations University of Canada. He holds a degree in anthropology and a PhD in linguistics from Laval University. He works on the morphology and semantics of East Cree (Algonquian), on teaching materials for Nakota (Siouan) and on the grammar of Southern Auvernhat (Romance). He is also interested in historical semantics and the ethnohistory of Indigenous populations of North America.

Amy Dahlstrom is associate professor of linguistics at the University of Chicago. Her research deals with issues of morphology, syntax, and information structure in Meskwaki and Plains Cree.

Brandon J. Fry is completing his Ph.D. in linguistics at the University of Ottawa. His research agenda is based on syntactic theory and his work to date has focused on agreement, especially in Algonquian languages. He is also interested in biolinguistic issues such as language evolution.

Erik D. Gooding is a professor of anthropology at Minnesota State University Moorhead.

Michael David Hamilton is an assistant professor of linguistics in the Department of Languages, Linguistics, and Comparative Literature at Florida Atlantic University. He received his PhD in 2015 from the Department of Linguistics at McGill University.

Meredith Johnson received her PhD in linguistics from the University of Wisconsin–Madison in 2015.

Kyumin Kim is an assistant professor in the Department of English Language and Literature at Cheongju University, South Korea. Her primary area of research is theoretical syntax, and her recent research topics include aspectual structure and syntax of number in Blackfoot (Algonquian) and East Asian languages.

Carol-Rose Little is pursuing a PhD in linguistics at Cornell University. She has been doing fieldwork on the Algonquian language Mi'gmaq since 2011. Her research interests include syntax, morphology, semantics, and fieldwork methodologies.

Hunter Thompson Lockwood is a PhD candidate in linguistics at the University of Wisconsin–Madison. His research focuses on Algonquian language documentation; he helped produce the first authoritative dictionary of Potawatomi and is writing a descriptive grammar of the language as his dissertation.

Éric Mathieu is Associate Professor at the University of Ottawa. He works on the syntax and morphology of a number of languages, including Ojibwe. He is interested in agreement phenomena, the structure of the noun phrase, interrogatives, and gender, among many other issues. He has published in journals such as *Linguistic Inquiry*, *Natural Language and Linguistic Theory*, *Lingua*, and *Studia Linguistica.*

Cherry Meyer is a doctoral candidate in linguistics at the University of Chicago with a focus on Anishinaabemowin. She has worked on topics such as discontinuous constituents, word order, information structure and, most recently, gender and classifiers.

Will Oxford is assistant professor of linguistics at the University of Manitoba. His research focuses on the morphosyntax of the Algonquian languages from comparative and theoretical perspectives.

Richard A. Rhodes has centered his work on topics relating to American Indian languages, particularly those of the Algonquian family. He has worked on the Ottawa dialect of Ojibwe, on Métchif, and on Sayula Popoluca, a Mixe-Zoquean language of southern Mexico. He has written extensively on the descriptive syntax and syntactic typology of Ojibwe, on the historical linguistics of Métchif, and on lexical semantics and lexicography in American Indian languages. His current research focuses on the intersection of language, history, and geography.

Bryan Rosen received his PhD in linguistics from the University of Wisconsin–Madison in 2015.

Melissa Tantaquidgeon Zobel is the Medicine Woman and Tribal Historian of the Mohegan Tribe in Connecticut. She was trained in Mohegan traditions by her great-aunt, the late Medicine Woman Gladys Tantaquidgeon (1899–2005), and received her BSFS in history and diplomacy from Georgetown University's School of Foreign Service, her MA in history from the University of Connecticut, and her MFA in creative writing from Fairfield University. Zobel's writings include a biography, titled *Medicine Trail: The Life and Lessons of Gladys Tantaquidgeon* (2000) and a young adult murder mystery called *Wabanaki Blues* (2015).